Praise for *Experiencii*

"Matthews leads the reader on a tour of the biblical world, as incredible as it is visceral. Through its command of biblical literature, archaeology, and the texts and cultures of the ancient Near East, *Experiencing Scripture* enlivens the world of the Bible for a contemporary audience, shedding light on the sensory experiences of Israelite society and the centrality of the senses in biblical literature."

—Erin Darby, University of Tennessee

"A truly evocative study from a veteran social scientific critic. Cassian and Augustine proposed interpreting the four *senses* of the Bible—literal, allegorical, moral, and mystical. Their method dominated scholarship until Baruch Spinoza launched historical criticism—the method of choice throughout the 20th century. Ironically, their four *senses* were not senses at all. They were anchored in the brain, not the body. Now Matthews proposes interpreting the Bible using the five *senses* that send information to the brain—touch, sight, hearing, smell, and taste. If you only read one book this year, make it *Experiencing Scripture*. It will revolutionize the way you understand and appreciate the world of the Bible."

—Don Benjamin, Arizona State University

"In this vivid and illuminating work, Victor Matthews distills a career of cutting-edge scholarship on the social world of the Bible into an elegant study of the sensory experiences that informed these ancient writings. He leads us on a journey of how it felt to live in the lands that lay behind biblical storytelling, thereby drawing us closer to those who told these stories in antiquity and the audiences for whom they were performed. In doing so, the insights offered in this book on the sensory aspects of biblical literature make us more sensitive, empathetic readers of what these texts claim."

—Daniel Pioske, University of St. Thomas

Experiencing Scripture

Experiencing SCRIPTURE

The FIVE SENSES in Biblical Interpretation

Victor H. Matthews

Fortress Press
Minneapolis

EXPERIENCING SCRIPTURE
The Five Senses in Biblical Interpretation

Cover image: Steve Johnson on Unsplash
Cover design: Savanah N. Landerholm

Print ISBN: 978-1-5064-7960-6
eBook ISBN: 978-1-5064-7961-3

To Carol, Don, and Carey,
whose encouragement made this volume come to life

Contents

Introduction

Senses matter. Human societies in every age experience their world through their senses, and the "sensescape" consists of both the natural and the built environment.[1] If we wish to re-create or envision life in biblical times, it is essential that we begin by acknowledging the fact that humanity in every time and place is constantly immersed in sensations and derives meaning by crystallizing sensual experiences and translating them into understanding.[2] Thus, it is necessary to explore what the ancients heard every day, smelled in their homes and their villages, and saw as they walked to their fields. The biblical text only provides hints about these impressions, but when it focuses on one or more senses, that is an indication they are valued. For instance, when the author of 1 John declares the ability to speak authoritatively about the incarnation of Jesus, the claim is based on the human senses of hearing, sight, and touch.[3] When the biblical text mentions the smell of incense and perfume, the sight of birds and the sound of their songs, the taste of various foods, the sight of stamping horses eager to go into battle, and the feel of clay being worked by a potter, it is possible to get a glimpse of the people's world. All these data are available to the careful reader who lingers long enough on the text to truly see how the elements of the narrative are being presented. It only requires that we slow down to better appreciate the feast of information waiting for us to explore and, of course, use our imagination to help re-create their ancient world.

While it is possible to isolate references to each of the senses in the biblical text, that is not the way that humans experience their environments. Even those with disabilities that rob them of the sense of hearing or sight make use of their other senses, sometimes in an enhanced manner. Thus, the blind prophet Ahijah can hear the footsteps of Jeroboam's wife when she comes to his house in Shiloh to ask about her son's illness. He can then surprise her with a greeting and take charge of the scene despite his disability.[4]

The chapters in this volume encompass the various living environments of ancient Israel. They range from the village to the city and delve into life-altering events like warfare. In addition, the ways the people's communities were shaped by law and religious practice are also explored. In every chapter, there is a systematic attempt to focus on each sense in turn. However, efforts have been made whenever possible to examine the full sensual experiences described in narratives, in poetry, in prophetic speeches, in Wisdom literature, in religious rituals, and in legal statements.

Over the course of my professional career, I have written a great deal about the social world of ancient Israel. I have tried to tap into how the people lived in a less-than-accommodating environment due to the climate and their physical placement between two superpowers (Egypt and various Mesopotamian empires), often leading to disaster or the invasion of hostile armies. However, it was their adaptation to external conditions that shaped the character of the people who initially inhabited the Canaanite Hill Country and eventually spread from Dan to Beer-sheba as they emerged as a recognizable people and nation. The wide variety of ecological conditions within a small region (125 miles north to south and 60 miles west to east at the widest point), from the barren wilderness of the Negeb to the terraced fields of the Hill Country to the rich farmlands of the Coastal Plain and Shephelah Plateau, created widely different living experiences and challenges. As a result, the sensory impacts of their physical environment play significant parts in the depictions of their own local areas. And their awareness of their physical environment comes out in their narratives and poetry. For example, in the encounter between YHWH and Adam and Eve in the garden of Eden, the scene begins with the remark that the time of their meeting was during that refreshing time of the day when the "evening breeze" cooled the heat of the day—a perfect time for a visit.[5]

Like people in every time and place, the inhabitants of ancient Israel perceived their world through their senses. The clash of drums, the smell of dinner cooking that filled the house, the sight of a loved one coming home from the fields, and the taste or even the memory of the taste of a favorite dish all allowed them to be centered and to feel that they knew a bit about their surroundings. There are constant references to sensory aspects of their world in the biblical narratives, legal formulas, Wisdom literature, and poetry. It will be the task of this volume to point out, interpret, and provide or restore a fuller meaning to the text, including common metaphors that center on the people's sensory experiences. I also will highlight the value of taking a sensory approach to the biblical text as an extra dimension to understanding the world of ancient Israel. It is my hope that you will enjoy the journey and be more aware in the future of the essential role of the senses in interpreting ancient and modern societies.

1

Village Life
Commonsense Adaptations to the Land

IT IS HELPFUL to envision the sights, sounds, and smells experienced by the people as they worked in their homes and in their fields, with their herds, and on various crafts such as weaving. The sights and sounds of their little piece of the world were simply part of life, and they often went unnoticed. The cooing of a dove would be expected, as would the hammering of the local carpenter. The eye and the nose can become muted when everything is as it should be and tend to react only to the unusual or the unexpected. The hints about the senses found in the Bible provide some information on what the people experienced. These hints, however, are masked in some cases by the emic (insider) perspective of the writers.[1] They tend to omit what is well known to the audience, and that leaves a great deal to the imagination and supposition of modern readers. Visualizing the hardships associated with living an often subsistence-level existence in an environment that was not all "milk and honey" requires us to consider the effects of drought, the extremely warm temperatures during the workday in the fields and on the terraced hillsides, and the heavy labor required to build and repair houses and other facilities.

Since a large proportion of the population of ancient Israel lived in villages rather than cities like Jerusalem, Lachish, Shechem, Megiddo, or Samaria, the focus will be on the various sensory impressions that would have been typical for village households. Archaeological evidence of the presence of an identifiable people referred to as *Israel* in Canaan begins with the Egyptian inscription of Pharaoh Merneptah dated to 1208 BCE. The economic and political disruption of this region that occurred after the invasion of the Sea Peoples shortly thereafter provided an opportunity for loosely affiliated early Israelites to establish themselves in the previously underpopulated areas of the Canaanite highlands, running north to south from the Galilee to the Negev.[2]

A village's economy would be based on the aspects of the physical environment that served as the boundaries of the people's living space. Terraced hillsides, wells and other water sources or channels, and various physical features all functioned as borders or lines of existence within which the villagers' daily lives were played out.[3] The space they occupied would determine what they could produce to feed themselves and their animals. In good years, when the climate favored their efforts and there were no raids to disrupt their lives, this meant that they could also set aside seed grain and store surplus grain for the inevitable drought and famine that arrived every three to four years on average. Each section below, as will be the case in subsequent chapters, will explore the five senses as a means of getting a better idea of what life would have been like in these ancient villages.

Sight

The villagers saw the same faces, sheep, goats, hills, valleys, and fields every day. Life was devoted to preserving the very existence of their community in an environment that was not always predictable. Nonetheless, what they saw during the day and at night was the expected, including the sun, stars, and phases of the moon. They were alert to major celestial changes and to shifts in the weather that could signal the coming of the north wind bringing rains or the rising of a harsh, dry wind out of the deserts to their east and south.[4] They would notice a particularly useful plant that could be used for medicinal purposes or to spice up a stew, the flight of birds or birds of prey settling on a corpse, or the prowling of a predator like a lion too close to their village. These sights were familiar, and villagers could respond appropriately based on experience.[5]

Only when something unusual required examination did villagers set their sights on that new thing. That also extended to strangers. To identify someone as a stranger meant that they looked different enough to be labeled as not part of the villagers' group. Perhaps it was the clothing they wore or the style of weaving or its condition, the length or cut of their beard, or even the carving on their staff that distinguished them. Interestingly, a change in clothing by a member of one's household could serve as a method of deception. When Tamar exchanges her widow's garments for the normal garb of an eligible female, she fools Judah, who only sees her clothing and ignores her other features.[6] Thus, seeing is not always believing.[7]

News tended to be passed by word of mouth. A great deal of the education of the young included telling the stories of ancestral figures and thereby providing a foundation for the basic aspects of their identities as members of their local communities. Very often that educational experience was based on being shown what needed to be done or what was important for children and fellow workers to see around them. That is not to say that everyone was illiterate. One "schoolboy" exercise was a recitation of the Gezer Almanac, which contained agricultural tasks associated with each season. Practical knowledge was coupled with basic writing skills.[8]

In a world in which work required the able-bodied to carry their weight, the loss of sight from disease, aging, or injury would be a calamity, but not one that totally removed persons from daily life.[9] When this occurred, a person simply had to rely on their other senses, as the blind prophet Ahijah does when he recognizes that he has a visitor by the sound of her footsteps.[10]

Villages were perched on the summits of ridges large enough to accommodate houses and work areas. They were in places that provided natural protection, available water sources, arable land, and accessible roads. For safety, the houses were built on defensible high ground and where villagers could see visitors or raiders approaching. Assuming that they would be in contact with friendly neighboring villages for purposes of barter, marriage arrangements, and defense, there was probably a signal fire that could communicate danger to the surrounding villages.[11]

Neighboring villages were ranged along ridges in sight of one another or facing one another across valleys, like Elah in the story of David and Goliath.[12] Some villages may have excelled in pottery making, weaving, or carpentry. Others may have had more abundant harvests of grain, olives, or grapes. Trading on a small scale could take place, but there may also have been conflicts over the use of natural resources like wells located between villages.[13]

There were walls connecting the houses as a form of defense, but villages did not have monumental structures tied to massive gate areas like those found in cities. A modest entrance into a village or nearby threshing floor would provide the elders a place to gather, like they do in Bethlehem in the story of Ruth.[14] The most prominent physical structures in villages would be the pillared houses. Although they did not all follow the exact same blueprint, it is possible to say that most measured thirty-three to thirty-nine feet long and twenty-six to thirty-three feet wide. Each one contained a broad room extending across the back end of the structure that was thirteen feet wide. The central living area comprised three long rooms that were separated from one another by walls or rows of pillars that also supported the ceiling and the second floor.[15] Village houses tended to be larger than those found in cities because they needed to accommodate the spatial needs of the extended family. Since all the rooms in a house could be accessed from the central space, this allowed for maximum interaction with all portions of the building while at the same time creating sufficient privacy so that space could be set aside for menstruating women and work areas.[16]

Each house had two stories and a flat roof covering the entire structure. It is likely that the upper floor was the principal living space for an extended family comprising at least four generations: grandparents, parents, married and unmarried children, and outsiders or people adopted by the household.[17] The story of Elisha and the Shunammite woman demonstrates that the roof could also be used as a living space.[18] The ground floor's pillared chambers allowed for the allocation of space for food processing, small craft production, the stabling of some domestic animals, and storage.[19] The first-floor walls were constructed with field-stone, while the upper floor was built with mud bricks laid and chalked with lime plaster. The exterior walls were usually about three feet thick, and windows were placed in the walls of the upper floor, from which smoke could escape, providing ventilation for the house.[20] The floor space was either beaten earth or in some cases lined with fieldstones to assist with drainage.

The walls were plastered with lime to seal them and prevent erosion of the mud bricks. However, that meant heating blocks of limestone in a kiln to a temperature of approximately 900°C to create quicklime.[21] A gradual deforestation of the slopes of the surrounding hills occurred as the need for fuel grew. Population growth added to the need to create arable land for cultivation by clearing the forests. Timber was needed for rafters and beams to support the ceilings of houses, and that further depleted the woodlands.[22] In time, there would be few large groves of trees other than the olive and pomegranate trees planted for their fruits. A lone old-growth oak, terebinth, or pomegranate tree might well have served as a visual landmark for travelers or as a meeting place for the assembling of warriors.[23]

The villagers' diet was primarily tied to the "Mediterranean triad" of bread, wine, and oil.[24] To provide a little variety, women planted kitchen gardens that contained lentils, chickpeas, and beans on the terraces or just outside their houses.[25] Where it was environmentally possible, cucumbers, garlic, leeks, and onions were planted to spice up daily meals.[26] Even when the supplements of fruits and vegetables were available, the villagers would often be short on rations and suffer vitamin deficiencies due to lack of sufficient rainfall, crop losses caused by insects and wild animals, and raids.

The slopes of the hillsides would be ringed from top to bottom with terraced fields to provide additional arable land.[27] Observing them recalls the level of cooperation and the amount of heavy labor required of every able-bodied person in the village.[28] The ground first had to be cleared of stray vegetation and stones. The terraces consisted of walls constructed with stones that had been dislodged as the villagers worked their way down the slope. The terraces were then backfilled with soil dug from the hillside or transported up the hill from where it had eroded into the valley.[29] Once a terrace was finished, the villagers diligently cultivated olive and fig trees and planted their vineyards, sometimes trailing the vines into the lower branches of the trees rather than constructing trellises. Strips of land in the valley at the bottom of the slope would be dedicated to raising wheat and/or barley depending on the salination levels of the soil.[30]

The Mediterranean climate, with rain only falling during the wet months from late October until March, meant that the annual days of rain would be between forty and sixty days.[31] Dew also served as a welcome source of moisture, helping the crops grow even in the dry months.[32] While cloudbursts could fill streambeds, the water quickly evaporated or settled into the porous limestone of that area, leaving the wadi dry for much of the year.[33] Villagers, therefore, carved bell-shaped cisterns into the native limestone to store as much water as possible. Other water sources that could be drawn on included wells and nearby springs, but that involved additional labor by the women, who transported jugs of water back to the houses twice daily or brought their animals there to drink.[34] Groups of women and girls tramping back and forth with their jugs would be a common sight. They left their homes early in the day and then again after the sun's heat had lessened in the evening to draw water and to fill the troughs from which animals would drink.[35]

Wine and olive oil were the staples of the ancient economy. Each village would have both a winepress and an olive press for processing its harvest of grapes and olives as well as pits and large pottery jars to store the hundreds of gallons of oil that they produced.[36] The story of Gideon demonstrates that a winepress could also be used to hide the processing of grain by villagers who were being bled of their resources by marauding peoples.[37] In good years, vineyards contributed grapes, raisins, and wine to the people's diet. Olives, especially their oil, provided fuel for lamps, a base for lotions and cosmetics for the skin, cooking oil, and a lubricant for the preparation of herbal medications.

Every settlement had a threshing floor located outside the village on a flat surface that was open to a prevailing wind. Here the stalks of harvested grain were brought for processing and distribution. A wooden threshing sledge studded with chunks of flint cut through the grain and was pulled by a team of oxen, whose feet contributed to crushing the stalks. Then men with winnowing forks would cast the debris into the air, where the prevailing wind could blow away the chaff, allowing the heavier heads of grain to fall to the ground.[38] Sieves were then used to separate the grain from sticks and stones, after which the grain was piled into heaps to dry. The air must have indeed been filled with dust and particles of chaff, swirling about the workers and adding a layer of dirt and irritating slivers to their skin. The oxen pulling the sledge must have also been chafed by the yoke around their necks as the hot day of work progressed.[39]

The distribution could then begin. A portion was set aside to support widows and orphans and to supply the needs of the villagers for another season.[40] The threshing floor, like the gate, also became a site associated with business transactions and legal procedures. Its economic importance to the village and the fact that it was a communal space regularly used by the people provided it with greater authority.[41] Here "elders," including postmenopausal women and heads of households, would consult on matters of disagreement in the village and come up with consensus decisions.[42]

As for the hardworking villagers, their life span was approximately forty years for the males and ranged from twenty-five to thirty for females, who were susceptible to complications of childbirth.[43] The ceilings of their houses were generally about five to six feet high, which suggests the stature of the residents would be between five feet and five feet, five inches tall. Their limited diet and daily grind would also mean that few of them would be considered overweight.[44]

Expressing their emotions took a variety of forms, including physical gestures. One standard response to a disagreeable sight was to wag or shake their heads, hiss, and clap their hands or sniff in disapproval. When frightened, they might quake or tremble, and when sad, their faces could turn red. When they were filled with joy, they could weep and shout and clap their hands in celebration. Adults could laugh at a humorous statement or to express an appreciation of good times. Children at play must have shown their joy with loud voices and laughter when released from the tasks of the day.[45]

Tanned brown by the sun, the men would be heavily muscled from hard work. While they were in the fields or with their flocks, they dressed in only enough to cover their loins and their heads from the sun and wore roughly made sandals to protect their feet. Since they could wear out, it seems probable that sandals were removed in the house and that children played without them. For the wealthier villagers, walking barefoot was also one of the signs of mourning. Women wore loose-fitting robes that covered their heads but shifted to "widow's garments" when they lost their husbands. What these garments or those worn by the other villagers looked like, other than that they were made of wool, is never said in the Bible. Some plant-based dyes were available, but village clothing was not dyed. Still, the styles and makes of the clothing must have been distinctive enough to set the widows apart from the other women.[46]

Clothing marked widows as well as orphans as bereft and "wards" of the village to be provided for from the harvest.[47] In the village culture, it is unlikely that the people wore linen clothing, since flax was not always available, and linen would be expensive and less durable. In later periods when Levitical priests were in residence to perform sacrifices, they were required by law to wear linen undergarments.[48]

Sound

Only in rural areas could someone approximate the range of sounds that occurred in the villages of ancient Israel. Even then it would be necessary to walk out into the fields at a time when irrigation systems, tractors, harvesters, and other motorized vehicles were not present. Only then would it be possible to hear the call of birds, the chirping of small animals, the buzz of insects, and the bellowing of cattle or other farm animals. With that in mind, it is necessary to become attuned to the villagers' world. Village sounds will therefore be divided between those encountered in the immediate vicinity of the houses and those that were heard in the fields and nearby grazing areas. Because these were the most familiar sounds encountered, they tended to blend into the general background noise rather than elicit or require a reaction. If the rhythms of a house, including identifiable voices and everyday activities, were heard, the assumption would be that all was as it should be. It can be said that sounds contributed to the identity of a household, and the sounds emanating from the house were considered signals or sentinels of its condition, whether healthy, prosperous, or in decline.

Typically, the house would be filled with the sounds of people and animals moving within and just outside it. That also would include the voices of those present and the bleating of sheep and lowing of cattle in their pens, as well as the songs of birds like the mourning dove or the flittering of sparrows.[49] The pitch, the depth, and the tempo of each person's voice would be recognizable.[50] The villagers spoke the same dialect, and if anyone spoke with a different inflection or vocabulary, they would immediately be spotted as a stranger and potential enemy, as is the case when Jephthah requires the Ephraimites to pronounce "Shibboleth."[51]

Household sounds varied based on the time of day. The rustling of people waking up and preparing to go to work or begin food preparation in the early morning would produce a particular set of sounds. Shortly after the normal work routine of cooking began, the sounds associated with the various cottage industries could be heard. Then, at the end of the workday, the sounds of weary field-workers and herders would be heard as they returned for their evening meal. Once all had been done and the animals were settled down for the night, their owners at last could prepare to return to their own beds, perhaps filling rooms with their snores or restless movements as they dreamed or their bodies adjusted to the aches and pains of their heavy labors.[52]

The villagers would have to adjust to new circumstances only when these expected sounds stopped suddenly or were interrupted by new or unexpected ones. In some cases, the response was to join in the songs and shouts tied to a victory celebration.[53] A mother or an adolescent sister may have had to drop what they were doing to deal with the strident cry of a hungry infant.[54] The whole community may have had to make quick preparations in response to a shouted warning, and it would be natural for attention to be shifted to address this new happening or to look out for some approaching danger. The simple fact is that these small villages were subject to the predations of raiders and were too often familiar with the sounds of war.[55]

There was a difference between the sounds made by men and those associated with women.[56] In the domestic sphere centered on the house and its immediate environs, women worked on a variety of tasks—from preparing food and rearing children to weaving cloth. That in turn meant that sounds were not always continuous but varied depending on the tasks at any given moment. This variation stood in contrast to the work assigned to men, except during the harvest season, when both men and women were required to complete the job of gathering the bounty from the fields, vineyards, and olive orchards.[57] For most of the year, however, work in the fields or with the herds would be continuous throughout the day, and the sounds it produced would be silenced only when an accident occurred, a wild animal attacked, or a repair was made necessary by the erosion of a terrace wall.

Women processing grain and bread making contributed quite literally to the "daily grind." Up to three hours per day were spent processing enough flour for the household's needs.[58] The sounds generated by this activity include scooping grain from storage jars and mashing the kernels with a mortar and pestle. Archaeological evidence from several sites indicates that some stone mortars shaped like cup holes were embedded in the floor of the preparation area. A handheld grinding stone that had been shaped to the size of a hand was then used in a back and forward motion to grind the grain on a saddle quern, producing a constant grinding noise.[59] The much larger lower stone upon which the flour was produced was preferably made of hard volcanic basalt when it was available in the area. Unfortunately, the flour also contained stone dust that contributed to the gradual wearing down of the people's teeth, which probably added more sounds in response to the pain associated with having bad teeth.[60]

After mixing the flour with water and a pinch of salt to compound the dough, yeast could be added from a previous batch of bread as a leavening. Unleavened dough was used when time was pressing. In either case, the mixture was then kneaded on a flat surface and baked in a clay oven. In some cases, the cakes of dough were pressed against the sides of a *tannur*, an oven located either within the house or in the courtyard area.[61] The aroma of baking bread would have filled the house, attaching itself to the women as a form of domestic perfume and masking other less appealing odors.

Because dough will not keep for long, bread making was a daily activity. Loaves of baked bread were kept in baskets until they were presented as offerings to YHWH or consumed by the household. The hand grinder would have become a valued implement, perhaps a legacy from mother to daughter. It is not surprising, therefore, to find a woman carrying one with her when her village is endangered and even using it as a weapon against Abimelech in a story from the chaotic period of the judges.[62] Unfortunately, the loss of her grinder means that her household will starve unless it is retrieved or replaced. A similar situation occurs when Jael hammers a tent peg into the forehead of Sisera. She would have been familiar with the task of setting up a tent, and the hammer and peg would have been items attuned to her hand.[63]

A horizontal loom for weaving woolen clothes was among the most common items within every house. Modern-day archaeologists can recreate the shape of a loom based on the pattern in which its weights fell when it was destroyed by fire.[64] The looms were approximately five feet high and "warp-weighted," with the threads attached to the long axis of the weave (= the warp) and suspended vertically with the loom weights. Then the thread (= the weft) was passed horizontally in and out of the warp to create the weave pattern. The sounds tied to this creative activity would have reverberated throughout the dwelling throughout the day. The style of the cloth produced provided a visible marker that, like the voices and common dialect of the people in a village, spoke to membership and group identity in a community.[65]

Weaving was primarily women's work, and weavers would gather and talk about the events of the day or instruct younger women on the skills they would need to learn to manage their households.[66] After washing the fleece of sheep's wool or goat hair, it was carded or plucked to separate out individual strands of thread. The thread was prepared for weaving by drawing it into long strands using a wooden distaff and spindle to entwine the fibers into balls. The quickly moving fingers of these women fabricated cloth for a variety of uses. There would be a steady sound of the spindle whorl as it twirled against the floor.[67] That sound was joined with the swiftly moving shuttle as the thread was first bound and knotted to the frame of the loom to begin the weaving process, much like Delilah's careful binding of Samson's hair to her loom.[68]

In addition to meal preparation and weaving, every household would be engaged in various crafts. Specialization of labor was seldom possible in a village setting, and therefore basic duties such as making pottery, constructing wooden frames for a loom, fashioning mud bricks for a house, or performing simple metalwork would have added tasks to the workday for each household. They also served as educational opportunities to teach the children skills they would need when they became older. The mix of sounds included a potter's wheel pushed by the foot, the hammering associated with shaping implements of copper or iron, and the drilling and sawing produced by a carpenter.[69] The hum of activity must have been a reassuring background noise that spoke of a village's industriousness and its dedication to performing the necessary tasks at hand.

The people of the village found it necessary to diversify their economy by engaging in both farming and herding sheep and goats. The sound of the animals' hooves as they were driven from the village and the shouts of the shepherds, with the clattering of their staffs, would have simply been part of the general background noise. Every day the animals were taken to pasture, and then, to keep them from scattering or getting stolen, they were returned to the fold either near the village or in their pasturelands. The sheepfolds also served as places where the nursing ewes could care for their lambs and the animals could breed as they drank from troughs set in separate pens.[70] It is not surprising that the prophets used shepherding as an analogy for YHWH's promise to return the people from exile.[71]

Those spending time in the open grazing areas might have heard the flapping of an eagle's wings as it took flight or other birds singing out as they hovered against the blue of the sky. Children were stationed in watchtowers to cry out and drive the birds away to prevent damage to the fields or orchards. More ominously, there might be the roar of a lion as it approached the sheepfold, causing the sheep to respond with nervous bleating while the shepherds raised their voices to calm them. Out in the open throughout the year, the villagers would also be alerted to changes in the weather, like storms indicated by the crashing of thunder over the heights or falling temperatures that brought swirling, icy wind, snow, and hail.[72]

The sheep were sheared in April and May before the summer heat became too oppressive. The flocks would be brought together at a central point where enough men would be gathered or hired to perform the slow job of removing the fleece with a sharp blade. There would be a great deal of noise and commotion as the sheep were rounded up for this yearly event. The object would be to hold the sheep in place to remove the fleece, if possible, in one piece. Careful handling resulted in a quiet animal once it had been flipped.[73] A gathering would also be the occasion for a feast; a loud, drunken celebration; and in some cases, a reckoning of scores, as Amnon discovers during his half-brother Absalom's shearing banquet.[74]

Once the winter rains had begun to loosen the sunbaked, hard soil and made the ground ready to absorb moisture, men and boys commenced the three-month planting season. While the rains moistened the fields, there were two plowings before the soil was sufficiently pulverized and smoothed for the sowing of seed.[75] The initial scratching of the wooden plow, sheathed with its bronze or iron plowshare, would have made a distinctive sound, and one very different from the second cutting of the furrow. The oxen pulling the plow would snort in their efforts and occasionally would be encouraged by the voice of the plowman as he employed his ox goad, which was also used to break up clogs of earth.[76] And there would be times when a cry of pain rang out after the plowman or his sons stepped on a stone or turned an ankle.[77]

Once the field was prepared, sowing would take place, and the rains continued to fall during the season, smoothing out the furrows and germinating the seed. Attention to the weather became an aphorism for farmers, who needed to observe the direction and strength of the wind before sowing.[78] Although there is no reference in the Bible to the sounds of those who sowed seed, it can be assumed that they would sing or chant to help maintain a steady rhythm to their distribution of the seed and to ask YHWH for a prosperous harvest.[79] They may also have shouted at the birds that flocked in to eat the seed.[80] From that point, the principal and backbreaking task prior to harvest would be to minimize the loss of germinated grain that would be squeezed out by thistles and other weeds.[81]

Other hazards faced by these farmers included mildew and blight attacking the plants and, worst of all, the periodic swarms of locusts. In their various stages of development, from wingless "cutters" to "hoppers" and finally to winged insects, the locusts literally would eat everything in their path. The sound of the insects' wings as they swarmed in their multitude must have generated alarm among the villagers as they saw their efforts being consumed. It is not surprising to find comparisons in the biblical narrative between these voracious insects and the sounds of invading armies, who also stripped the land of its bounty.[82]

The harvest of the cereal crops was literally tied to the survival of the village, and everyone who was physically able would be involved. Egyptian tomb paintings from Beni Hasan provide a pictorial sequence of events from the field to the threshing floor.[83] Starting early in the morning, the dew began to evaporate in the heat. It rose from the field, and it would have been possible to see the waves of moisture mingling with the hot air that quickly parched the workers as they began their labors. A freak burst of rain during the harvest would have been a welcome, if temporary, relief. Ordinarily, however, jars of water were placed at the edges of the field to refresh the thirsty harvesters. The harvest sequence began with the workers grasping the stalks of grain and then swinging sickles with flint-edged blades to cut the stalks.[84] The swishing sound of the sickles created a rhythm that may have been joined by a chant or work song by the workers to help their labors. It would have been only natural for these people to rejoice when they experienced a bountiful harvest that would have met their needs for that season and the next. Of course, drought or invaders could have reduced the harvest and silenced these sounds of celebration.[85]

The final stage of processing the harvested grain took place at the communal threshing floor, where the farmers could separate out the kernels of grain and participate in the distribution. The sheaves were transported by donkey or cart. A wooden threshing sledge studded with sharp chunks of flint and pulled by a team of oxen or donkeys was driven over the stalks while the teamster cried out to encourage their efforts. The animals' hooves would add to the crunching sounds as the stalks were thoroughly crushed.[86]

Then men with winnowing forks or shovels would cast the debris into the air, where the prevailing wind could blow away the chaff, allowing the heavier heads of grain to fall to the ground. With the air filled with dust and particles of chaff whirling about the workers, their coughing and sneezing would have added one more noisy consequence of their labor. The oxen pulling the sledge must have reacted to the chafing of the yoke around their necks as the hot day of work progressed. When the winnowing was done, sieves were then used to separate the grain from sticks and stones, after which the grain was piled into heaps to dry and to be guarded until it could be properly distributed and placed in secure ground storage.[87] There is sufficient archaeological evidence of pits dug for grain storage to indicate this was a common practice. Some were lined with lime, but in other cases, they were prepared by burning chaff or older grain to provide a layer of ash that prevented insect infestation or microbial contamination that would have caused the grain to rot or become moldy.[88]

The other major harvests during the year involved the grape vineyards, the olive groves, and the fig trees, which were situated on the terraced hillsides. The villagers pruned their vines and hoed the ground throughout the year to remove vegetation that could have stolen the precious moisture. The fig trees would be tended prior to the harvesting of the ripe fruit in June and again in August and September. The olive trees, prized for the oil that was pressed from the ripe fruit, were harvested in September and October. The workers, both men and women, beat the branches with long sticks, creating a racket. The ripe fruit plopped onto large cloths strategically placed around the trunks of the trees. The fruit at the top of the trees was left to be gathered later by gleaners.[89]

Once the grapes had been harvested, the next stage involved treading a portion of them to produce the juice that would be used for syrup or to make wine. As the grapes filled the vat, they were crushed underfoot, staining the garments of the workers. The gurgling liquid would be drained into another vat, from which the future wine was taken to store in jars to promote the fermentation process. Naturally, a rhythm was maintained, since several workers trod the grapes together and would not want to unnecessarily bump into one another or waste energy, and that meant they kept the process going and perhaps less boring with work songs or chants. Singing these songs may also have served as a form of instruction, designed to instill the memory of YHWH's bounty and blessings as described in the Song of Moses.[90]

Olives were too hard to tread, and the first extraction of oil was done by crushing the fruit under a stone roller, which produced the best quality. The grating sound as it rolled over the olives would have been mixed with the grunts of those pushing the stone or the donkey attached by a harness to a beam inserted into a stone drum.[91] Subsequent pressings of the pulp involved placing it in wicker baskets attached to a levered press and counterweighted with heavy stones. The creaking of the baskets as they were flattened and the hiss of the liquid going into the storage vats must have heartened the farmers, as these sounds demonstrated their hard work was producing a product that had many uses in cooking, oil for lamps, ointments, and cosmetics.[92]

Once the harvest was gathered, processed, and stored, it was time to feast, celebrate with "festal songs," and dance to the sound of tambourines, pipes, and lyres. These feast days would be especially welcome as a balance to a life filled with hard work and too often with sorrows. What better way to celebrate than to eat, drink, laugh, and enjoy fellowship? It also was the right time to give thanks to YHWH in rituals and sacrifices less grand than in the cities and towns. A pilgrimage to a local shrine might also be appropriate to make an annual acknowledgment of what was due to YHWH.[93]

Life in the village included moments of joy and sorrow. Villagers would be familiar with the sounds of a woman giving birth, who "writhes and cries out in her pangs" as she labors to bring a new life to the village. They would keen laments[94] while tearing their garments or putting on sackcloth as they mourned the premature death of a woman who had given birth.[95] Her death might have been the result of complications that overwhelmed the skills of the midwife or due to shock.[96] Calamities like a stillborn infant and the premature death of an adult due to illness or injury would have been common enough for the villagers. Their private weeping and public acts of mourning would be recognizable and understood by all. Even the happy sounds of musical instruments, generally mentioned in relation to celebrations or festivals, could be retuned or played in a desultory manner to reflect the emotions of those who were experiencing a loss or weeping.[97]

Clearly, these villagers would not be afraid to express their emotions openly. They knew that there was a time to weep and a time to laugh.

And sometimes an event was so horrible that they could not contain their emotions. Thus, in her despair after being expelled from Abraham's encampment and struggling to survive in the wilderness, Hagar weeps without hope.[98] Jacob also weeps, but with joy, after discovering his future bride Rachael following his journey from Canaan back to Harran. After the sacking of David's village of Ziklag, David and his men weep until they have no more tears.[99]

Not every sound would have been associated with work or pain. There were many occasions for which singing and dancing to the sound of tambourines and lyres were appropriate. For example, Laban wistfully chastens his son-in-law Jacob for leaving without providing the people with a farewell celebration that would feature mirth and songs. When YHWH manifests divine power or after a successful military engagement, the women "sing with joy, and with musical instruments," or the people establish a rhythm to their songs of joy by clapping.[100]

Villagers also expressed their opinions with a variety of gestures and sounds. For example, they would clap their hands, stamp their feet, gnash their teeth, and hiss to show disapproval or condemnation of persons or places. Such displays were also designed to show their disdain for fallen enemies. Apparently, even passing by despised locations could elicit signs of scorn, with people scoffing at ruined sites.[101]

Storytelling was a major form of entertainment after the workday was done. In this way, the foundational stories of the people were passed on to the next generation in a manner that stuck in the mind. They were most often associated with the joy of victory or a clever escape from their enemies. Thus, the story of Deborah and Barak's campaign against Jabin and Sisera is retold dramatically to the accompaniment of musicians.[102] Since much of the villagers' lives were filled with audible clues and communication, growing deaf in old age would rob them of the pleasure of hearing these stories or "the voice of singing men and women" as well as the sound of the voices of their friends and households.[103]

Households had to be constantly vigilant. Without a central government to protect the villages and with only a few adults able to bear arms in each community, they had to watch for the approach of strangers or raiders.[104] One response to this potential danger was the development and implementation of the hospitality protocol, which could at least temporarily transform a possible enemy into a guest for a short period of time. Thus, Abraham, while sitting before the door of his tent, sees three men standing near him and, as the head of his household, goes out and extends a welcome to them, offering the hospitality of his encampment, including water to wash their feet, a meal, and a chance to rest from their journey. With their expressed consent to stop, the social protocol goes into motion, including the exchange of news and, in this case, the prediction of a son for the elderly couple, which elicits a hearty laugh from them both.[105]

Smell

The "deodorization" of society, with its ties to public health, has literally showered away the Western audience's ability to understand or relate to the societal importance of smell prior to the nineteenth century.[106] Humans living in traditional societies such as ancient Israel seldom bathed or washed their clothes except to deal with ritual impurity or to prepare for a life-changing event.[107] As a result, body odor associated with the human and animal residents of villages would have been quite pervasive. Individual scents were discernable but based on a different range of smells. The different smells associated with members of the community and strangers were distinguishable, just as those between ripe and unripe grain or fruits. Any familiar smell could elicit a response and even could forecast changes in the weather.[108] Most important, flashes of memory could summon up the desire to taste and smell a favorite meal or conjure up the memory of a scent as an analogy to a smell that had just been experienced.[109]

Smells are culture-specific. The villagers would not have considered them particularly offensive or strange unless there was something new or overpowering in the air. It would take particularly foul smells—like the corpse of a rotting animal, the sweat of workers coming in from the fields, or a stable that had not been mucked for some time—to grab their attention.[110] For the villagers, the way to fit into their pastoral society was to smell like everyone else.

Bathing customs originated with the shortage of water. Naturally, their clothing smelled of sweat, dirt, animal dung, and cooking fires. In fact, a person's individual body odor, like their clothing and appearance, was part of their personality and immediately recognizable to others. A shift away from the norm was tied to a transition in life that marked the person as shifting into a new social status, such as marriage.[111] That may explain why prior to her supplicatory meeting with Boaz on the threshing floor, Ruth washes and anoints herself (probably with olive oil) and puts on her best clothing. Through this transitionary ritual, she first washes off her previous status as a widow and then gives a sign that she is prepared to take up her case with Boaz. She asks him to accept the role of "near kinsman" and bring her and Naomi into his household.[112]

Under normal circumstances, it would be expected that a shepherd would smell like his animals, a tanner would smell like tanned leather, and a farmer would necessarily smell like the fields in which he worked every day. If they did not have these distinctive aromas, they would be considered frauds masquerading in their declared professions. Value judgments were based on the simple maxim that people were most comfortable with the ordinary. Things should be as expected, and life in the village, despite its hardships, should be according to what has "always" gone on before.

Literary Depictions of the Trades

The Egyptian Teachings of Khety provides a litany of reasons why a master scribe wishes his son to become a scribe.[113] In the process, he describes the tasks assigned to other trades and in some cases the physical appearance and smell of the workers:

> The coppersmith at work before the mouths of his furnaces, with fingers like the scale-covered claws of a crocodile. Reeking with sweat like the odor of rotting fish.

> The potter is buried alive in clay. He wallows in mud like a pig to mix the clay for his pots.

> The gardener bears a yoke. His shoulders slump as with age and there is a festering sore on his neck.

The deuterocanonical book of Sirach (38:24–34) parallels these descriptions of the trades while favoring the role of the scribe:

> How can one become wise who handles a plow . . . who drives oxen . . . and whose talk is about bulls?

The smith, sitting by the anvil . . . the breath of fire melts his flesh . . . the sound of the hammer defends his ears.

The potter sitting at his work and turning the wheel with his feet . . . he molds the clay with his arm and makes it pliable with his feet.

One example of the effect that smell had on these villagers is found in the story of blind Isaac. He smells Jacob's garments and identifies him as Esau, since they smell "like the smell of a field the Lord has blessed."[114] That could be the aroma of crushed wildflowers or a freshly harvested field. An analogy like this one becomes real to the original audience of the story when the author plays off an "embedded memory." In this way, he brings it back to life every time an aroma is encountered. Similar examples are found in biblical poetry and the prophetic speeches where garments and people who wear them have the scent of Lebanon, probably a cedar smell.[115]

There is an interesting transformation ritual in the Deuteronomic Code that requires a female prisoner of war to "shave her head, pare her nails, discard her captive's garb," and spend a month mourning for her parents before she can marry her captor. Such an irrevocable initiation allows her entrance into an Israelite household and terminates all association with her previous household.[116] At the same time, it removes, symbolically and physically, the aroma of both her previous familial association and her captive status. A parallel to this transformation can be found in the Joseph story when the former prisoner's garments are replaced with fine linen.[117] Yet another example is found at the conclusion of the Egyptian story of Sinuhe. When this former political refugee and exile is allowed to return to the Egyptian court, he bathes, shaves, and puts on "robes of fine linen" suffused with myrrh. He then discards his desert clothes, returning them to the sand where they belong, along with the aroma of the nomadic encampment in which he had lived.[118]

A prevailing wind swirling up from the valley would occasionally carry with it the smell of dust and vegetation. The wind might temporarily mask the smell of the urine and dung from the animals in their pens or in the houses. Animal dung was used as fuel for cooking and produced a distinctive aroma unlike a wood fire.[119] Human waste may have been deposited in latrines outside the village or heaped into dung pits trodden down with straw. Normally, however, people relieved themselves in the fields, since human waste had value as fertilizer.[120] The use of human waste as fuel is not attested in the Bible except in the instance in which the priest-prophet Ezekiel is scandalized by being told by YHWH to cook his meals over a fire made from human dung. He seems to be relieved when YHWH then allows him to cook with cow dung.[121]

The animals that were housed in the village had their own distinct odor. Male goats especially had a strong smell that they used to attract females who were ovulating. The village might have had a pair of oxen to pull a plow, although few could afford that luxury. If a team was available, it was likely that it was a communal asset shared in rotation by the villagers or was rented from another village.[122] More often, an ass pulled the plow, or in some cases, impoverished villagers were forced to assume that task. Donkeys were used to carry burdens and people and to pull carts. Like goats, she-asses in heat sniffed the air for traces of males' urine.[123]

Animal dung was the most common form of fertilizer used by ancient farmers. Shepherds like Joseph's brothers would often graze their flocks in harvested fields, leaving behind the dung that would enrich the next crop.[124] Given this reality, it is quite appropriate that "dung on the field" serves as a good analogy for unburied bodies left to lie and rot after a battle.[125] This dishonorable fate also applied to those executed like Queen Jezebel or the disinterred bones of Judah's kings and their court officials.[126] The lack of any mention of odor in these cases is due to either an emic omission by the storyteller or the loss of an aroma, as the dung dried out in the sun after just a couple of days.

Cooking smells would reflect one of the daily activities performed primarily by women.[127] The familiarly enticing and reassuring fragrance would appeal to the workers as they returned from the fields in the evening.[128] Beer, which provided needed calories and a check against the bacteria prevalent in drinking water, would have been brewed as part of the daily baking process. Egyptian and Mesopotamian sources describe how it was created by taking the lightly baked barley or wheat dough that had been infused with yeast and placing it in jars with a stopper that allowed gas to escape and resulted in a sweet liquid. The yeast facilitated the chemical reaction that converted the carbohydrates in the dough into an alcoholic beverage. The resulting aroma and the bubbling of the mixture indicated that fermentation had occurred and that it was ready to drink.[129]

For the most part, the villagers' typical diet would consist primarily of bread or porridge, cottage cheese or yogurt made from goat's milk, and a mixture of vegetables and fruits depending on the season.[130] Diet contributed to a person's individual body odor, as it mixed with the body chemistry and the breath.[131] When a "stranger" entered the village, their smell, based on a diet unlike that of the villagers and the places he had traveled, may well have marked him as different.[132]

Animals were too precious to the village economy to be butchered on a regular basis except as part of a sacrifice. Only wealthy landowners, like Nabal, were able to hire extra laborers during the shearing season and prepare meat to feed them.[133] When meat was available as part of the sharing of the sacrificial animal with YHWH, the "pleasing odor" experienced by the people's divine patron would undoubtedly have been shared by them as well.[134] Meat was usually boiled, giving off a distinctive smell as it simmered. Only the Passover meal required meat to be roasted, and that complied with the ritual associated with the hasty departure from Egypt.[135]

If the villagers butchered an animal as part of a sacrifice or festival or to celebrate a victory, the dung and offal would have added to the butcher's personal fragrance, overpowering the smell of shed blood and the press of people.[136] Even so, the joy associated with the feast, the aroma emanating from the cooking pots, and the accompanying drinking might well have submerged the worst of these odors.[137] The distinctive and lingering aroma of blood would have been present around the altar, as it undoubtedly is when Joseph's brothers present their father with the robe covered with goat's blood that serves as proof that Joseph has been slain.[138]

Skin infections would not have been uncommon given the working conditions faced by these villagers and the opportunity for infection to infuse wounds and abrasions.[139] Infected blisters, sores, or boils are generally referred to in English translations as *leprosy*, but in this context, they would also have contributed a distinct odor that indicated the person was unclean—no longer certified to participate in village life.[140] Simple remedies for these afflictions would be to wash away the bloody flux, soften callused skin with olive oil, and then bind them against further damage.[141] The differentiation among different forms of skin disease described in Leviticus 13 centers on the appearance of "raw skin," a rash or itch, and the color of the skin or the associated hair. If a person contracted a skin disease with a fungal infection, in addition to the red and suppurating skin, they would also have a distinctive odor. Sometimes a topical ointment was applied to the skin.[142]

The appearance of the disease in garments would be tied to dry rot or mold in the fabric.[143] The wool absorbed the pus exhibited by their skin disease after encountering the diseased person. In the village setting, clinical examination was probably the task of someone trained to create herbal remedies.[144] In later periods, these examinations were turned over to priests, who could pronounce a patient either "clean" or "unclean." The latter designation meant a period of confinement away from the community, and in some cases, the person would be ostracized permanently to live by begging outside the village.[145]

Industrial smells emanating from the village would vary depending on the tasks performed and the time of year. Thus, the overwhelming smell of urine and dung used in the tanning process would fill the air on occasion.[146] The potter's workplace would be filled with a muddy smell from working wet clay, and that would combine with the fumes from his kiln. A fuller who had repeatedly washed fleece to obtain lanoline ("wool grease") or to create a felted garment would have an oily or greasy smell, as would his workshop.[147] The smell of fermenting grapes that had just been crushed in the winepress as well as the smells associated with brewing beer from bread would swirl about in the air. If a garden midden, into which food waste and animal bones were deposited, was present, that too would add the smell of composting vegetable matter. Anyone who tended a fire for whatever purpose would smell of fire.

The fields of wheat or barley also had a distinct fragrance as the grain ripened. A wheat field ready to harvest had a "hoppy" or "bread-like" smell. The best wheat had a low moisture content, since it was less likely to rot during storage. Such a smell would be captured in memory and thus could evoke a reaction like Isaac's when he smells Jacob's garments.[148] The harvest was in the dry early summer months. An unexpected storm with the unnerving sound of thunder would have delayed the harvesters' work and potentially beaten down and ruined the crop.[149] There was also a hoped-for scent that would be common in semiarid regions—the scent of water. Job recites an aphorism about trees that revive when they catch the "scent of water."[150] Such anthropomorphizing parallels a similar reaction that thirsty humans often experience.

Most villages had a "high place" (*bamah*) on a nearby peak where communal sacrifice was performed by an elder.[151] The animal sacrifices on the altar would have had an odor of cooked and burnt meat that presumably provided the "pleasing aroma" that was acceptable to God.[152] While it is possible that a form of incense was also offered at the village altar, few would have been able to obtain luxuries like spices, myrrh, frankincense, and perfume in any great quantities, since these had to be imported and would have been costly.[153] These items were more typical of the urban settlements and will be discussed in that context.

Touch

Among the senses, smell and touch can be improved with practice. Both are associated with an awareness of the space that humans occupy. In terms of sensation, touch discerns both soft and hard, dull and sharp, and hot and cold, as well as the feeling of wind on one's face or the breath of someone nearby.[154] In addition, movements as simple as stretching one's arms or legs, walking, and swimming all involve both the feel of the body and its parts and the forces (gravity or buoyancy) that affect the ability to move.[155] The villagers of ancient Israel were certainly aware of their surroundings and given their daily physical exertions would be familiar with the aches and pains associated with hard labor. Even the blind, who would be limited in what they could do, would still be able to find their way around by "groping" against walls or by the feel of a path they had long trodden or by the feel of the wind against their face.[156]

On a personal level, affection and care are expressed by the human touch. When Hagar is instructed by YHWH to "lift the boy [Ishmael] up and hold him fast," she provides reassurance to a scared child. When Isaac caresses his wife, Rebekah, he is demonstrating his love for her. Jacob shows his joy and kinship feeling for his cousin Rachael by kissing her in much the same way that Laban kisses Jacob when welcoming him as his nephew to his household.[157]

There are several significant gestures that involve touching. Abraham's servant places his hand "under the thigh of his master" to complete the ritual of oath taking. Jacob indicates his choice of the more favored of Joseph's twin sons by crossing his arms and placing his right hand on Ephraim's head to give him the blessing that ordinarily would have gone to Manasseh, the firstborn. A person in mourning often tore their clothing to indicate their loss.[158]

The sense of touch also encompasses the sensations that affect the skin and the body. The heat of the day, so well known to these villagers toiling in the fields, is expressed as a unit of time,[159] a general characteristic of "those who work in the heat of the day,"[160] and one of many afflictions that they must bear.[161] Cold temperatures and winds were other sensations with which they had to contend. However, a cold drink could help revive the weary.[162]

During their daily tasks, women could tell when a cooking pot and its contents had been heated by the feel of its surface. They could also feel and see when the grain they were grinding in their mortars was of the proper consistency. Gleaners would stretch out their hands to pluck the remaining kernels of grain in the fields,[163] and it is likely that the plowman would strike the flank of the ox pulling his plow. Concern for animals was built into the law, allowing the ox to take a portion of the grain it was treading. The beast came to know its master because of the care shown to it as well as his voice and touch.[164]

Pain is also an extension of the sense of touch. Sometimes pain was the result of an imposed ritual surgery like circumcision.[165] The movement of a fetus in the womb or the pangs of childbirth would be both welcome and unwelcome experiences for women.[166] At other times, pain was based on the festering of a wound or an unrelenting aching in the bones. The constant irritation of an itch or boil also stole energy that was desperately needed to complete the day's work. Sensing pain is, of course, a protective reaction to prevent harm, but it is also part of the learning process, as was the case with all the sensory impressions experienced by the ancient villagers.[167]

Taste

Perhaps the most significant characteristic of the diet of these ancient villagers was its lack of variation. Despite the variety of imported spices that would eventually become common for the elite population in the cities, the villages depended on local sources for salt and native herbs like sage, thyme, garlic, onion, and fenugreek. The more exotic spices like cinnamon and saffron were indigenous to Southeast Asia and were transported to the Middle East over a very long trade route, making them quite expensive.[168] Hops, used as a preservative against bacterial growth in beer, were not available to ancient brewers and that affected the taste of beer, creating a very different flavor from that in modern European beers.[169]

Traditional cultures like those in the ancient Israelite villages tended to be conservative and slow to change. As a result, the way food was prepared and served could remain unchanged for generations unless they were faced with major environmental or cultural changes. Archaeological evidence in the form of carbonized plant remains, the assemblage of animal bones, and the lipid residues of food that are biochemically identifiable on serving dishes are helpful indicators of the local diet.[170] Examination of human skeletal remains also can point to nutritional deficiencies and body defects.[171] Added to this data are references to a relatively bland diet deficient in protein except for milk products. Meals seldom included meat except on special occasions.[172] Thus, the range of tastes beyond their "daily bread" only varied according to the seasonal availability of fruits (figs, grapes, and pomegranates), nuts (almonds, pistachios, walnuts, and acorns), and vegetables (lentils, chickpeas, peas, beans, and bitter vetch).

References to the various tastes associated with the food that was available to these villagers extend from those that were considered savory to those judged to be sour or bitter. Plants with a bitter taste included lettuce, dandelion, and chicory. To provide a contrast, "sour wine" or vinegar was used as a dip for their whole-grain bread.[173]

Additives such as mint, cumin, dill, or grown coriander seeds could spice up bread or an otherwise bland dish of stew.[174] A welcome sweetness came from honey, and it could serve as a stimulus for the energy-starved soldier, like Jonathan, whose eyes are brightened by the taste of honey. Apparently, based on the comparison with the taste of manna, wafers made with honey or "cakes baked with oil" were part of standard fare.[175] Figs, among the prized "summer fruit," took eighty to one hundred days to ripen. The fruit or its syrup added sugar to the diet whether eaten fresh or baked into fig cakes and served as a welcome change from the blandness of their daily diet.[176] Few condiments are mentioned in the biblical text, but Job does indicate that a "tasteless" meal can be improved with salt.[177] And the memory of a wider variety of food choices and tastes is encapsulated in the nostalgia expressed in the wilderness for Egypt's cucumbers, leeks, melons, onions, and garlic.[178]

A range of senses was employed by a person gathering medicinal as well as culinary herbs. Taste, smell, and touch could discriminate among a wealth of sensations and provide clues to the full range of sensory worlds.[179] Seeking out valuable plants would be among the practical skills passed on orally from parent to child. Spotting them growing may be based on previously locating the plant in a particular place near the village or in the grazing areas. Their color and shape would help identify specific species. The feel of the leaves and the taste indicate their identity and possible uses.[180] Of course, mistakes could be made in gathering plants for a stew, but an acute palate could detect when something harmful had been added, as in the case of Elisha's companions.[181]

Water was not always sweet to the taste or drinkable. After lying in the cisterns for months, water became stale and filled with fungi and bacteria. Pools of water during the evaporation process could become suffused with salt or other minerals in the soil, making it briny and unfit to drink. This phenomenon was common enough that both Moses at Marah and Elisha at Jericho ('Ain es-Sultan) have to take measures to "heal" the "bitter" water at the sites.[182] In Elisha's case, he casts salt into the water to make it potable.

Final Thoughts

The villagers experienced their world through their senses. They used these sensations to determine adjustments in their work and to take advantage of opportunities like the harvest and learned to pass information about sensory impressions on to the next generation. Since theirs was a small world, basically defined by the hills they occupied, the range of sensations would primarily be limited to their work in the fields and with their animals, their family and friends, and their responses to joyous and sad events. In the next chapter, which deals with cities in ancient Israel, that range of sensations will be broader but will still retain a memory of life in the village. That is made clear by the allusions to farming, herding, and harvesting that fill the prophetic materials.

2

Urban Life and the Senses
Abundance and Social Complexity

THE SENSORY EXPERIENCES of ancient city dwellers encompassed a wider and different world than that of the village and its environs. The smaller villages had a greater intimacy than was possible in cities with populations between two and ten times the number of people. The increased exposure to non-native products, persons, fashions, and dialects contributed to the creation of an urban perspective.[1] While the human senses remained the same, the range of sensory phenomena made this an entirely different culture. In exploring the sensory characteristics peculiar to the city, it is necessary to start with some introductory material to set the stage and then reflect on each of the senses in turn. Readers are encouraged to examine the additional examples and information contained in the endnotes.

Setting the Stage

Size did matter. While cities varied in size and could even be synonyms for tribal regions, their individual influence would also have varied based on their population size.[2] The usual measure of population density in the Iron II period (ca. 1000–700 BCE) was 250–500 persons per hectare (= 2.47 acres) within a fortified city. The reasons for locating a city in a particular place were like those of a village, but it was the swelling of a city's population that put a strain on the continued suitability of the site. For growth to occur, the natural resources must have included an adequate and reliable water source that could meet the growing needs of the settlement. In addition, these ancient cities needed nearby arable farmland to supply the needs of between five hundred and three thousand persons as well as enough nearby grazing areas for herds of animals. Proximity to a trade route was also important, since the economic life of the city would depend on commercial activity.

The sight of a fortress atop a hill that was wedded to its rising slopes would provide a psychological advantage to its defenders and a deterrent to raiders.[3] As these settlements continued to grow, the cities would expand down the hill and place a greater reliance on produce from nearby villages. For example, Jerusalem in the early Roman period probably had a population of around seventy-five thousand persons. The only way they could sustain such a large number was to draw on the resources of the surrounding area through either trade or taxation.[4]

The methods for determining the population size and occupation density in antiquity are based on the extent of the settled area covered by the site, estimates of family size (usually a multigenerational group), the square footage of housing within the walls of the city, and the floor area ratio of the buildings, indicating actual living space. For instance, the tenth-century Iron I city of Hazor, which was built upon the remains of the destroyed Late Bronze city, only covered a small fraction of the upper city on the Tell. However, the ninth-century site encompassed much of the upper city, indicating a much larger population and an expansion of both domestic and administrative construction.[5] Flotation methods employed within these living spaces provide indicators of the basic diet, the types of crops grown, how productive harvests were during a given period, and other indicators of domestic life (seeds, charcoal, bones, eggshells, beads, and microchips of flint).[6]

The growth and variable size of a city over time, therefore, require a flexible understanding of the sensory impact associated with the relatively larger number of inhabitants at any given time. Naturally, there would be a range of urban experiences from smaller cities like Mizpah (Tell en-Nasbeh), with a population estimate of about nine hundred inhabitants in the Iron II period (1000–700 BCE), to major population centers like Jerusalem, Samaria, or Megiddo.[7] During certain time periods, some sites were destroyed and abandoned, and others, like Megiddo in the ninth century BCE, were transformed from city sites into fortified centers with massive defenses and stable areas to help protect a region or a major trade route.[8] The larger the city, the more interaction, thus magnifying the range of sensory impressions.

A larger population that was not entirely devoted to agricultural and pastoral pursuits allowed for greater specialization of tasks, including administrative, manufacturing, and commercial functions. Instead of having to divide activities between the field and the home, skilled individuals would be able to spend the bulk of their time in their homes and workshops creating pottery, baking bread, processing products (olive oil or wine, for example) or preparing them for market day, working as artists or masons, or creating a variety of items for sale.[9] To meet the religious needs of the people, there would be a professional priestly community in charge of ritual and sacrifice.[10] In addition, a guild of scribes and other bureaucrats would be given the tasks of recording events and transactions, keeping track of stockpiles of grain and other necessities, and collecting taxes.[11]

Another distinctive aspect of urban life was the construction of monumental architecture. In fact, the idea that a city required large public buildings, a major temple, and palatial housing for high officials and the king was a common expectation throughout the ancient Near East. The massive stone structures built with carved ashlar blocks and decorated with rich furnishings were testaments to power and visual forms of propaganda, designed to give visitors and the representatives of foreign nations a sense of the majesty and authority attached to the place.[12] The maxim for these public displays was "The more awe inspiring, the better."

As noted later in the sections on sight and smell, a larger population living within the walls of a city in a more densely housed setting would tend to overwhelm sanitation facilities, creating a distinct aroma and a major health risk. Even in the Roman period, when water channels helped flush away some of the waste, the streets would be fouled with excrement and, by modern standards, less agreeable debris.[13] Public health was not as much of a concern as it is today, and medical treatment was less sophisticated. Thus, a modern visitor to an ancient city would be in danger of infection and certainly shocked by how incredibly filthy it seemed.

The feelings of fellowship in the close, kin-based society of a village may not have been as strong in the city context. As a result, it is common to find complaints by the prophets about violations of social justice, since the distribution of wealth and power would be more uneven in the urban setting.[14] The ideal of a homogenous, egalitarian community living under a common covenant with their divine patron and one another was just that—an ideal.

The inhabitants of a city were identified by kinship ties or a more general designation as the "people of YHWH," and they composed most of the community. They would be able to easily identify resident aliens as "outsider" groups (*gērîm*), who did not share common kinship or cultural ties. The very presence of these "outsiders" in the city would have been based on their contributions to the economy and social life of the city. For instance, Abraham's nephew Lot lives for a time in Sodom and achieves sufficient status to have a place where he can sit in the gate area, presumably transacting business.[15] In addition, transient visitors—including merchants from other areas of the Near East, like those of Tyre—would stand out based on their foreign garb, language, and social practices.[16]

Within a city's walls, the various zones would be cordoned off into industrial districts, temple complexes, administrative centers, and private businesses occupying distinctive spaces. The smells associated with a closely packed and quite limited living space would consist of a mixture of human and animal scents, cooking odors, smoke from cooking and manufacturing fires, incense, perfumes, and the muck in the streets. On most days, the people would hear the familiar sounds of neighbors talking, the marching feet of soldiers making their rounds through the city, the clash of a hammer on metal in a blacksmith's shop, and the cries of merchants trying to attract customers. The taste of freshly baked bread or wine brought into the city from surrounding villages would be mingled with the grit produced when mud bricks were repaired, a stonemason shaped a block of stone, or a woodworker caused sawdust to fill the air. And in this busy community, there would be constant contact with a variety of surfaces (paved and unpaved), animals, commodities in the marketplace or at stalls in the city gate area, and other people packed together in the limited space inside the walls. All this activity defines a city, and with this as an introduction to the setting of an ancient city, it is now time to turn to the individual sensory experiences as if the reader were visiting such a city.

Sight

What could an inhabitant of or a visitor to an ancient Israelite city expect to see? Typically, like their fellows in the village, those with normal vision could distinguish color, texture, and shape and identify the distinctive qualities of objects and persons. Sight would be more limited at night. They could only rely on sputtering oil lamps to provide some illumination in their homes, in public buildings, and in the streets. Simply walking around the streets of the city, there would be familiar sights. However, they would be much more varied than in a village setting. For one thing, the sheer number of persons walking about the city on missions of their own was a testament to a busy place. Even areas that provided shade could be seen and appreciated, especially by older men and women sitting in doorways who were visiting or just staying out of the scorching heat of the midday sun.[17]

The size and construction of the city walls, battlements, and gate areas spoke to its defenses and perhaps added to a comfort level that would not be available in the unwalled villages. In some cases, cities had casemate or hollow walls, which allowed for additional living space—like Rahab's dwelling that is said to be "within the wall" of Jericho.[18] These spaces also served as warehouses to store commodities and items essential to trade and to the defense of the city during a siege.[19] There is just something about massive city walls that creates an intimidation factor for potential attackers and a source of civic pride.[20]

People would be encountered everywhere within the city. Private dwellings separated by narrow, winding lanes would be clustered together in housing complexes without space for large private gardens or to house their animals. Unlike the major thoroughfares of the city, passage through these streets required careful attention to avoid obstacles and to keep from scraping against a wall. Given the need to take advantage of every inch of space, roofs and central courtyards of private homes were used for a variety of purposes. In Jericho, Rahab's drying stalks of flax on her roof serve as an excellent place to hide the Israelite spies.[21] Roofs, with the addition of walls and a few amenities, could also be used for temporarily housing guests. That is the case when the rich Shunammite woman supplies the prophet Elisha with a guest room on her roof.[22]

Excavations have demonstrated that changes occurred based on political shifts, invasions, disease, or famine.[23] It would therefore be shortsighted to assume that any Israelite city, once established, would remain the same throughout its history. Its basic outlines would change, and thus the sights would vary from one period to another. In periods of relative peace and environmental stability, the population increased, and that required the city to expand its boundaries to encompass housing areas that had previously been constructed outside the walls. After a particular phase of the city was destroyed, urban planning would basically reinvent the scope and location of housing and public buildings to fit a new situation. In addition, since this region is subject to earthquakes, reconstruction and abandonment of portions of a settlement are evident to excavators.[24] To provide a baseline, however, it was common in the initial stages of an Iron Age city for richly designed houses and public structures, including temples and palaces, to be constructed in the center of a site or near the gate, while the poorer sections were pushed to the periphery and out of the sight of foreign visitors.[25]

With the wealthy and more influential citizens gravitating to the most advantageous areas, the poor and those engaged in commercial or manufacturing pursuits were pushed into sections of the city with increased noise, unpleasant smells, or poorly constructed dwellings. Even if distinctive areas in the city shifted over time in their desirability based on an expansion of the urban site or a rebuilding phase, it seems logical to assume that those with wealth and influence would always commandeer space to their liking even if it had at one time been the site of a poorer sector of the city. In a similar fashion, when the wealthy shifted their residences and major buildings, the poor in turn would be shifted into the newly abandoned or run-down spaces.[26]

Suburbs would house families who did not have the resources or influence necessary to claim a space within the city proper. When the city was threatened, however, these people would have flocked inside the walls, swelling the population and threatening the city's food and water resources.[27] There would also have been contact with the people of nearby villages, the "daughters" that existed within proximity to the larger urban centers, supplying them with grain, oil, wine, and various other goods that could not be produced in sufficient quantity within the city.[28] For example, the fuller could be seen making daily trips to a major water source to engage in the processing of wool.[29]

The mix of people who lived in the cities of ancient Israel would compose a greater diversity, including a fair number of resident aliens engaged in commerce or, in the case of Jerusalem and other major cities, diplomatic activities for foreign states.[30] Men of substance, like Abraham's nephew Lot, would station themselves in the precincts of the city gate to transact business or to serve as councilors in legal disputes or commercial transactions.[31] The local elders, who represented households or even clans, were called to sit in the gate to hear legal cases until they were superseded by the judicial organization created by the monarchy.[32] A man with a well-ordered household was "known in the gates." Onlookers would nod their heads, recognizing this sight as evidence of a prosperous city.

In addition to the able-bodied and well-to-do, there would be a variety of persons present with disabilities or illnesses or who were identified as older by their gray hair and slower gait.[33] To some extent, that would be expected in any general population, but it also is an indicator that those with temporary or chronic diseases would be both a concern for a household and a common sight.[34] Of course, some illnesses, classified as "leprosy," did require exclusion from the city. These persons, who were declared to be "unclean" based on priestly evaluation and therefore a danger to the general populace, lived shadow lives, but they were still part of the landscape existing as beggars just outside the gates of the city.[35]

While persons with disabilities are common in all cultures, they were not to be singled out for abuse or disdain except in terms of participation in temple rituals.[36] Legal protections for those with disabilities forbade putting "a stumbling block in front of the blind" and cursed anyone who "[led] the blind astray on the road."[37] Apparently, the temple precinct was a likely place for those who were crippled to be placed and to beg for alms.[38] In essence, these persons, like everyone else, came to be part of the everyday scenery.[39] The assumption in the biblical text is that the "poor, the crippled, the blind and the lame" can be found in the streets of any city.[40]

Of course, disabilities were not restricted to any one class of persons. King Saul's grandson Mephibosheth is said to be "crippled in both feet," and Proverbs speaks of "a lame man's legs that hang limp," probably a common sight.[41] In fact, Israelite society appears to have valued those who gave special care to the needs of those with disabilities. In his recital of his virtues, Job claims that he "was eyes to the blind and feet to the lame."[42]

Social interaction of any kind produced its own set of visual images. Weddings and other social gatherings created festive scenes.[43] In the midst of celebrations, faces and body gestures could become quite expressive. Inflamed emotions and the effects of overindulgence showed on a person's face and body and even in an increased respiration rate.[44] Angry words could be accompanied by "flashing eyes" and a heart that became "hot" and carried a person to extremes.[45] Sorrow, accompanied by tears, reddened the face and left deep shadows under the eyes.[46] It was possible to identify those who habitually drank too much wine by their needless bruises, bloodshot eyes, and staggering gait.[47] No matter their social station (including priests), they also marked their drunken state by their unsteady movements and by covering the tables where they drank with their vomit.[48]

The clothing of city dwellers, while similar in cut and fabric to that worn in the village culture, reflected greater availability of items, styles, and colors and the higher standard of living, at least among the elite.[49] For example, the mantle that draped over the body and was fashioned with a belt or pins would be common to both locales. While a belt was a common accessory, a finer quality was available and prized.[50] However, an elaborately embroidered hem like that of a priest or king marked a person of a higher station.[51] One indication of the richer garments that could be found appears in Sisera's mother's expectation that when he returns from his campaign against the Israelites, he will bring her "highly embroidered garments" to wear around her neck.[52] The list of trade goods that passed through the markets of Phoenician Tyre included clothes with blue and embroidered work.[53]

Personal adornment also included an array of jewelry, braided hairstyles, and fine garments.[54] Among the flashing precious stones mentioned in the biblical text are sapphires, pearls, and rubies.[55] Those worn by the wealthy of Jerusalem are chronicled in Isaiah's prophecy of YHWH taking away their "finery."[56] The registry of items, with their accompanying sounds and sights, includes tinkling anklets, headbands, dangling crescents and pendants, jingling bracelets, scarfs and headdresses, amulets, gauzy and linen garments, turbans, and veils. Ezekiel also provides a list of the various forms of rich fabrics and jewelry that adorned the body of a wealthy woman.[57]

When Hosea decries Israel's idolatry, he describes the fine garments and other apparel worn during festival days. By adorning themselves with rings and jewelry, they "went after lovers" (= other gods) and participated in the worship of false gods like Baal.[58] In addition to being objects designed to serve as status symbols and generate personal delight, jewelry also functioned as a form of exchange and as part of the negotiations over a marriage contract between families. For instance, Laban quickly calculates the value of the gifts of silver and gold jewelry presented to Rebekah by Abraham's servant.[59] On their wedding day, both the bride and the groom would display their joy and the wealth of the family decked in garlands and jewels.[60] Particular items such as club-shaped bone pendants may also have been ethnic markers. Such pendants have been discovered in southern Levant contexts from the Iron Age and have been identified by archaeologists as distinctive to Israelite settlements.[61]

Sound

The most basic function of the ear is to notice vibrations in the air that produce a specific frequency, amplitude, and phase that we call sound. The mind then translates what the ear detects and identifies it as familiar, strange, pleasant, or dangerous.[62] In the city context, the most familiar sounds of everyday life would be mixed with a constant hum of background noises. Note, however, that the ancients would not experience the sounds of sirens or trucks and automobiles that distinguish modern cities. Ancient or modern, however, the mind is constantly filtering out these sounds for a person to concentrate on those words or noises of immediate importance or relevance. For a mother, that might be the cry of her baby or the sound of a meal cooking, and for a soldier on duty on the city wall, it could be the cry of another sentry who had just spotted the approach of a messenger or an enemy. That occurs when the sentinel tells David about the approach of two runners and identifies one, Ahimaaz son of Zadok, by the way he runs.[63]

When a sound cuts through the normal background noise, such as the cry of someone being attacked or robbed, the expectation is that the people will go to investigate and help the victim. That helps explain the legal situation in the case of the betrothed young woman who is raped within the city walls. She is condemned along with her attacker on the assumption that she acquiesced to his advances because she did not cry out for help.[64]

What, then, would be the most distinctive sounds in the ancient urban setting? With a larger population than a village, the buzz of voices would be a constant.[65] The tread of sandaled feet and even the clicking of a man's staff as he walked or hobbled, depending on his age, would become part of the aural character of any town.[66] It was expected that children would be playing in the streets when not required to assist with chores in the home, and their rambunctious cries, shrieks, and laughter would reflect their joy.[67] Excavators have found clay objects (figurines of horses and riders and model chariots) that may have been children's toys but may also have been used for cultic purposes. However, there are references to jumping rope, running races, playing hide-and-seek, and engaging in wrestling matches in Mesopotamian texts, and these might well have fit the ancient Israelite context and have added to the swell of sound.[68]

The everyday commercial activity would include the sounds of persons haggling over merchandise or hawking their products and calling on customers to come view their wares.[69] Ben Sira cautions the customer to beware in dealing with merchants who seek profit and whose sales patter may shade the truth to increase their gain. At the same time, he notes that no one should be judged prior to their speaking, since the measure of a merchant's honesty is to be determined by his words.[70] Too easily the unwary can be tempted by persuasive speech to purchase unnecessary items or engage in unwise acts.[71]

Daily, the groaning of laden wagons and the creak of leather harnesses on donkeys could be heard as they brought oil into the city for lamps and cooking. Adding to the sounds of commerce would be the use of a whip on a horse pulling a wagon, the jangling of a bridle on a donkey, and possibly the application of a rod on a foolish worker.[72] Each would produce a distinctive sound. Stables housing horses would resound with their movement about in the stalls or their neighing for a filly in heat.[73] The stalls of the city's market would contain grain, fruits, and wine from surrounding farms. Dried fish transported from the coast and the Sea of Galilee also would have been available for sale amid the bustle in the market square.[74] Beggars, crying out for alms in the marketplace or near the temple, intentionally stationed themselves in these high-traffic areas and added their pleas to the general mix of sounds.[75] References to children begging for bread are reminders that hard times did strike the cities and their inhabitants.[76]

Within the chambers of power in the palace, the "smooth" words of political advisers could be heard vying for the attention and favor of a king or governor.[77] The contest for influence and authority within David's royal court is showcased in the conflicting advice given to Absalom by Ahithophel and Hushai after the young man has driven David from Jerusalem. It centers on the position of striking while the iron is hot in disposing of David as a threat (Ahithophel) and the more cautious position of taking the time to consolidate power before moving against David's forces (Hushai).[78] In this encounter, all that really matters is whether one voice is heard and accepted over another. The acceptance of the truth or probability of one position or the other hinges entirely on the naivete of the inexperienced Absalom, the natural tendency to delay, and the ability of the adviser to persuade.[79]

Back in the city and away from the power brokers, there would also be the repetitive sounds created by workmen engaged in their daily labors. Potters could be heard working clay on their wheels.[80] Masons and carpenters would make chiseling and sawing noises as they were kept busy repairing houses and shaping stones for the temples and the city walls when they needed repairs.[81] In some cities like Tel Dan, evidence of metalworking and fabrication has been found. These remains suggest the sounds of a bubbling crucible, the crackling of the coals in a furnace, or the hammering of metal objects into shape that would also become part of the voice of the city.[82] And perhaps just as loud would be the moans and cries rising from the houses of those suffering the pangs of childbirth or the insufferable pains of illness or injury.[83]

Facilitating the ability to hear sounds clearly are the acoustic qualities of any given place. An echo thrown back by the physical shapes of hills and valleys is a natural phenomenon.[84] Taking advantage of a natural amphitheater, Moses stations himself on the slopes of Mount Sinai when speaking to the assembled Israelites. Jesus delivers the Sermon on the Mount utilizing an elevated site that allows his voice to be projected down to the crowd and amplified by the terrain.[85] The stone backdrop of the palace at Jezreel plus the height of the window from which Jezebel confronts the insurgent general Jehu when he enters the city provides sufficient amplification for both her taunting words and his defiant response.[86]

Similarly, the architectural design, construction materials, and placement of some buildings or public facilities may be associated with anticipated public gatherings and the need to be heard by priests, prophets, and kings.[87] That helps explain why there are so many scenes in which a public address is delivered in the city gate, before a temple, or in a public square.[88] Given these circumstances, it makes sense for government spokespersons and prophets to position themselves in places where the largest number of people can hear their voices. In particular, the gate of a city was designed to function as both a defensive structure to repel enemy attacks and a focal point for public events.[89] The city gate often witnessed the tramping of soldiers as they assembled before their leader and then went forth to battle.[90]

City gates also served as public places to hear legal disputes that involved the giving of testimony before the city elders and on occasion echoed with the thudding of stones striking persons sentenced to execution for their crimes.[91] It seems likely that the public square associated with the inner gate at Tel Dan also contained an elevated podium where a local official could sit and functioned as a place for announcements of all kinds.[92] Unfortunately, not every word pronounced in these places of assembly was deemed to be the truth or represented justice, for sometimes "truth stumbles in the public square."[93] It is on the ability to discern truth that Ahab and Jehoshaphat sit on their thrones in the city gate of the Israelite capital at Samaria. In this public display of executive authority, these two kings hear the pronouncements of four hundred court prophets and Micaiah, the independent prophet of YHWH. Since the court prophets and Micaiah have competing messages, Ahab eventually is forced to test their words by going into battle against Aram in disguise. His ruse fails, and he is mortally wounded, demonstrating the veracity of Micaiah's prophetic message.[94]

In a similar example of prophetic performance, Jeremiah makes use of the public nature and acoustic qualities of the city gate when he processes through the streets to Jerusalem's Potsherd Gate, which overlooks the Hinnom Valley. He is accompanied here by a crowd curious to see what he will say or do. His subsequent condemnation of the city and enactment of an execration ritual conclude when he smashes a pot that he had been carrying during his procession. Obviously, his dramatic gesture would not have been very effective if only the people directly around him could hear his words.[95] It is likely that the natural amphitheater created by the Hinnom Valley contributes to funneling Jeremiah's words to the crowd assembled by the gate.

Although it did not happen every day, street theater, major announcements from the battlefield, or political posturing would create both entertainment and excitement among the people of the city. Thus, when a runner enters Shiloh to report the loss of the ark of the covenant to the Philistines, the city goes into an uproar.[96] The cries to come see what is happening would rise to a crescendo as they approached the scene being created for them. That surely is the case years later when David enters Jerusalem with the ark. His mass of soldiers following the procession of the Levites carrying the ark—along with songs accompanied by lyres, harps, tambourines, castanets, and cymbals—would bring out the entire population of the city.[97] David takes advantage of the opportunity, dancing before the ark before installing it in a tent and staging a banquet for the people. Only his wife Michal, the last voice of the house of Saul to be raised against him, offers a sour note to the occasion, but David quickly silences her and revels in the acclaim given him by his subjects.[98]

Interestingly, silence is also a function of the sense of hearing—not just as the opposite of noise but as a choice, a gesture, or a way that demonstrates wisdom or maturity rather than resorting to voiced interaction.[99] An example of remaining silent in the face of a tragedy is Aaron's stoic reaction to the death of his sons.[100] This case demonstrates the maxim that movement is one function of sound, but silence, while producing no audible sound, still resounds as a means of communication.[101] It is therefore possible to interpret stillness or silence as one point on the spectrum of sound and human activity. It does not mean that sound is not possible when someone is immobile, but instead, audible sound is at rest or in a state of expectedness—perhaps like Elijah's perception of YHWH's presence in the silence at Mount Horeb.[102] Prophetic speeches that contain a "world-turned-upside-down" theme also include unnatural silence, like dogs (= city sentinels) that do not bark but instead lie asleep dreaming of remaining watchful.[103] Thus, in an examination of the sense of hearing, it is necessary to explore the full spectrum of possible sounds, from silence to clamor, and the reactions to them.

Smell

Aroma is an indicator of human activity and health and a memory trigger for everyone with a functioning sense of smell. It was possible for a person to walk from one section of an ancient city to another and identify exactly where they were by sight and smell and be able to tell when a new district had been entered. So, with that in mind, it can be said that anyone walking through the streets of a city in ancient Israel would experience a wide range of aromas.[104] There is some question about how noticeable these smells would have been to the inhabitants, although there would be some odors associated with specific professions or social classes that would confirm one's identity.[105] Scent has been described as the "mute sense." When entering a familiar or known place, people would expect certain aromas to be habitually present and therefore just part of the general atmosphere of that space.[106] For instance, in commercial and manufacturing districts, the smell of sweat emanating from the bodies of those working in the heat of the day would be more overpowering than in sections where the inhabitants were more sedentary and perhaps better perfumed.[107] A sign of the temperatures and the different expectations for classes of people can be found in the injunction that Levitical priests should only wear linen garments and avoid "anything that causes sweat."[108]

The everyday scents of the city would include the smells of the press of people, rotting fruits and vegetables, and unpaved streets, with their accumulation of garbage.[109] All these odors mingled with the scent emanating from the usual mire that consisted of human and animal waste and any other debris cast aside by the residents.[110] The pungent smell of urine would whiff up from walls or side streets, where opportunistic males and dogs relieved themselves.[111] The common fog of sweat from infrequently washed bodies would permeate the air everywhere one went. Animal pins associated with the temple district or slaughterhouses added the aroma of frightened livestock with all these other wastes. Adding to the clamor and crowding on festival days, large numbers of animals would have been herded into the city to be slaughtered as part of the festivities.[112]

Private homes could be identified by the smell of cooking fires and small incense altars. Many of these domestic hearths and ovens preparing bread and other dietary items had to rely on animal dung collected from the street as a supplement to charcoal, since it burned cleanly and left little residue.[113] Offensive odors from these ovens would attract insects and produce gases and vapors that were added to other hygienic problems. Some readily available plants with aromatic qualities, such as laudanum and various gums and resins, could be used even by the poor to dispel the worst of these odors.[114] While it is uncertain if the small incense altars found in domestic contexts were used for cultic or noncultic purposes, the prevalence of these objects, some of them highly decorated, indicates they were common fixtures in the homes of the wealthy and may have assisted with masking domestic smells.[115] The citrusy smell of cedar oil, imported from Phoenicia, wafted up from some homes, since it was used as both an insect repellent and a means of controlling strong odors.[116]

The smell of the roasting flesh from animal sacrifices rose from the altar within the temple complex, adding to the city's signature perfume.[117] While these offerings are said to create a "pleasing aroma," that is more likely to be an assurance that all the proper rituals had been performed and thus the sacrifice would be pleasing and acceptable to YHWH.[118] The Jerusalem temple area would have been suffused with the smell of a distinctive, restricted blend of incense that made it clear that persons were entering the vicinity of the temple complex. The exactitude of its mixture of ingredients—including special spices, frankincense, and other ingredients—and the restrictions placed on nonsacred use created a sensory boundary within the city for official religious practice. By association, the scent of this blend of aromas would characterize the sacred precinct and the activities of the priests.[119]

In the industrial districts both inside and outside the walls of the city, the odors associated with various trades would add a mixed blend to the air and may well have sparked a coughing fit or encouraged people to move along more quickly.[120] Among these processes would be tanning, laundering clothing, the shaping and firing of pottery, and the burning charcoal furnaces of metalworkers and jewelers. Tanners, with their soaking vats of urine or briny water for removing the hair from animal skins, were forced to conduct their noisome business on the outskirts of inhabited areas or outside the walls of the city.[121] While dyers produced less noxious vapors in their work with clothes, they often were forced to locate in areas that were less congested because of the potential for fire igniting the chemical baths in which cloth was permeated with the dyes.[122]

Joining the general background smells of the city would be the fumes produced by various forms of manufacturing and the accumulated smell of many people living in proximity. A variation on the standard index of fragrances would be found in cities on the Mediterranean coast or near a river, where the smell of rotting fish and garbage would emanate from the waters.[123] In both types of cities, there would be the smells of the domestic animals, especially donkeys and asses, that also occupied space within the city walls and worked at tasks like powering a grinding stone or transporting goods or people. The odor rising from their urine, dung, and sweat may have simply been an acceptable or unavoidable addition to the background smells of the city.

In the city context, the volume of human waste would be too great to be disposed of according to the injunction in Deuteronomy to take it outside "the camp" and bury it.[124] As a result, until the Roman period, when running water was funneled beneath public baths, latrines, or ditches located outside the immediate environs of houses, chamber pots were dumped into the street each morning, but that added to the general miasma of smells.[125] Carved stone toilet seats have been discovered in urban settings where they sat above cesspits whose contents could be covered with lime.[126] However, these probably belonged to wealthy households and would not be indicative of most city dwellers.

Less pungent aromas were brought into the city markets each day on the wagons carrying grain, fruits, and salted or dried fish.[127] No urban center could produce all the food needed, so by necessity, they had to rely on produce brought in daily by local farmers from surrounding villages and merchants traveling the region. Naturally, this redistribution of food from local producers to urban inhabitants would not be evenly balanced. Royal courts and members of the elite classes in the cities would have a more sumptuous table spread with a greater variety of foods.[128] However, even the humblest household in normal times would occasionally take advantage of the availability of these items. As a result, the palaces, temples, and dwellings within the city would produce the appetizing aroma of baking bread and stews, along with the scent of olive oil, beer, and wine coming from private residences or bakeries.[129]

Incense, along with perfume, was burned in many of the houses as a fumigant and on private altars, from which the rising smoke created a channel connecting the household with the divine plane.[130] Of course, temples kept up steady streams of incense throughout the day as offerings to YHWH and perhaps to mask the smell of blood and the burning flesh of animal sacrifices.[131]

Smell is also a social indicator. People in the same community expected other persons to smell the same as they did unless they were engaged in a specialized task like tanning or herding that gave them a distinctive and pervasive odor. In the more cosmopolitan character of the urban setting—with its mixed population of freemen, slaves, citizens, and nonresident aliens like merchants—smell also became a way of identifying different social classes or the stranger.[132] The greater availability of fragrances among the elite also contributed to a social divide and may have contributed to a mental sense of superiority that allowed the wealthy to perpetrate the social injustices that are decried by the prophets.[133]

Aromas, including expensive perfumes, fragrances, and incense, may be deemed to be pleasant in one culture or one segment of a culture but abhorrent to another.[134] As luxury items, perfumes may have been desirable to urban dwellers, but they would generally only be available to the elite who could afford luxury goods.[135] For that reason, they may not have been socially acceptable for general use; rather, they may have been intended to be used only within the confines of one's house or for a special occasion. In that sense, perfumes or perfume boxes were less likely to be associated with dispelling all bad smells and instead considered an enhancement of the body's attractiveness.[136] Some may have received praise for either presenting a pleasant scent from the use of perfumes or evidence of clean or fragrant breath.[137] The promise of a fragrant bed perfumed with myrrh, aloes, and cinnamon may have also made an adulteress's invitation more enticing to the unwary.[138]

Unlike some luxuries such as jewelry or precious stones that had a lasting value from one generation to the next, perfumes as well as scented oils used to anoint the body had a short shelf life.[139] Fragrances were designed for afternoon or evening events and perhaps as a means of attracting a lover or admirer.[140] For a longer-lasting effect, some spices may have been ground up and placed in a sachet to be worn around the neck.[141] The love songs in the Bible also mention the use of incense and various fragrances to perfume clothing, bedding, and bodies. Presumably, these substances were designed to both freshen and mask the odors associated with long usage or sexual activity.

Illness and injuries were the primary causes of new and unwelcome smells. One of the first signs of illness may have been a fever or a change in the body's odor.[142] Gangrenous or festering wounds and lingering ailments such as the bleeding disorder suffered by the woman who touches Jesus's garment to obtain a cure created pervasive and pungent odors.[143] A disease also could result in a change in the scent of a person's breath, and that could lead to others avoiding them or having them seek out a diagnosis from the priests.[144] The lack of personal hygiene contributed to skin diseases, but regular bathing is seldom mentioned except to deal with ritual impurity or as a part of a transformation ritual associated with idolatry.[145] Since few bathed themselves often, it was considered normal and would not have raised eyebrows or led to condemnation.

Touch

Like taste and smell, the sense of touch can be both refined and improved. Even infants can discriminate among various tastes and react with a reddening of the face, blinking eyes, a pursing of the lips, or vigorous sucking when tasting something sweet or agreeable. However, peer group pressure and the availability of some foods often serve as the foundations for what is considered acceptable cuisine.[146] Furthermore, since touch contributes to the basic awareness of the body and the space in which one lives, it can be divided into categories of sensation.[147] Among these are the detection of pressure, pain, pleasure, moistness, dryness, thickness, texture, weight, vibration, smoothness, and temperature.[148] As is the case with the loss of sight when one ages, some tactile sensations are modified or even lost. For instance, in his old age, David "could not keep warm," and his elderly vassal Barzillai decries the loss of his sense of taste.[149]

While the ancients may have not been fully aware of the causes of pain unless a wound, a blemish, or swelling was particularly evident,[150] it is known today that there are distinctive physiological mechanisms in the body's nervous system that can detect and react to these sensations.[151] In addition, the nerve endings in the muscular system provide an awareness of movement, and the vestibular system in the inner ear provides gravitational orientation and a sense of balance.[152] Thus a runner like those sent on a mission to report a victory makes an effort to maintain speed and agility while running, avoiding hazards, and adjusting to the changing terrain. In addition, there is an awareness of the strength needed to continue the race, and that contributes to a style or gait that is recognizable to others and expresses the joy of the race.[153] In a similar way, a sailor acquires "sea legs" when handling the sails and rigging on a ship in all types of weather.[154]

The ability to distinguish the placement of objects through touch is of particular importance to the blind, and the lack of sight can be tied to the darkness actually being "felt."[155] Thus, when Samson is blinded by his Philistine captors, he feels for the pillars of the temple of Dagan, ostensibly to balance himself, but in fact to give himself the necessary grip to pull down these supports and kill his tormentors.[156] The very familiarity with the blind having to grope along a wall to find their way becomes part of a curse against unfaithful Israelites, who in the state of blindness will also be subject to robbery and abuse.[157]

The physical qualities of objects can be examined through touch and are associated with gaining life experiences as well as the acquisition of the skills necessary for one's occupation. Thus, the tailor would learn to distinguish and grade the smoothness of cloth or leather and determine the strength and ornamental quality of the stitching.[158] In a similar way, a woman intending to purchase material for a garment would also feel its texture and examine it carefully for flaws.[159] A warrior realized through trial and error the best grip on a weapon,[160] a craftsman learned how to hold a mallet or a saw,[161] and women determined the best grip on their grinding stone to process grain into flour or the correct consistency of dough after it had been kneaded.[162] Experiencing the changes in weather and the touch of a dry, hot wind on the skin became a life lesson and one that thereafter was spoken as an aphorism: "When the south wind blows, you say 'It is going to be hot.'"[163]

While touch is a distinct sense, it very often is paired with other senses to enhance perception. For instance, if a garment was fitted too tightly in the hot climate of the Near East, it could chafe the body, and its bacteria-laden fabric could lead to infection.[164] The robe also would be more subject to attracting stains or becoming soiled. Another example of combining the senses occurs when one extends the hand to feel the heat of a flame and then sees what happens to a strand of fiber when it is touched by the fire.[165] In like manner, the practice of pouring oil on the heads of participants in a banquet or other gathering produced a cooling sensation as the oil soothed the scalp, and all those present would be able to see the calming or joyous facial expressions of the participants.[166]

Tactile gestures involve several of the senses. Thus, when Zipporah circumcises her son and then touches the bloody foreskin to Moses's feet and cries out that he is a "bridegroom of blood" to her, she foreshadows the blood painted on the doorposts in Egypt during the tenth plague.[167] And sometimes an aggressive act like rape becomes the basis for a prophetic interpretation or political transformation. Thus, Amnon's grasping and raping of his sister Tamar set off a series of political events that leads to his death at the hands of his vengeful half-brother Absalom.[168] A similar case occurs when Saul reaches out to stop Samuel after the prophet tells him that YHWH has rejected him as king. The prophet's robe tears, and Samuel uses the sound of the tearing to verbally expand on his condemnation of Saul and then predicts another man will become king.[169] Ahijah uses another version of this tactile gesture by tearing a new cloak and giving ten pieces to Jeroboam while declaring that he will become king of the ten northern tribes of Israel, thereby initiating the division of the kingdoms.[170]

Taste

Taste provided a savor to everyday urban life, especially in narratives that describe banquets and the flavor and aroma of food. The lavishness of a banquet was an expression of the wealth and generosity of the host. Thus, Ahasuerus displays his power and wealth by hosting multiday banquets in which wine is drunk from golden flagons "without restraint."[171] But an insensibility (= a heart made merry with wine) brought on by such indulgence can provide an opportunity for mischief or revenge. Absalom takes advantage of a banquet to have his men kill his half brother, Amnon.[172]

Aroma is coupled here with taste, since the enjoyment of a meal is often enhanced by its delectable smell. In fact, the palate can be trained to differentiate the quality and nuances of the taste and texture of food and drink.[173] It does require practice identifying specific smells and colors and distinguishing basic tastes like salty, sweet, bitter, and sour and their balance in prepared cuisine. The gustatory pleasure can be magnified by increased testing and knowledge of each item in the available diet.[174] The ability to appreciate specific foods is coupled with the degree to which a person is hungry at the time. Food just tastes better when someone is hungry and loses some of its flavor and attraction once satiety is reached.[175] Wisdom literature uses this idea, noting that the person whose appetite has been sated will even decline honey, while those who are ravenous find "even the bitter is sweet."[176]

One example that immediately presents itself is the taste and fragrance of wine. Since this is a product that, like olive oil, was intimately tied to the economy of ancient Israel, it is not surprising to find many references to vineyards, harvesting grapes and processing them in the winepress, and serving wine as a beverage of choice during many occasions. Demonstrating the different characteristics and savor of wine, the steward in the story of the wedding of Cana can discern the better quality of the wine that Jesus creates.[177] The juice from grapes ferments on its own due to the presence of yeast organisms that break down the sugars present in the fruit and transform them into alcohol and carbon dioxide.[178] Careful attention to the process produces palatable results.

Common practice, especially in the households of the poor, was to water down the wine for everyday use to make it go further and to lessen its alcoholic effects. Knowing how it can affect the intellect, Wisdom literature declaims that "mixed" wine would allow the participants to keep their faculties together during the banquet and be more attentive to instruction.[179] Still, wine is said to create a "merry heart" as it flows freely at a banquet.[180] Real appreciation of a fine wine, however, is found in its delectable character, worthy of comparison to the taste of a lover's kisses that are like "the best wine that goes down smoothly, gliding over lips and teeth."[181] The author of 2 Maccabees, in his epilogue to readers, proclaims that a well-styled story is like wine mixed with water that is sweet and delicious.[182] Despite how much it may be treasured, a warning about wine's attraction is also tied to the overindulgence of the drunkard, who wastes time lingering over his cup and is cautioned not to look too longingly at red wine even if it "sparkles in the cup and goes down smoothly." The warning continues with the admonition that an addiction to wine is like the "bite of a serpent" and is the basis for hallucinations, a loss of balance, and an insensibility to normal sensations like pain.[183]

Seasonings could enhance the taste of a meal, but that depended for the most part on the availability of salt and plants indigenous to Syro-Palestine. There are mentions of imported condiments such as saffron and cinnamon, but their cost would have limited them to the wealthy elites.[184] While natural deposits of salt were available from the Dead Sea area and sea salt was extracted along the Mediterranean coast, ready transport to other parts of the region was probably not common until the establishment of the monarchy and the rise of more cities. Still, its desirability as an enhancement to a meal is attested in Job, who notes that tasteless food requires salt to be appetizing.[185]

A selection of plants commonly found in ancient Israel—like lettuce, black cumin, chicory, and dandelion—provided additional flavor to food or to salads, and some may have been the basis for the "bitter herbs" in the Passover meal. Brown coriander seed, planted along the fringes of barley fields, may have been added to bread and is a common addition to meat and rice dishes in the modern Middle East.[186] However, it is best to keep in mind that a dish prepared today, with access to the full range of spices and in stainless steel cookware, likely would not taste the same as that prepared in a clay cooking pot in ancient Israel.[187]

In a world in which there was no chocolate, the ancient Israelites had to resort to what nature provided. Thus, in the biblical text, honey in the comb is prized as a delight to the tongue and serves as the basis for numerous metaphors reflecting the pleasure that results from gaining wisdom or a greater understanding of the commandments of YHWH.[188] As an alternative to beer, which had a bitter taste, a sweet wine or liquor was fermented from pomegranates.[189] Bunches of raisins and cakes made from figs also provided sweet tastes, especially between harvest seasons, and would have been popular commodities in the city market.[190]

As a counterpoint to sweetness, sourness is also mentioned in the biblical text. In some cases, it can be attributed to sour grapes, perhaps caused by unfavorable environmental conditions in a particular season or due to the mishandling of the fruit during the harvest, which causes decaying organisms to become imbalanced and spoil the wine during fermentation. Grapes that are not yet ripe also create a sour taste so keen that it serves as a metaphor in both Jeremiah and Ezekiel, who remark on how sour grapes cause the lips to pucker, which, by extension, is even felt by anyone who sees them eaten.[191] The taste is like vinegar and would bring a grimace of irritation to the face of anyone who bit into the grapes.[192] Vinegar does have its purposes as a dip that provides a bite to the taste of bread as well as a medicinal rub.[193] Other than those tied to the bile associated with reflux problems, references to gall, with its bitter taste,[194] probably are based on poison hemlock, whose seeds can be mistaken for cumin or celery seed.[195] Since gall is a painkiller that attacks the nervous system, that may explain why it is offered to Jesus during the crucifixion.[196]

Final Thoughts

Some aspects of urban life have been intentionally abridged in this chapter. More extensive examinations of the effects of warfare, international affairs, legal statements, and religious practice will appear in subsequent chapters of this volume. Each of these topics deserves closer attention than can be provided in a general survey focused on a single setting.

3

Sensory Aspects of Warfare
*The Taste of Battle and the
Sights and Sounds of Violence*

IT WAS AN unfortunate fact of life for the people of the Near East that military conflict was a very common occurrence. While that was not always a matter of large armies invading another region, even raids like the one on David's small village of Ziklag by a group of Amalekites had a traumatic effect on inhabitants.[1] Thus, for ancient Israel, war was a constant companion, always nearby or just over the horizon. The biblical text and the agricultural calendar tell us that warfare had its seasons (spring in 2 Sam 11:1, after the planting of the crops and when roads were once again passable), but there were always exceptions given a determined opponent. Army commanders and scribes who recorded events to please their employers tended to use rather flamboyant rhetoric. The biblical text's focus generally highlights the exploits of kings and their generals, but sometimes an unusual or unexpected hero is featured.[2]

The strategies of warfare demonstrate that sometimes simple ambushes rather than the sophisticated movement of large groups of troops around a battlefield are to be preferred.[3] The motives that lead to armed conflict—both good and bad—are on display, as are the ambitions of those who use war to rise to power.[4] A wide variety of weapons and war engines are either described in the biblical text or depicted visually on the walls of royal monuments and palaces.[5] And perhaps most poignant are the multifaceted examples of human emotion and sensory reactions to their experiences: courage, fear, and pain, all of which contribute to the mosaic we call war.[6] In those brief periods when hostilities were absent, very few regretted that fact.[7]

By examining warfare's sensory aspects, it will be possible to better understand the impact it had on the people and why the role of YHWH as the Divine Warrior became such an important factor in their own military endeavors.[8] In the course of our examination of warfare, it will be necessary to draw on texts and iconography from throughout the ancient Near East, since we have little in the way of visual evidence from ancient Israel other than the remains of fortified cities and a few examples of their weapons. Nevertheless, we will explore each of the senses as they relate to this very human activity, from preparations to participation to the aftermath in all types of military activity. With that in mind and to help demonstrate the value of this approach, elements associated with the village community, the urban setting, and those battlefields divorced from human occupation but valued for their strategic placement will be analyzed.[9] It is necessary to consider the events leading up to the actual confrontation as well as the battle itself and its aftermath. Therefore, this chapter will follow the pattern of those on village and city life, but since warfare lends itself to displays of multiple senses, there will be more examples of the mixing or combining of senses in the examples provided below.

Sight

The visual perspective of the viewer is a major factor to be considered in the context of warfare. What could be seen would differ widely depending on whether the viewer was in a village or a city. While both would be in danger of attack, the scale of the potential threat was relative to the size of the community. A village lacked all but the most rudimentary defenses other than topography, being located on a hilltop, and had few trained defenders.[10] It certainly could not be defended for long in the face of an approaching army or even a determined raiding party. Thus, the perspective of a viewer in this case after the alarm was sounded would be focused on the people looking for escape routes into the hills or to a nearby city willing to take in the villagers while their homes were being overrun and despoiled.[11] That is likely the case with the flight of the inhabitants of Gebim and other villagers in the face of the approaching Assyrian army during the Ashdod Revolt of 711 BCE and a century later when Jeremiah warns the people of Judah to flee for safety to Zion (= Jerusalem).[12]

The combined might of an approaching army or sizable raiding group would be one of the most frightening sights for village communities. It meant that many of those persons who were not killed would be taken away as slaves or conscripted into the conqueror's army.[13] Those who survived the attack and wished to rebuild their village saw the disastrous results of their terraced fields and vineyards being destroyed. Their grief at what would be lost is captured in Micah's lament in which the rural prophet wails and howls like a jackal, mourning the devastation of a group of twelve villages in the Shephelah.[14] In some cases, the capture of a village meant the total displacement of its inhabitants and its resettlement by its captors. That is the case with the migrating Danites who capture the city of Laish and then rename it Dan.[15]

In the cities, sentinels stood on the walls, in a tower, or on the roof over the gate to warn the people of a threat to the city.[16] Their vantage point allowed them to view the area within the city as well as beyond the city to the horizon and to provide a shouted warning or blow a trumpet to raise the alarm.[17] Looking away from the city, a sentinel might spy the dust raised by an approaching messenger, as is the case with the lookout on the wall above the gates of Mahanaim, who reports to David that he has spied two runners coming with news of the battle against Absalom's forces.[18] Sentinels would also be expected to watch for signal fires ignited on hilltops or at regional fortresses like Azekah to warn of the approach of enemy forces or to relay distress signals.[19]

Kings or governors of threatened cities would find it politic to be seen walking around the walls of their city to inspect its defensive readiness or to determine if its water resources had been protected. In this way, any flaws that might present themselves could be repaired in preparation for a siege, and at the same time, the inspection could serve to bolster the morale of the defenders.[20] For example, the inspection tour by King Ahaz of Judah serves the practical purpose of looking for potential weaknesses and also shows the leadership of the king and his advisers.[21] Unfortunately for Ahaz, his public display is spoiled by the confrontation with the prophet Isaiah and the prediction of both the demise of his enemies (Israel and Syria) and the immanent impoverishment of his own people during the Assyrian campaign.

Part of what an inspector would be considering in preparation for military action would be the readiness of the city's defenses, including its gate system and defensive towers, the size and depth of its walls (sometimes both an inner and an outer wall), and its battlements.[22] The condition of the defensive ditch and the slope of the glacis, which would require an enemy to construct a ramp to approach the wall, would also be focuses of any inspection.[23] These latter installations were designed to prevent an enemy's siege engines or battering ram from making a close approach to the walls. They also kept sappers from trying to weaken or undermine sections of the walls. Depictions of the siege of Lachish by Sennacherib's army in 701 BCE appear on the walls of the royal palace in Nineveh.[24] Although the artist tries to capture several elements of the siege, it is not totally realistic but rather a composite representation of events that resulted in the fall of the city.[25] Still, the magnitude of the siege, the various stages of the assault, and the portions of the city defenses are quite clear in this propagandistic rendering of Assyrian military might.

Looking back into the city from the walls allowed a wide panorama of its houses, streets, and public buildings. The usual bustle of activity would be present, along with smoke rising from cooking fires, workshops, and the altars within the temple complex. A sense of whether times were normal or becoming stressful could be seen in the movement of the people. If there was anticipation of an imminent siege, there would be furtive efforts to store food, weapons, and other supplies; cisterns would be filled; and troops would step up their drilling and refurbishing of swords and spears.[26] If a siege had already begun and had been in place for some time, the energy level of the people would be reduced by their anxieties, mounting health and sanitation issues in an environment that simply could not cope with the larger number of persons within the walls, and the growing scarcity of food.[27] Signs of starvation and malnutrition would be evident, and the growing desperation of the people could be seen in their worried expressions.[28]

Turning the scene around, there was the perspective of the person or host that was approaching a walled city in preparation for a battle. As the army got closer to the environs of the city's metro area, its features became more evident depending on the time of day and the amount of sunlight available. A massive, fortified city may have been an intimidating sight for the approaching army. Conversely, the array of an army in attack formation that suddenly appeared at dawn with the sun at their back could be a very intimidating sight for the people of a city. Abimelech uses this strategy in investing the city of Shechem by stationing his troops in four companies and only making them appear to the inhabitants as the sun rose.[29]

The portrayal of a city being besieged often includes the description of the defending army arrayed in full armor and brandishing their weapons before their city gates.[30] To magnify this visual and oral threat, Thutmose III begins the investment of the city of Megiddo by stationing segments of his army at different points, making it appear even larger. In a similar case, when the Israelites attack the city of Gibeah, the arraying of their forces before the targeted city was designed to intimidate the populace and served as an invitation for the city's soldiers to be drawn into battle away from the city walls, where they could be ambushed or flanked.[31]

The admittedly biased rendering of the siege of Megiddo by Egyptian scribes notes that the Egyptian forces surrounding the city first processed in formation before the pharaoh and so frightened their opponents that they fled their positions before the gates of Megiddo. They abandoned their horses, chariots, and possessions, and many were then hoisted up the walls with robes hung over their sides while exposing their genitals to a taunting Egyptian army.[32] Defeat is therefore depicted with the visual image of an army streaming back to the entrance to the gate.[33]

From the perspective of the soldiers in the invading army, the campaign began for them with activities associated with preparing for the journey and the topography to be traversed in traveling to the specified target for that year's campaign. An interval would be needed to muster the needed troops, in some cases through forced conscription or by hiring foreign mercenaries. David's thirty-seven "Mighty Men" include several non-Israelites, including Uriah the Hittite.[34] Organizing an army in ancient Israel is given only scant attention beyond the simple phrase that kings "assembled" large armies or "mustered" troops.[35] At least on some occasions, the mustering involved sounding the trumpet/shofar to indicate the need to meet a military threat.[36] Once assembled, the logistical aspects of an army on the march would be crucial to the success of the expedition. The soldiers would have to be equipped with weapons and other gear, a pack train would have to be put together to transport supplies, and fodder would have to be gathered and stored on the wagons to feed the pack animals.

Of course, the longer the distance that the army had to travel, the greater the requirements for requisitioning stores from vassals along the way and eventually living off the land. That meant smoke rising from burned cities and villages, with their animals slaughtered, their fields stripped of grain, their vineyards looted, and where necessary, new wells dug to supply water.[37] In some cases, a marshaling of the troops from different areas of the land or allied regions would be necessary, and they would be ordered to meet at a staging point from which the whole army would then begin its march. That would explain the euphemism proclaiming the beginning of a military campaign: "War was within the gates."[38]

A good example of this spectacle is outlined in the twin accounts of Deborah and Barak's expedition against Jabin and Sisera. After a call goes out to rally against the Canaanite foe, those tribes who chose to respond meet at Kedesh, Barak's hometown in the Galilee, before proceeding south to Mount Tabor and ultimately engaging Sisera's forces. It is possible that this site is well known to the commanders of the army and nearby villages for its topography, a single volcanic mountain that stands out from the plain and as a setting for previous battles. The choosing of a battlefield could also be based on information obtained from scouts/spies about the movements or encampment of the enemy force.[39] There are significant topographic differences between the prose account in Judges 4 and the poetic version in Judges 5. In the latter, there is more emphasis on the work of the Divine Warrior, who manipulates the waters of the Wadi Kishon to drown the Canaanite soldiers—a parallel with what happens to the Egyptian charioteers in the crossing of the Red Sea.[40]

Turning back to the line of march, the scene would shift continuously for the army, and therefore the soldiers' sensory impressions along the way changed over time. Since most of these soldiers would be moving through unfamiliar territory and were increasingly far from home, their basic sense of place was altered, and this was magnified by night terrors in unfamiliar territory.[41] That may explain the turmoil of the Midianite camp when it is attacked at night by Gideon's tiny force. The flashing torches, trumpets blasting, and smashed pots simply add to their fears and make the darkness even more terrifying.[42]

With all their senses being called upon to make mental shifts in how to perceive this new world, continuous adjustments to the terrain were needed to identify safe locations for their encampment. They would also have to spot nearby sources of water and fodder for their animals. As they proceeded, they had to adjust their pace based on the rockiness of the path and narrow pathways that would constrict their movements. For example, in the description of Pharaoh Thutmose III's campaign against Megiddo, narrow passes contribute to a sense of anxiety, as they funnel the army into spaces that limit the soldiers' maneuverability and make them more vulnerable to attack.[43] Scouts would provide information on these hazards and help spot landmarks that could be used to guide the way. Even with this as a guide, the army inevitably encountered steep places where soldiers would be called upon to assist their baggage wagons to climb over hills or prevent them from losing control on the downslope.[44]

The soldiers in an invading army often were following a route that was unfamiliar ground, even if it was within just a few miles of their home territory. During their march, the troops would experience a sense of mental and spatial dislocation. It is a common axiom that if someone does not know where they are or where they are in relation to where they would like to be, they can experience a very disquieting feeling.[45] No longer being centered in a place where they had spent the bulk of their lives, the soldiers were apprehensively forced to assume they were surrounded by enemies who evoked different sensory impressions. They spoke a different language, wore clothes of a different style, and cooked meals that produced new and unsettling aromas. Given these conditions, the army had to maintain a continual awareness of the potential that the topography provided for ambushes, even when the way was smooth.[46]

As they marched, armies contributed to visual and environmental changes that radically altered the landscape. They trampled fields of grain and vineyards, destroyed or stripped fruit trees, and systematically destroyed the houses in the villages in their path in order to deprive the people of their own sense of place and the means to survive in a devastated land.[47] For example, in the Assyrian emperor Sennacherib's account of his first campaign against Merodach-Baladan of Babylon, there is a grandiose boast that his army "destroyed, devastated, and burned [their towns] and turned them into forgotten tells."[48] Similar language appears in Isaiah's account of the devastation of Judah by "aliens" who burn the cities and devour the land.[49]

There were traditional or perennial battlefields or city sites with histories of being besieged. That was based on the tendency to establish cities at points designed to defend roads and guard natural resources and the fact that Canaan was a relatively small region.[50] Among the most frequently listed sites are Megiddo and the adjacent Jezreel Valley. Because of its placement, Megiddo became a frequent target of armies who wished to control an important trade route or prevent other countries from using it for their military activities. For instance, Josiah attempts to stop the advance of Necho II's Egyptian army by meeting it at the bottleneck in the Jezreel Valley near Megiddo in 609 BCE, but he is slain in the attempt.[51]

The topographical challenges of the Jezreel Valley became clear in Thutmose III's First Asiatic Campaign in 1457 BCE. The pharaoh was faced with the combined forces of several Canaanite rulers, and to reach their destination, his advisers suggested possible routes that would bring them in contact with the assembled enemy at Megiddo. Thutmose chose to discount their advice and took a route through a narrow pass that required the horses and soldiers to walk single file and be continually subject to attack. The unexpected route surprised the enemy and ultimately helped contribute to the Egyptian capture of the city.[52]

Once the armies had reached their selected battlefield or the siege of a city had begun, strategies would then center on the spatial qualities of that place. In the case of disputed territory, it is possible to point to the Philistine and Israelite forces during Saul's time that respectively occupy opposite ridges overlooking the Valley of Elah, an east-west corridor through the Judean Hill Country that is the key to control of the Shephelah.[53] While neither side is likely to attack the other's "high ground," the Israelites also do not want to meet the heavily armed Philistines in the more open confines of the eastern Valley of Elah. They instead station themselves above the narrow western entrance to the valley, where they can ambush the Philistines from their vantage point without resorting to combat on the floor of the valley.[54] It is clear from this example that an army and its commanders needed to be aware of the capabilities of their troops and confident in their ability to meet the demands of combat within the dimensions, topography, and weather conditions of their chosen battlefield.

The visual realm of political preparation for war included poised demonstrations of power and authority by kings, generals, heroes, and other leaders. For example, kings made use of significant spaces like the city gate to stage events that were designed to show that they were in charge. That is clearly the case when Kings Ahab and Jehoshaphat place their thrones in the gate of the city of Samaria, giving them even greater authority because they were on the former site of a threshing floor.[55] The kings are planning to go to war against Aram/Syria to regain lost territory, but they want to make it clear that the Divine Warrior / YHWH will bless their efforts.

As a preliminary to going to war, Ahab calls on his four hundred court prophets to provide assurance of divine support. Topping off their efforts, their leader Zedekiah performs a pantomime with a pair of iron horns designed to evoke the power of the deity to defeat the Aramaeans.[56] Jehoshaphat still raises some doubt about these assurances of divine assistance, so Ahab arranges for the independent prophet Micaiah to be brought before him to confirm that prediction. The staged scene gets away from Ahab when Micaiah maneuvers him into receiving a contradictory prophecy that could have derailed the king's military expedition. Even after the king's prophet slaps Micaiah as a visual punctuation of his disdain, Ahab, to maintain his authority and to encourage his troops to proceed with the fight, publicly rejects Micaiah's prediction of doom and has him imprisoned. Despite this show of bravado associated with place and public performance, Ahab's death in the resulting battle demonstrates that rhetoric alone is not enough to win a war.[57]

A similar potential loss of face is found in the episode of Absalom's rebellion against his father, David. That revolt ends with a startling visual image: Absalom caught by his hair in the limbs of a tree as he attempts to flee the battlefield.[58] Learning of his son's demise, David is overcome with grief and sequesters himself to mourn him. That display of grief and the apparent snub of his army nearly lose him the loyalty of his army. His mistake is to forego the typical ritual performance expected after a military victory that requires the king to make a public appearance to thank them for their support.[59] It is only when David's general Joab shames the king and warns him that he is flirting with disaster that he reluctantly seats himself in the city gate at Mahanaim, confirming his intention to resume his role as king of Israel and allowing the victorious soldiers to parade before him in review.[60] The entire narrative hinges on David's resumption of proper protocol with this public gesture and emphasizes Joab's role as the king's more practical counselor.

While it is not typical of Israelite warfare accounts, the boastful challenge of the immense Philistine warrior Goliath to meet one-on-one with Saul's champion creates quite a scene.[61] Only the matched duels between Joab's and Abner's "young men" near the Pool of Gibeon approach this type of posturing by warriors.[62] There is an element in both cases of a trial by combat in which the god of each side judges the contestants and determines the ultimate winner while the assembled armies provide the audience for their struggle. A sensory analysis, however, focuses on the spectacle, the clear differences between a heavily armored warrior and a young unarmored man spinning his sling with the hope of striking a vulnerable spot.[63] Once David's stone stuns Goliath, the memorable visual image focuses on David's taking Goliath's head as a prize of war. Coincidentally for the narrative, it also serves as a visual demonstration of his right eventually to become king when Saul's reign ends.[64] As a follow-up to David's victory over Goliath, during his "outlaw period," when he goes to Nob to retrieve Goliath's sword, he obtains yet another visual image to display his credentials for the kingship.[65]

Common props that served as multipurpose visuals on the battlefield were the battle standards, visual images of armies or their nations. They functioned as totems or identifying banners for individual units and as rallying points during the battle when the dust made it difficult to see and the press of combat forced units to regroup.[66] It is likely that they were used along with trumpets as a means of signaling movements to the troops.[67] Both would be necessary when the army was divided into separate attacking units.[68] However, if the fight went against them and their officers abandoned their standard, that was tantamount to defeat, since it disheartened the troops and sent them into flight.[69]

Another visual aspect of warfare was grisly piles of hands, heads, or other body parts. They are sometimes said to have been placed strategically before the conquered city or hung on the branches of trees. Such displays had both a psychological and a propagandistic effect and served as means of determining or exaggerating the body count. The Assyrian annals regularly include these details, and these records are augmented in complementary pictorial and textual displays in the decoration of Assyrian palaces. Their regularity and gruesome detail suggest that it was either a de rigueur practice or a scribal convention to be added in the appropriate place in the account.[70]

A similar form of military propaganda was the erection of monumental inscriptions. Once a war had been won and territory captured, it was common practice for rulers to set up a stele or other monument to both commemorate their victory and serve as a continual reminder to the conquered city where it was erected of their subservient status. Prime examples of this visual form of propaganda are the ninth-century BCE Mesha Stele from Moab and the Tel Dan Inscription. The Mesha Stele provides an alternate version of events that also appear in 2 Kgs 3:4–27, but more importantly, they illustrate the type of interregional conflict common in this period as well as a shared perspective on the role of the divine patron of Moab. In this case, it is the god Chemosh who first allows the Moabites to be subjected to Israel's rule and then contributes to their liberation and a series of military victories.[71] Fragments of the Tel Dan victory stele were found in excavations of the city of Dan detailing the capture of the city by the king of Aram, probably Hazael, in the eighth century BCE. Although the populace of Dan may not have been able to read the bragging claims of the Aramaean king on this basalt stele, just having it displayed for all to see in the gate area of the city communicated to them a shameful event and probably explains why it was eventually broken into pieces and reused as flagstones in the plaza before the gate.[72]

To complete this discussion of the visual realm, it is worth mentioning the role that the battlefield served after the conflict was done. Some descriptions paint a gruesome picture of the dead lying in massive piles to the point that the combatants even stumble over the bodies.[73] Since these bodies were not always buried and were left to be scavenged by birds and animals, the skeletonized remains could easily be described as "very dry."[74] They and the battlefield eventually became a visual testament, a living memory, and a site of memory.[75] It is quite possible that in addition to these bones, relics of battles would continue to emerge from old battlefields as they were plowed or eroded. In the case of Israel's history, these bones serve as a reminder to the living of their immediate past and a warning of the dangers of a future lived at the crossroads of major powers and their political ambitions.

Sound

The rhythm of an ancient army as it marched produced many different sounds. The most familiar sounds to the soldiers' ears would include the tread of their sandals over sandy or rocky ground and the jangling of their weapons and equipment as they banged against their sides. If there were cavalry or chariots, they would hear the beating of horses' hooves on the turf, the rattling of quivers attached to horses' sides, the rumble of chariot wheels, and the shouts of their officers keeping them moving.[76] As long as these sounds remained within tolerable levels, the army could concentrate on its regular tasks and the pace of the march. It was when the unexpected arose or a troubling sound was heard that panic could drive the soldiers apart and send them into retreat or flight, and their fear could only be harnessed when their officers were able to rally them to do their duty.[77] In one instance, the Aramean army abandons its encampment after hearing what the soldiers think is the approach of a "great army," and they succumb to the fear that the Israelites have allied themselves with the kings of the Hittites and Egypt.[78]

An army traveling any distance from its home territory required the use of pack animals and supply wagons, since they could not always depend on foraging for food along the way. The result was the sounds of the shuffling feet of donkeys or oxen and the creaking of the wheels of those wagons.[79] In addition to the unfamiliar sights along the way, another major factor requiring psychological gymnastics was the adjustment to variations in the sounds of everyday life.[80] For soldiers, normal sounds centered on the familiar noises produced by their companions and the pack animals. However, something as simple as different bird songs or the buzzing of unfamiliar insects could be unnerving. As noted in previous chapters, it was not uncommon for people to filter out or even ignore expected sounds, but their sense of place was disrupted when unusual or threatening tones entered their immediate environment.[81] It was possible that new sounds or even an unnatural silence could make them more alert or require them to prepare for battle.

Many ancient armies included chariots pulled by teams of horses. In battle, these would be employed against massed troops and served as platforms for commanders and for archers.[82] The friction of the wheels and axles would have had a distinctive tone punctuated periodically when hit by a stone or when one broke under the impact. Accompanying the movement of personnel at every stage of the march or in battle would be the shouts of officers encouraging or threatening the soldiers who were lagging or had fallen out of the formation of battle.[83]

During the march through enemy territory, the soldiers clung to those persons, objects, sounds, or smells with which they were most familiar and therefore were most comfortable or meaningful to them. Since many ancient armies included soldiers from conquered or allied peoples, groups of soldiers would tend to cluster with contingents from their own ethnic backgrounds.[84] In that way, the language spoken as they marched would be their own, and they could feel a sense of camaraderie even if their officers were strangers to them.

Their leaders, from long experience with other campaigns, would know that keeping a strict routine was the key to maintaining the morale of their troops. The simple practice of remaining in step with one's companions helped create confidence and bonding while producing a definite cadence and tempo as they marched along.[85] Although a postexilic reference, there is a mention of Jehoshaphat employing singers to march before his army to praise the Lord, and it is possible that this chant served the purpose of invoking the help of the Divine Warrior and providing a steady cadence for the troops.[86] There would also be the sound of familiar commands being issued, helping create an almost self-contained world for the soldiers. The established order of march would also follow a prescribed pattern, with regiments formed into units and one designated as a rear guard, all responding to the spoken orders of their officers.[87]

That feeling of belonging to a distinct enterprise with a specific purpose would be further reinforced through the daily tasks associated with setting up temporary encampments.[88] While little is known about the life of these soldiers, it is easy to imagine them sitting around their crackling campfires at night with shadows dancing and men boasting about their exploits or laughing at a joke or the ineptitude of their enemies.[89] Heroic stories like the tales associated with Ehud or Samson or David's "Mighty Men" could be told to pass the time and provide entertainment.[90] Officers would circulate through the camp issuing orders for the next day or an individual unit's role in an attack.[91] Camp life also included ritual performances and sacrifices to gain the help or affirmation of their god(s), and these were accompanied by formal addresses by their commanders or priests.[92]

More startling to witnesses would be the sound and the sight of a foreign army as it made its way toward the city or battlefield and then arrayed its forces for all to see. That fits the situation described during one of David's campaigns when the "sound of marching in the tops of the balsam trees" alerts his forces to the approach of the Philistine army in the Valley of Rephaim.[93] Once the army did reach its intended battlefield or target city, all the sounds were magnified. Based on several examples in the biblical narrative, the preliminaries to battle also included shouted taunts and challenges as each army worked itself up to fight and hoped to unnerve its opponents.[94]

Perhaps one of the first sensory cues foretelling the coming conflict would be the ominous sound of swords being drawn from sheaths.[95] The bending of their bows would produce a twanging sound as arrows were released, filling the sky with flights that flashed downward into the midst of the enemy army.[96] Slingers accompanied the archers, and the whirling of their sling stones sent the ominous sound of hail hurling toward the enemy or a city's walls.[97] As the blast of the trumpets was sounded, the army raised its battle cry and rushed into battle with the volume of the roaring of the sea.[98] Trumpets also served as a form of communication, sometimes to signal the charge into battle or as a call to cease operations.[99] Hearing these piercing blasts would elicit a range of emotions, from fear and apprehension to a quickening of the pulse in anticipation of the action to come.[100]

The sensory details and metaphors contained in ancient accounts give a picture, if somewhat exaggerated, of the sights and sounds of battle as it engulfed the participants. Once the armies at last engaged, the scene was filled with sometimes chaotic sensory references and postconflict propaganda exaggerating the sizes of the armies. Where the terrain allowed them to freely maneuver, chariots are said to be so numerous that they were like a locust swarm.[101] As it built up its powerful momentum, the army was described in metaphorical terms as a storm or an enveloping fog sweeping its way across a widening battlefield.[102] On the flip side, when an army had been routed and its soldiers fled, that frame of reference broadened, as the chase was on and the combatants spread across the land in pursuit.[103]

As the troops went into combat, they rattled their javelins against their shields and added their voices to the cacophony of sounds with their battle shouts along with the commands barked by their captains.[104] For those less skillful or unlucky enough to be cut down in the conflict either on the field or in the city, their cries for help and their groans as they lay mortally wounded would have added to the din of battle.[105] The fleshy sound of a spear being jabbed into an opponent's body or a dagger or sword being thrust into their stomach or chest would be regularly repeated throughout the struggle.[106]

It is unlikely that any individual soldier was aware of the totality of a battle scene. He would be too consumed with his own survival and his opponent to visualize and analyze the entire picture. Instead, his experiences were composed of the deafening sounds around him, and his sensual impressions would be those of proximity, primarily touch and smell. Even afterward it would be difficult for him to describe fully the sight of the mutilation of bodies and the horrific events in which he was one small part.[107] As for the inhabitants of a city under siege, their senses of proximity as they experienced these events included a variety of sounds. There would be the rolling of the wheels of the siege engines as they were maneuvered toward the city walls, the thumping of the battering ram and the ring of axes driven into the gate, and the frightening slapping of assault ladders being raised on the wall.[108] It must have been unnerving to witness the sights and sounds of these efforts on the part of the attacking army, and that contributed to the energy expended by the defenders to at least try to slow their progress, including sending a hail of sling stones into their massed shields.

Biblical narratives and prophetic pronouncements contain many heroic images. For instance, among the warriors who joined David during his outlaw period were Gadites whose faces were as fierce as those of lions and who were swift as gazelles.[109] There are also stirring depictions of horsemen charging into battle with flashing swords and glittering spears raised and scenes dominated by the whirlwind sound of charging chariots and galloping horses with hooves flashing like flint.[110] In some of these poetic accounts, the Israelites are assured that YHWH will help them triumph. They are told that God will break the flashing arrows, the shields, the swords, and the weapons of war of the enemy. The Divine Warrior will also join the conflict by casting fiery arrows of lightning and a flashing spear. These missiles will speed across the sky, dazzling the eyes of the enemy.[111] Of course, when the Israelites are the target of YHWH's wrath, all this energy is turned against them, and like an enemy army, YHWH destroys city walls, breaks the bars of the gates, and causes laments of anguish by widows and the few survivors to be raised.[112]

Somewhat more realistic were the smaller sounds associated with the battlefield, including the rattling of quivers attached to warhorses' sides, the rattling of lances and strapped-on equipment as the soldiers marched or ran into battle, and the rumbling of chariot wheels.[113] In the evenings, warriors would fill the air with the sound of sharpening their arrows and swords.[114] The snorting of nervous horses pawing the ground and the neighing of stallions as they anxiously awaited their opportunity to plunge into the fray would add to the general climate of prebattle preparations and anticipation.[115]

Once the fighting was done, sounds associated with both victory and defeat could be heard. The victors, who were now free to loot the camp or city of their foe, raped and burned without a check on their actions. Some accounts even refer to ripping open the bellies of pregnant women in their frenzy, and there is also visual evidence of this practice on the reliefs from Ashurbanipal's palace.[116] They mocked their victims with laughter or showed their disdain for their broken enemies with hisses, wagging heads, or clapping hands while their victims groaned in despair.[117]

Some of the prisoners may have experienced torture at the hands of their tormentors. There are many examples of the mutilation of men and women. Horrific forms of execution of prisoners appear in the Annals of the Assyrian kings as well as on the pictorial reliefs on palace walls and in the biblical record.[118] While some prisoners' lives were spared, many were mutilated in such a way that they became walking advertisements of their foe's victory.[119] Aside from the psychological effects of these practices, it is likely that the mutilation of prisoners and of the dead was intended as a means of publicly shaming the enemy.[120] In any case, the screams of these victims, some impaled on stakes before the walls of their city, must have echoed throughout the area.[121]

A victory over their enemies ascribed either to the hand of the Divine Warrior or to the efforts of the army would be celebrated by women singing and dancing while they beat their tambourines and cymbals and rattled their timbrels and castanets.[122] For example, when Saul and David return victorious after defeating the Philistines, they are met by women singing, dancing, playing musical instruments, and chanting a rhythmic phrase that compares their leaders' prowess.[123] For the losers, however, there was no celebration. Some would have fled at the sound of the approaching soldiers into the thickets and caves to hide, while others wailed at the extent of their loss and envisioned their fate as enslaved prisoners.[124]

Another aspect of warfare that did not involve actual fighting was the diplomacy that preceded conflict and then dealt with the details of the aftermath when conflict became necessary. It had both visual and oral dimensions. In some cases, an army or a migrating people may not have wished to fight their way through the lands that they wanted to enter. Negotiations were initiated that may have included promises not to harm fields or vineyards and to pay for the use of water rights in exchange for safe passage. The success of these efforts may have depended in large part on the military might of either the migrating force or the nation involved.[125]

Oral performances may also have taken place during a war. A classic example is the speech of the Assyrian diplomat, the Rabshakeh, who stands before the walls of Jerusalem and cries out in sarcastic terms about the futility of Hezekiah's people's standing against the might of the Assyrian emperor Sennacherib during his siege of the city in 701 BCE.[126] Such a staged scene is not unique and is paralleled in other accounts of Assyrian ambassadors.[127] A similar, swaggering demand is made by the messengers sent by King Ben-Hadad of Aram to King Ahab of Israel in 1 Kings 20:1–6, and Josephus recounts a speech by Agrippa calling on the people of Jerusalem to end their revolt against Rome.[128] These speeches represent both an effort to intimidate a city into surrendering and a propaganda display that serves as a warning to other cities in rebellion.

Diplomacy, however, did not always work. That is the case when the king of the Ammonites dies, and his son succeeds him. David sends an official delegation to the new king as a diplomatic gesture intended to assure that political ties between the two peoples would remain intact. It was the practice in the ancient Near East that messengers were considered to be surrogates for their political masters, and they were to be treated in a manner similar to their kings.[129] Transitions of power were delicate periods for new leaders, and in the case of the new Ammonite king, it allows him to be susceptible to the voices of his royal council who caution that David's men were actually sent as spies and that the Israelites were planning a military invasion.[130] Diplomacy is then transformed into political theater when the Ammonite king orders that

David's delegation be publicly shamed and emasculated, cutting off half of their beards and a portion of their garments to expose their genitals. David, of course, cannot let this provocation go without a response, but he also cannot let men who are his representatives be seen in this shameful condition. They must be allowed time to regrow their beards and reclothe themselves so that they once again can serve as David's messengers. The result of this diplomatic slight is a war that devastates Ammon and prevents the Aramaeans from a future alliance with them as well.[131] In this case, both sound and sight combine to provide a backdrop to conflict.

Smell

Of all the senses, sight and scent are most associated with memory. They can take a person back to previous events or help them recall instances that may be pleasurable or disturbing. A veteran soldier or his commander may have marched on previous campaigns over the same ground, and as every mile passed, they may have mentally ticked off their memories as they were recalled through familiar sights or smells. Armies consisted of thousands of soldiers and their auxiliaries. Their route of march to their intended battlefields or targeted cities could range from less than seventy miles (Jerusalem to the Jezreel Valley) to hundreds of miles (from Nineveh on the Tigris River to Syro-Palestine) over a wide variety of terrains and elevations. Since these military expeditions occurred in the heat of spring and summer, when they would not be impeded by rain and storms, the stink of unwashed men's bodies mingling with their sweat as they relentlessly marched and fought in the hot sun would be quite familiar to the soldiers—a background factor that was an expected consequence of their efforts.[132] In addition, the sores created by the chafing harnesses on the draft animals that pulled the wagons and chariots created their own distinct odor. Left untreated, they could easily fester.[133]

While most references to smells associated with the activities of ancient armies are related to the odors of battle, it is also worth considering the stench created by thousands of men who regularly had to relieve themselves. To maintain a basic modicum of hygiene in the camp, they would have had to dig latrines away from their encampment that could be filled in and thus tamp down the worst of the odors.[134] Such a gathering in proximity to one another also could have bred illnesses from either contaminated water or infectious disease. The reference in Amos to a military camp that has been struck by plague summons up mental images of the smell of men who have lost control of their bodily functions as well as the stench of rotting corpses waiting to be buried.[135]

As the army approached the site of the battle, the not-so-subtle smell of fear emanating from both sides would fill the air.[136] The trepidation as well as the urgency to begin the conflict was also experienced by the horses that had been trained for combat. They could smell the heightened emotions being produced as well as the horses of their opponents.[137] They would quiver with anticipation and snort as they prepared to "plunge headlong into battle."[138] Interestingly, horses have poor depth perception and must turn their heads to focus on objects. That may explain why the description of the warhorse in Job does not mention its sight but instead emphasizes its ability to smell and hear the approaching conflict.[139]

When the time came to engage in combat, massed soldiery was not the only aspect of a battlefield. Individual combat produced its own brand of smells, although it can be assumed that these odors were simply produced on a smaller scale than the entire battlefield. One such depiction is found in Sennacherib's Bavian Rock Inscription, where the scribe records how the kings of Elam and Babylon became so frightened that they defecated in their chariots. While this may have been a shaming jab at these enemy nations, it also invites the reader or the audience to share in this whiff of personal agitation.[140] Biblical examples tend to focus on the one-on-one details of assassination. For instance, when Ehud assassinates King Eglon of Moab, stabbing him in his stomach, the narrative describes how his entrails poured out, creating a stink that the king's guards mistook for the monarch relieving himself.[141] The evisceration of a victim produced massive bleeding that splashed onto his attacker and produced an odor that would last for some time.[142]

Furthermore, the continual references to putting a city or all the men of an army "to the sword" suggest massive casualties and the resulting odor of dismembered bodies.[143] The huge body count associated with these battlefields is framed as a scene of mass quantities of the rotting corpses scattered about the site, leaving a stench like dung on a field.[144] However, even though the massive shedding of blood during the battle must have created a distinctive and pervasive smell, there is no mention of that feature of the conflict in the biblical narrative. It may be that the smell of blood was a familiar feature due to the offering of regular animal sacrifice or the slaughtering of animals in the villages and towns and that it served as just another expected (emic) background to everyday life—or in this case, death.[145]

Touch

Skin is the primary medium for the sense of touch.[146] It provides the ability to feel the warmth of a fire and to distinguish between smooth and rough surfaces. In the case of warriors, it helped them perceive how sharp their arrowheads, swords, and spears were as they prepared for battle.[147] A blunt sword required more effort to inflict a telling blow and may not have had the cutting edge to pierce armor or a shield.[148] An astute warrior took great care of his weapons, since they could be the difference between life and death. In the case of those who used slings as their primary weapons, it is possible to point to David, who chooses smooth stones for his sling, knowing that they will be more likely to fly true to his target, Goliath.[149]

For soldiers, the sense of touch included the awareness of bodily movement as they marched. That also included the hazards of long marches, such as swollen, sore feet; inflamed muscles; strained backs; and blisters caused by exposure to the sun and ill-fitting foot gear.[150] Maintaining their balance as they moved over uneven, rocky ground was a function of sight and the nerve endings in their muscles that provided a sense of gravitational orientation through the inner ear.[151] A lack of either of these senses or sufficient daylight combined with weariness from carrying their equipment could have resulted in injuries and stumbling against one's fellows.[152] Plus, marching through lands without adequate water sources weakened the soldiers' stride, and their tongues would be parched with thirst.[153]

Feet were often associated with military activities as well as their aftermath. One visual and tactile gesture of supremacy over an enemy was to place one's foot on the neck of the defeated king.[154] A similar metaphor was to describe how one's enemy has fallen under one's feet.[155] Another sign of submission and supplication involved grasping and kissing the feet of a ruler.[156] And, mixing the visual with the tactile once again, David describes how Joab had murdered Abner and Amasa, with the bloody evidence found smeared on his belt and sandals.[157] When

Uriah the Hittite returns to Jerusalem from a military zone, David encourages Uriah to go to his own house and wash his feet, signifying his separation from hostilities and a return to domestic life with his wife.[158]

Soldiers entering or running into battle would have to carry their shields and keep a firm grip on the shafts of their spears or the handles of their swords.[159] As part of their preparation, they would learn the proper way to handle a bow and the muscle strength needed to string their bows and to pull back the bowstrings to send their arrows sailing straight.[160] In fact, the training necessary to be an effective warrior would have hardened the body and raised its stamina level to undergo the physical hardships of military life.[161]

Casualties in war were inevitable. In the melee, soldiers would constantly be cut down and either crawl away from the fighting, crying out in pain, or be left to expire on the field. That was the fate of the common soldier who, unlike Ahab or his son Joram, did not have a chariot to carry him to where his wounds could be treated.[162] They would feel the slice of a sword into their flesh or the piercing pain of a spear thrust into their body.[163] While some battlefield wounds were bound up with dressings and treated with soothing oils, lotions, and balms, the healing process was uncertain due to infection and the festering of their injuries. Some had the skill to drain a wound or boil, but that was not always successful.[164]

Prisoners were taken in war, and some became slaves of the temple or were put to hard labor or incorporated into the army of their captors.[165] While there are numerous visual images in reliefs in the Egyptian hypostyle hall at Karnak and in the royal Assyrian palace at Nineveh depicting lines of prisoners roped together, it is the sense of touch that portrays their suffering and humiliation.[166] They were deprived of rank and in some cases their clothing. This latter state is depicted in Isaiah's enacted prophecy of parading around as a naked prisoner to show the fate of Judah should Hezekiah join the Ashdod Revolt against Assyria in 711 BCE.[167] Some prisoners were eventually freed from slavery, such as the young woman described in Deuteronomy 21:10–14. In her case, the sense of touch comes into play when she is required to undergo a transformation ritual that includes shaving her head, paring her nails, discarding her clothing, and mourning her parents for a month in the house of her captor before she can marry him. By stripping her of those physical qualities that had made her attractive to the Israelite, this ritual also provides a cooling-off period before he makes a final decision to marry her.[168]

Taste

A soldier's diet often seems to consist of nothing but the dust raised during their march. In fact, the metaphor for defeat in battle is for them to "lick the dust" in obeisance to their conquerors.[169] Of course, an army, ancient or modern, must be fed, and the larger the number of soldiers, the greater the logistical problem in feeding them. Records describing the Assyrian military campaigns in the reign of Sargon II (ca. 714 BCE) describe collecting animals as tribute from the lands through which the army passed, including horses, cattle, camels, and sheep. Some of these animals were used to transport gear or pull chariots, but the inclusion of cattle and sheep is an indicator that meat was part of the diet. Vast amounts of grain were also needed. Some calculations suggest the need for as much as 70,500 liters of grain per day to feed an army of thirty thousand.[170]

For an army on campaign, adherence to a standard diet of food and drink was essential to the maintenance of morale, since it provided a common experience and a sense of continuity. When supply lines were stretched to the breaking point, however, it became necessary to supplement the soldiers' ration with local fare or abandon their own stores that had become moldy or inedible. In many cases, that meant taking grain and animals from the local villagers, stripping their fields and storage facilities. Not surprisingly, these local people wished to preserve as much of their food as possible and therefore created stratagems like that used by Gideon, who was beating wheat in a winepress to confuse his Midianite enemies.[171]

During battle, when a soldier's energy could begin to flag, it would be common enough for them to forage in the baggage and tents of their enemies when they were in flight. That seems to be the basis for Saul's unwise oath in which he denies his men the chance to eat anything during the battle.[172] By handicapping his army in this way, Saul blunders by attempting to force the Divine Warrior to intervene and give him a military victory over the Philistines.[173] In the context of the sense of taste, the text is clear that Saul's men see a honeycomb within the enemy camp, and their mouths water for the sweet taste, but they are too afraid of Saul to indulge. However, Saul's son Jonathan is absent when Saul proclaims his oath and therefore—unlike Achan, who intentionally violates the Jericho *ḥerem*—unwittingly violates his father's oath. He dips his staff into the honey, and when it reaches his lips, his eyes brighten as he savors the rich taste, and his energies are refreshed.[174] And once they defeat the Philistines, the famished soldiers indiscriminately loot their camp, slaughtering sheep and oxen and not taking the time to drain the blood before consuming the meat, a violation of the dietary laws.[175] Trying to mitigate this sinful act, Saul sets up a temporary altar upon which to slaughter the animals properly. Saul's original oath thus sets in motion a ripple effect that causes harm to his own soldiers both by depriving them of a taste and then by setting them up to fail in their duty to the law. It also nearly costs him his son.[176]

Final Thoughts

There was perhaps no single experience more trying and more impactful on the people of the Near East than warfare. It turned lives upside down whether it was on a small scale, involving bands who raided villages, or the more systematic destruction described in the Assyrian Annals of Sennacherib, in which he boasts of conquering forty-six fortified cities and "countless villages" during his march through Judah in 701 BCE.[177] The cycle of destruction, adjustment, and restoration found its way into the fabric of their lives, became the basis for theological reasoning about the will of god(s), and served as a warning that this undoubtedly will happen again.

4

Law and the Senses
Right Behavior and Consensus

LEGAL STATEMENTS IN the Hebrew Bible provide a wealth of sensory information, but they need to be examined within the context of the ancient society that produced them as well as the thought processes and nuances of the original language.[1] Since they are predicated on the regulation of human activities, they account for each of the senses, and many of them encompass several of the senses. The laws contained in Near Eastern law codes and the Bible are indicators of the principle that communities that are not under the direct control of more powerful entities choose to regulate themselves. They also choose to bolster the authority of their legal pronouncements by declaring that they are a gift from the gods.[2] That contention works best generically, but the case laws found in these collections are aimed at individual or hypothetical situations that relate in some way to overriding legal and social principles. Thus, the apodictic commands contained in the Decalogue or portions of the Holiness Code form a legal foundation for the more specific cases contained in the Covenant and Deuteronomic Codes. They all express a society's concerns and judgments on human behavior and their attempt to present a solution that is designed to prevent a repetition of what is deemed to be improper or shameful behavior. And overall, they are constructed to protect life, property, and the social order.

It should also be noted that there is no direct evidence that the biblical laws ever functioned as case laws used in determining actual legal situations in ancient Israel.[3] That is not to say, however, that they are not based on legal rules and procedures that were being used to establish justice.[4] In addition, it is unlikely that the biblical text contains a full accounting of the legal principles that helped guide ancient Israelite society. There are some sections of the law that seem to be more complete and that may be reflective of the seriousness of criminal behavior such as homicide and the overreaching effects of liability when applied to property or harm to persons or animals.[5]

Law is the way that a community expresses its values and regulates behavior. Ancient Israel operated as an honor and shame society. That meant that households maintained their acceptable standing in the larger community by encouraging every member of that household to seek to engage in honorable behavior and to avoid anything that would bring shame upon that household. In effect, this was a survival of the fittest strategy, with the most honorable households being recognized as the most viable and therefore those with which other households would be willing to do business and to point to as models of behavior. Those deemed to be shamed households would be banned from free participation in the community's affairs and ultimately would be forced to physically move out of the community or become extinct. Acceptance of community standards, then, required the creation of a set of norms to which all could and would abide. Having given this set of principles the authority of group consensus, it then became necessary to establish a means whereby law could be maintained and enforced. Occasionally, that required the calling of a forum led by the elders representing the households in that village or city to meet to form a consensus on cases or situations. Consensus in turn became the justification for physical restraints to be placed on people who otherwise were judged to be a danger to society.

The charts found in the appendix detail the legal pronouncements in the Decalogue and other legal collections and how they can be tied to sensory analysis. Note that in some cases, the sensory connection is quite explicit, and in other cases, it is more implicit in character. It is also evident that many legal situations involve more than one of the senses. Each legal statement will be discussed below in the sensory category to which it belongs.

Sight

The sense of sight within the legal corpus begins with the restrictions on worshipping other gods. In the Decalogue, that principle is underscored by the prohibition against making and worshipping idols. It is repeated many times in other legal statements and in the prophetic materials, making it a consistent theme throughout the rest of the Hebrew Bible.[6] The idea that the people needed to see their gods and that the gods needed to be seen by their worshippers, at least in the form of idols, permeated the cultures of the Near East, although ancient Israel was unique in its official statements prohibiting that practice. Perhaps most telling in terms of a sensory reflection of this legal position is found in Psalms: "They have mouths, but do not speak; eyes, but do not see. They have ears, but do not hear; noses, but do not smell. They have hands, but do not feel; feet, but do not walk; they make no sound in their throats."[7]

The sense of sight as it appears in the collections of legal materials generally involves the examination of evidence, performance of public legal procedures, and obligations associated with awareness of one's surroundings. Since most legal issues center on a response to an accusation, they will be discussed below in the section on sound. However, ancient Israel was very optically oriented, and thus the proof of innocence or guilt hinged on both the spoken statements of witnesses and physical evidence that could be examined by the elders before judgment was pronounced or punishment imposed.[8]

Many of these incidents in fact involve sight, sound, and touch. For instance, in the case of a childless widow who has been spurned by the man who owed her deceased husband levirate obligation, the scene is very public, as is the drama involved and the implications of his refusal to carry out his familial duties.[9] While his motives may be based on an effort to increase his own share of the household's inheritance, the case in the Deuteronomic Code is not unique. Both Onan in the Judah and Tamar narrative and the next of kin in the story of Ruth and Boaz also refuse to do their duty ostensibly for personal economic reasons.[10] Yet the rights of the dead man and his widow are upheld to an extent in the Deuteronomic injunction. She is allowed to bring a charge against the reluctant levir before the elders at the gate. When he reiterates that he will not marry her, a ritual of humiliation is initiated in which she removes his sandal, spits in his face, and declares for all to hear that he refuses to build up his brother's house. Such an angry display must have been shameful for him, but his willingness to endure the public disdain for himself and his family must have been worth it and may have been based on a personal aversion to the widow and an assertion that he may not be forced to marry without his consent.[11]

Sight is the trigger for action in several laws tied to property rights and the obligations of a neighbor. Thus, when an Israelite sees a strayed animal, he must return it even if it is owned by an enemy, and he must free a donkey that has been overburdened by its load and is lying exhausted in the road.[12] Theft of property is explicitly forbidden in the Decalogue, but proof of theft depends on finding the animals or other items in the possession of the theft, and that in turn results in a stiff fine.[13] For a charge of rape of a betrothed virgin, which is a violent act and is a form of theft in the sense of infringing on the sexual/property rights of the father, the couple must be witnessed in the act. The consequences of his crime are to pay a fine equivalent to the bride-price. The Deuteronomic law requires that he must marry her without the right to divorce later, but marriage in the Covenant Code remains the purview of the father.[14] In this way, the household is compensated for the lost value of a virgin daughter, and the young woman is guaranteed a husband, something that otherwise might not be possible to arrange.[15]

An adulterous couple engaging in a sexual act is a violation of the command in the Decalogue.[16] It is considered a capital crime injurious to the public at large, and therefore both parties are sentenced to die by stoning in the gate area and by the hands of the community. Their condemnation assumes that they were both consenting parties and that their action was witnessed by others. There is one mitigating factor included that depends on whether their sexual misconduct occurred in the town or in "open country." In the latter case, the assumption is that the woman attempts to resist his advances, but her cries for help could not be heard.[17] However, that does not consider the possible extent of coercion being applied by the man and the potential to which her fears might have stifled her voice from being a factor.[18]

Finding or viewing evidence of a crime is a factor in a number of these legal statements, especially those involving theft. For example, if stolen livestock is found in the possession of a thief, that is sufficient evidentiary basis for a substantial fine or the thief's being sold into debt slavery to satisfy the financial loss of the owner.[19] The addition of physical evidence that can be viewed and examined may be an editorial extension of the original law that dealt with evidence based on the sale or butchering of the animals.[20] While the further injection of a time factor into theft may relate to the stealing of animals, it may also refer to a separate case of housebreaking. Thus, if a thief is caught trying to break in (whether an animal corral or a house), there is a "castle law" that applies that removes bloodguilt from the homeowner should the thief be beaten to death.[21] The fact that bloodguilt in this case is dependent on the time of day is interesting, since it is based on whether the criminal could be seen and whether neighbors could be called to help apprehend him.

There are times when the physical evidence of the crime of murder exists, but there are no witnesses to the crime and no clear lead to finding the murderer. That is the case of the discovery of a corpse in open country between settlements that requires the use of a "ritual of elimination" to absolve the bloodguilt associated with the spilling of innocent blood.[22] It must first be determined by careful measurement by the judges and elders which town is closest to the site of the crime.[23] Then to deal with the impurity and bloodguilt, these elders must take a heifer that has never been used for work and break its neck over running water and in this way avoid shedding blood. Their act in a place of unfulfilled potential slaying a heifer whose vitally has never been tapped is symbolic of their acceptance of a similar fate if the oath that they take is false.[24]

The ritual is completed when the elders of the affected town, before an assemblage of Levites, wash their hands over the body of the heifer and speak an exculpatory oath that they were not a party to shedding innocent blood and should be considered guilt-free. The additional layers of authority figures beyond the elders involved in this procedure are an indication of restrictions being placed on local leaders and more direct oversight being imposed by the central authority after the establishment of the monarchy.[25]

Ultimately, the object here is to deal with the pollution of the blood of the dead man and the bloodguilt, since it cannot be eliminated without punishing the murderer. They do this by symbolically transferring the polluting blood to a visibly uninhabited and uncultivated spot and away from the elders' own town and cultivated field.[26] A similar intent is found in the prohibition of leaving the corpse of a hanged man on the tree during the night, since that also defiles the land.[27] Presumably, public execution is designed as a visual deterrent to future felons, but the requirement that the body be taken down is an acknowledgment that the sight is equivalent to the range of improprieties that must be dealt with when evening comes to prevent YHWH's curse being imposed on the land and the people.[28]

Sound

The failure to hear or obey the voice of authority was a major violation of societal norms and one that placed the community in jeopardy. That is made clear in situations involving human interaction in the generic case of the stubborn and rebellious son who is accused of continuously denying the authority of his parents when they attempt to verbally discipline him.[29] The foundation for this case is embedded in the Decalogue's command to honor and obey one's parents.[30] When all of their spoken remonstrances and efforts to educate him fail to bring him back into a pattern of acceptable behavior, they physically take him to the gate of the city and publicly testify before the elders that he is an unrepentant glutton and drunkard. This declaration labels the son as both disobedient and unpredictable and one who wastes his parents' property and his own potential as an asset to the community.[31] When consensus is reached by the elders on this case, the rebellious son is stoned to death as a means of purging his evil influence from infecting others.

A similar case and one that names the father and the offspring is found in the story of Eli's two sons, Hophni and Phineas. After having sexual relations with women serving before the tent of meeting, Eli's sons refuse to listen to the voice of their father even though numerous verbal reports had come to him about their behavior.[32] Compounding these reports, Eli is visited by an unnamed "man of God," who voices the displeasure of YHWH decrying the corruption of the Shiloh priesthood and pointing to Eli's ungovernable sons who greedily and unlawfully take a larger portion from the sacrificial meat than customarily would be allowed.[33] Failure to obey the voice of a parent usually results in the death of the culprit(s), and both Hophni and Phineas are killed during the battle with the Philistines. However, in this instance, it also is the house of Eli and his line of priests who are to be extinguished, while a non-Levite, Samuel, emerges as the prophet-priest leading the Israelites prior to the beginning of the monarchy.[34]

On a communal level, the Israelites are repeatedly enjoined to obey the voice of YHWH. The covenant promise that serves as the contract between YHWH and the Israelites first evolves from the command to Abram to obey the deity's voice in order to receive a legacy of land and children.[35] Obedience to YHWH's voice is further codified once they reach Mount Sinai in a reiteration of the terms of the covenant and linking the Israelites present at that time back to the "house of Jacob."[36] And that in turn becomes the basis for warnings to and curses on those who choose not to obey the voice of YHWH.[37] That reverence for the deity also includes prohibiting use of the name of YHWH in a curse. Those who curse God are subject to communal execution, with all persons who heard this curse to participate in stoning the culprit.[38]

In later periods, the Hebrew prophets have a prime directive to call the people to remember what YHWH has done for the people. They exhort the Israelites to maintain or return to obedience to the covenant and thus to the voice of their God who has provided them with direction and commandments.[39] It is the affirmation of obedience by the Israelites at Mount Sinai to "all the words and all the ordinances" of YHWH that places an obligation on all future generations to listen carefully and continue to obey these statutes.[40]

The wedding of law and obedience is central to the identity of the Israelite community and is firmly seated in the Decalogue's injunctions to worship only YHWH and to honor the name of the deity when speaking a vow.[41] The most explicit examples in which YHWH's voice condemns the Israelites for their succumbing to idolatry are found in the Israelites' worship of the Baal of Peor and Ezekiel's enumeration of Israel's systematic violation of the law in his depiction of the "bloody city." The wilderness incident at Shittim contains one of many examples of how easily the people could be led astray, especially when they encountered local people (Moab in this case) and their worship practices.[42] Ezekiel's prophetic oracle contains a checklist of violations ranging from idolatry to contempt for parents to adultery and taking bribes.[43] Presented as proof texts for disobedience, both instances end badly for the Israelites. Their failure to uphold their obligations under the law results in a quick lesson that includes both divine and mundane penalties for infidelity.[44]

In the ancient world, taking a vow involved invoking the deity's name, thereby making the god a contractual partner while focusing on the reciprocal relationship between the penitent and the deity.[45] This sometimes occurs in moments of psychological tension, like prospective military activity or the shame and distress of a childless woman like Hannah.[46] While her vow is clearly based on her personal need and could be described as a childbirth vow, it is likely that she is not the first to express such a vow, and in fact, it may be based on a common practice at the shrine by childless women.[47] In contrast, Jephthah's vow is spoken as a way of enticing the Divine Warrior to grant him a victory, but his precipitous statement, a form of a conditional vow that requests something and offers something if the request is granted, costs him his daughter.[48] While the Israelites' vow to YHWH promising to destroy the city of Arad if they are given a victory is similar, it differs in that the Israelites forego personal gain and instead dedicate the city and its loot to YHWH.[49] At least in Jephthah's case, it is evident that there is an inherent danger in what is contained in the vow, since it must be fulfilled even though it costs him his daughter and his posterity.[50] That helps explain the admonitions against making a vow if there are second thoughts about fulfilling it.[51] In other words, be careful what you ask for and what you promise to provide. There is also evidence of vows taken in less extreme conditions and even on a regular basis. That would apply to Elkanah's yearly pilgrimage to Shiloh to sacrifice and pay his vow.[52] The injunctions on making a vow (by both men and women) that appear in the priestly literature suggest that it was a common enough practice.[53] In fact, the discovery of a votive seal impression indicates that the fulfillment of a vow could be documented in the repeated use of the ring containing the votive inscription.[54]

Also radiating from the legal statements in these codes are injunctions demanding social justice for all persons, regarding concern for the poor and vulnerable, and honoring each generation for their contributions to the household and the larger community.[55] Social stratification and the emergence of elite members of the society took place after the establishment of the monarchy. That tested the societal principles of equal justice under the law. Counterbalancing the tendency to indulge their desires and abuse their power are examples in which a prophet confronts the powerful and forces them to face the consequences. Nathan's voicing of an example of social injustice to David, which is a thinly veiled reference to the king's adultery with Bathsheba, is an excellent case in point.[56] So too is Amos's cry against the "cows of Bashan" (= wives of wealthy merchants in Samaria), who see no issue in calling for more for themselves while others starve.[57]

Other legal statements are designed to protect the rights of those who are part of the landless poor or those who lack a head of household to protect or care for them: widows, orphans, and strangers / resident aliens.[58] The Covenant Code singles these individuals out for protection but does not make any explicit demands on the people, only warning them against oppressing them and warning that their cries for help will be heard by YHWH.[59] In the Deuteronomic and Holiness Codes, however, they are given material assistance, allowing them to glean from vineyards, olive orchards, and fields of grain.[60] One explanation for this expansion of the law may be found in the elimination of local shrines that may have provided for the poor when Jerusalem became the central repository for the kingdom of Judah.[61]

Concerns for the poorest members of Israelite society also are expressed in the laws on debt slavery. It is possible for persons to be temporarily sold into slavery to satisfy a debt. That period of servitude is required by law to end after six years, and a male can then go free.[62] The first iteration of the law in the Covenant Code simply ends at that point, but a later expansion in the Deuteronomic Code requires that he be given a portion from the flock, the threshing floor, and the winepress so that he does not go out empty-handed and susceptible to recidivism into slavery. The Holiness Code refers to these persons as "hired or bound laborers," not slaves, and requires them to be released in the Jubilee Year.[63] Where sound and touch enter this process is in a codicil in the earlier versions of the law that allow the man to remain in slavery at his own request, seeing this as a better option. If he makes a public declaration to that effect, noting his "love" for his master, he is brought before Elohim, is taken to the doorpost of his master's house, and has an awl driven through his earlobe. In this way, a physical connection is made between him and that household—tying the ear, the organ associated with hearing, to his perpetual obedience to that household.[64] It also marks him with a piercing that testifies to his permanent social placement as a slave.[65]

Coupled with these concerns over social injustice are the laws that deal with false witness and false testimony.[66] The Covenant Code provides the initial injunction beyond that in the Decalogue, forbidding anyone from spreading false reports or malicious gossip or simply joining

the majority when it perverts the justice process regarding the social status of the one charged.[67] At issue is whether the community can trust a
person's spoken word. To prevent a lack of trust in the judicial process,
the standard for conviction is based on the testimony of two or more
witnesses and is anchored to the evidence presented.[68]

Those being charged with a crime are assured that a thorough investigation will take place by the judges and priests and that the case will
be brought before YHWH as well. It is possible that "before YHWH"
means before the deity's human representatives rather than at a local
shrine, since they have been abolished according to the reforms of Hezekiah and Josiah.[69] In addition, the accused is assured that a false or malicious witness will receive the same punishment imposed on the convicted
person.[70] However, in the Psalms and in narratives that are dependent
on these legal protections, there are also strategies that use the law to
their benefit when two witnesses are suborned to speak falsely.[71] That
is the case when Jezebel arranges the judicial elimination of Naboth in
order to obtain a piece of land for her husband, King Ahab.[72] In this
instance, the injustice done is loudly denounced by the prophet Elijah,
and the condemnation of Ahab and his family ultimately results in a
coup led by Jehu.[73]

The damage caused by false charges is illustrated by incidents when
dissatisfied husbands claim that their wives have been unfaithful. In the
first case, a man, after consummating his marriage, slanders his wife by
claiming that she was not a virgin at the time.[74] That charge places an
obligation on the bride's father to demonstrate publicly the proof of her
virginity by testifying to her innocence and producing before the elders
the bloody sheet indicating the breaking of her hymen on the wedding
night.[75] In this way, the senses of hearing and sight are employed to settle the matter. And if the evidence of her virginity is not presented, she
is condemned to be stoned at her father's doorstep both to punish her
for prostituting herself and to shame the household that has committed fraud in arranging a marriage that did not adhere to the established
terms between the families.[76]

The other instance in which a husband raises the concern that his
wife has committed adultery is referred to as the Sotah ritual and deals
with both familial issues and matters of ritual purity. In this case, there
is no witness to testify to the matter, so a form of trial by ordeal is
employed.[77] The woman is physically taken to the priest by her jealous

husband, and she is required to take an oath before YHWH and consume a potion mixed from water and dirt from the floor that is infused with a divine curse. The labeling of this concoction as the "waters of bitterness" may be a reference to its taste or more likely a reflection of her husband's dangerously jealous attitude.[78] The implication is that if she is innocent, no harm will come to her after drinking the cursed mixture, but if she has been unfaithful, she will experience extreme pain, and her ability to reproduce will be permanently damaged by a prolapsed uterus.[79] Her submission to this ritual, while perhaps attributable to her duty to be obedient to her husband's word, contains an element of violence and collusion on the part of the priest, since both males assume that she is guilty. That conclusion is reinforced in the summation of the law, which, unlike other cases where the principle of talion retaliation is present, does not contain any consequences for the husband, who is simply redeemed by the implication that he has been overcome by a "spirit of jealousy."[80]

Both the Covenant Code and the Deuteronomic Code are quite explicit in forbidding taking bribes, blinding the eyes of judges to the fact of a case, and shedding innocent blood.[81] Unfortunately, bribery appears to be a common practice, subverting the judicial process and accommodating the wealthy and powerful. The verbal negotiations with judges that result in verdicts favoring those with the most to offer are condemned in Wisdom literature and in the prophetic materials.[82] However, private law for the powerful continued to be a reality, as indicated by Amos's refrain about those who feel free to "trample the head of the poor into the dust of the earth"—a metaphorical reference to the sense of touch.[83]

Smell

Smell is not explicitly mentioned and does not serve as a distinguishing factor in legal statements in the Hebrew Bible. However, because smell is a cultural factor with associated values that classify it as either pleasant or foul, an examination of its legal role can only be deduced through context.[84] Aroma, therefore, can be implied from several items in the codes. For example, the injunction that persons must relieve themselves "outside the camp" so that their excrement does not defile space that must be kept holy not only meets hygiene standards but also isolates the

odors to a designated location away from other people.[85] Since several
of the laws do involve homicide and accidental death, it can be assumed
that the discovery of the rotting corpse of a victim would fill one's nostrils with the stink.[86] The metaphor "like dung on the field" used for
bodies left unburied raises a memory and would quickly evoke knowledge of the odor of fields fertilized with dung.[87] When arson is committed and a field of standing grain is destroyed by the blaze, the smell
of the smoke would serve as an alert and evidence of criminal mischief
that requires full restitution of the value of the grain.[88] The "leprous
disease" and bodily discharges described in the Holiness Code must
have emitted a smell distinguishable by others and the priest examining
the individual.[89] However, since these laws reveal more information on the
role of the priesthood, they will be dealt with in the chapter on religious
practice.

Touch

When a person's skin contacts objects or another person, the receptors in
the skin that produce the sense of touch help translate or provide meaning to that contact and, to an extent, their world. They may say that
this contact is rough or smooth, soft or hard, round or square. And to
lose the sense of touch becomes a real handicap, since it also determines
the proper grip on a tool or weapon, the degree of pressure applied to a
task, or how to maintain balance while walking or going downstairs.[90]
In a legal sense, to touch involves the full range of contact with persons
or property: theft, sex crimes, physical violence, premeditated murder
and unintentional homicide, restraint or apprehension of individuals,
property rights and liability, physical punishment of felons, and codes
designed to prevent harm to persons or animals. There are also laws in
the law codes that deal with touching unclean things or persons, but they
will be dealt with in the chapter on religious practice, since that also
involves the intervention of priests.[91]

Theft of property includes the stealing of animals, goods given in
trust, and produce of the land. Since the theft of livestock has been
dealt with above in the section on sight, the issue of broken trust will be
examined here. The Covenant Code lists animals and moveable property in this category. At issue is whether the person to whom these items
have been entrusted is responsible should they go missing or, in the case

of animals, die. Touch comes into the picture in terms of the transfer of property from one person to another, along with the sense of responsibility for the items held in trust. Symbolically, the hand of liability hovers over them, and should harm or loss occur, restitution is required except in those cases in which there are no witnesses or an oath is taken before YHWH.[92] A similar level of liability is found in the law dealing with borrowing or hiring livestock.[93]

Theft of dignity and exploitation of the weak are at issue in the legal statement concerning the return of a cloak taken in pledge. Day laborers were required to turn over this outer garment to the owner or foreman as surety that they would work a full day in the fields. The law then requires that the cloak be returned at the end of the day so that they could wrap it around themselves against the night chill.[94] The humane character of the statute is clear, but the cloak, however humble in weave or fit, is a physical sign that the laborer is a freeman even if he is landless. Unfortunately, there is evidence that abuse of these members of the poor working class and flouting of this law did take place in ancient Israel. Amos's condemnation of the people of Israel includes those who take garments in pledge but sleep on them instead of returning them to their owners.[95] A similar instance that plays upon the values and customary norms expressed in the law is found in a seventh-century BCE letter written on a broken piece of pottery (an ostracon) that details the plea of a worker whose cloak is being unjustly held by the foreman who hired him.[96] The case made in the letter, which is an extrajudicial petition for justice, presumes knowledge of this legal principle, and like the plea of the Eloquent Peasant in Middle Kingdom Egyptian Wisdom literature (2040–1640 BCE), it calls on the powerful to deal justly with the people of the land.[97]

Coercion can take the form of kidnapping or taking someone into custody prior to a judicial hearing. Kidnapping, like rape, is a form of theft by force and is classified as a capital crime in large part because it undermines a sense of trust within a community when an "insider" acts like an "outsider" by stealing individuals for profit.[98] Human trafficking is certainly not a new phenomenon, but within the ancient Israelite context, its inclusion within the list of thirteen capital crimes is based on its foundation in the Decalogue command against stealing.[99] It also fits into this category based on its equivalence to premeditated homicide by stripping away an individual's life and its associations with rape, which also strips away personal volition and feelings of worth within the community.[100]

Similar abuses of power are found in laws forbidding the mistreatment of neighbors, the weak, and persons with disabilities. The injunction that forbids moving a neighbor's field's boundary stone first appears as a protection of property rights. It is tied to the allotment of land given under the covenant promise to each Israelite household by YHWH.[101] It is then amplified with a curse, and in Wisdom literature, it includes the command not to move the boundaries of an orphan's or a widow's field.[102] The placement of this law in the legal collection next to a curse on anyone who misleads the blind on the road suggests that misdirection is deemed equivalent to fraudulent rearrangement of boundary markers. Another injunction warning that the deaf are not to be ridiculed and no one is to put a "stumbling block" in the path of the blind not only reflects an attitude forbidding degrading the value of a fellow Israelite but also cautions against endangering the disabled through speech or physical misdirection.[103]

Physical violence, exclusive of warfare, occurs when tempers flare or when premeditated harm is intentionally planned. Harm can take the form of refusal to accept authority. For instance, striking a parent regardless of whether injury has occurred not only violates the injunction to honor parents in the Decalogue but is termed a capital crime in the Covenant Code. It is possible that this injunction reflects an earlier legal collection such as the eighteenth-century BCE Code of Hammurabi (#195), although in the Babylonian law, the son is to have his hand cut off.[104]

The prohibition of murder so succinctly stated in the Decalogue and in the Covenant Code cries out for clarification.[105] Perhaps for that reason, the definition of a murderer found in the priestly legislation is instructive based on how many permutations are covered. Thus, the judgment of murder is to be returned if the assailant strikes another person with an iron object, a stone in the hand, or a weapon of wood that can cause death. Murder is also assigned to cases in which a person is shoved to their death or attacked by someone lying in wait. In each case, the determining factor is intent or uncontrolled hatred that results in the death of another person.[106] Maintaining the legal balance here are corresponding references to unintentional or accidental harm that results in death.[107] The Deuteronomic Code expands the list of instances in which a person may unintentionally cause the death of another, providing a plausible example in which the ax-head of a forester comes loose and strikes someone.[108] In each case, the situation is removed from further legal proceedings and is classified as a blood feud. The sentence of death is to be carried out by the "avenger of blood," a close male relative of the deceased, rather than in a communal execution, since the crime has been committed by one household against another. Placing the case in the hands of a kinsman provides a finale as well as a limit to any further violence that might occur if the honor of the household is not satisfied.[109]

In the case of unintentional homicide, the law codes provide a means of escape for the culprit by creating a series of cities of refuge to which an unintentional murderer can flee until the families and the blood avenger have had time to cool off.[110] The development in the legal definition and reference to the number of cities of refuge that first appears in the Covenant Code with its reference to taking asylum at YHWH's altar seem based on the shift to Jerusalem-based cultic practice in the Deuteronomic Code and the need to make sure that a refuge city is within a reasonable distance.[111] For the purposes of the sense of touch, which includes motor skills, that means that safe haven is possible for a person with a normal ability to travel. Note also that taking refuge at an altar—that is, holding on to the horns of the altar within a temple—only applies if it is determined that the person claiming asylum did not willfully commit murder. In the aftermath of Solomon's assumption of the throne as David's successor, his brother and political rival Adonijah's holding on to the horns of the altar temporarily forestalls his execution. Joab, having backed Adonijah's claim to the throne, is struck down within the shrine based on his past murders of his rivals Abner, Amasa, and Absalom.[112] In his case, political expediency and the laws of homicide combine to remove a potential threat to the new king.

The designation of the principal heir is framed in the law and in the biblical narrative. Interestingly, the principle of primogeniture is not the principal determinant in the single legal statement that deals explicitly with heirship. Instead, it is predicated on a situation in which there are multiple wives and multiple children, and the point being made is to protect the rights of a son of an "unloved mother." It seems clear that a father has the prerogative to divide his estate among his progeny, but there is a preference that grants a double portion to the firstborn son of the principal wife, regardless of the personal feeling of the father toward that son's mother.[113] That runs counter to the narrative in which Jacob blesses Joseph's sons Manasseh and Ephraim but gives preference to the younger son despite Joseph's objections. He even crosses his hands to make this choice clear, touching Ephraim with his right hand.[114]

Issues of obedience to a parent's wishes or solemnizing a relationship through an oath are found in the custom of taking an oath by touching the thigh, a euphemism in this case for touching the male genitalia. While the examples of this practice come from the Ancestral Narratives, the reliance on oath taking is solemnized in the Decalogue and mentioned frequently in other legal statements (see above). The first example of touching the thigh occurs when Abraham instructs his servant to return to Nahor in Aram-naharim to obtain a wife for his son Isaac.[115] In this case, the oath is sworn in the name of YHWH. A similar use of this gesture is found when Jacob, on his deathbed, commands his son Joseph to swear that they will return his body to Canaan, where it can be buried in the family tomb.[116] Finally, in what has been mistranslated as an oath taken on the "Fear of Isaac" (it is better rendered the "thigh of Isaac"), Jacob twice berates his father-in-law, Laban, for unfair dealings and invokes the traditional meaning of the gesture that involves swearing on the power of the family ancestors and on the "God of Abraham."[117]

In cases dealing with bodily harm and the resultant liability for that injury, there are several separate incidents put forward. Each of them hinges on a person's moral responsibility for their actions whether they are overt or based on inattention to public safety.[118] One simple example could be termed a building inspector's code, since it requires the placement of a safety rail on the upper story of a house to prevent someone from falling.[119] A similar safety measure is found in the Covenant Code that deals with leaving a pit uncovered, presenting a hazard to animals.[120] The classic example of liability law is the case of the goring ox, which is found in both the biblical text and two other Near Eastern legal collections.[121] The similarity and divergences of the language in these legal statements suggest both familiarity with the earlier legal materials and a biblical reworking that helps explain the sharp distinction in terms of sanction between the Mesopotamian laws and the Covenant Code.[122] Since a goring or, more properly, "errant" ox is a probable feature of any agricultural society, it is not surprising to find this case among the principal laws dealing with liability.[123] At its heart is the failure on the part of the owner who has been warned about his ox's predilection to stray from its tasks and to harm other animals and persons. What is particularly interesting is the hierarchy of persons affected by the ox's actions, with a descending degree of punishment going down to payment of a fine for harm to slaves as opposed to capital punishment for a freeman or woman or child.

Another level of liability attends to the harm done to another person during a struggle. In a series of laws in the Covenant Code, a variety of scenarios are outlined, including injury, both lethal and nonlethal; loss of a fetus when a woman is struck; and issues involving injury to slaves. In the first case, when injury is not fatal, the liability results in compensation for time lost during the injured person's recovery.[124] If a pregnant woman has been injured inadvertently during the fight and subsequently miscarries without further harm to herself, compensation is set by the woman's husband at a figure based on the loss of an economic asset for the household.[125] In cases involving slaves, there is no liability for striking a slave, assuming that it is simply a form of punishment and that the slave has not been devalued as a result of the loss of a tooth or an eye, but if the slave dies, there is an unspecified punishment making this law similar to those that relate to misuse of property.[126]

The degree to which individual scuffles took place must have been sufficient to require further elaboration within the legal collections. The Deuteronomic Code includes a statement about a woman intervening in a fight between her husband and another man. If she reaches out and grasps the other man's genitals during the struggle, even if it is inadvertent, her hand is to be amputated.[127] A similar example in the Middle Assyrian Laws (#8) hinges on physical damage to the man's testicles, requiring amputation of the woman's fingers or having her eyes gouged out if both testicles are harmed.[128] Like the law in which there is a loss of a fetus, damage to the male genitals could result in sterility. Even though the Deuteronomic version does not qualify the difference between touching and actual physical harm, it may be implied that there is potential for damaging the man's later ability to sire children.[129]

Taste

While there is little explicit information on the sense of taste in a legal context in the Hebrew Bible, the dietary laws may provide some insight into this area, especially about the creation of a social identity through the development of a cuisine that also involved the exclusion of certain foods.[130] In one case, it can at least be assumed that the taste of produce taken from a neighbor's field is satisfactory and nourishing.[131] While the intent of the law is to prevent wholesale harvesting of grapes or grain and explicitly forbids "putting a sickle" to the neighbor's standing grain, the humanitarian nature of the law is like the law governing gleaning.[132] The restriction against eating meat mangled after being attacked by wild beasts both speaks to the issue of purity and suggests that the meat is likely to be either contaminated or rotten.[133] Similarly, the restriction banning the boiling of a kid in its mother's milk invokes a concern for mixing meat and milk as well as creating an abhorrence for the taste of that dish.[134] Since the law appears in different social and historical contexts and there is no conclusive explanation for this dietary taboo, it may have had different origins based on an illicit mixture that includes blood for cultic purposes.[135] However, once a dietary preference or restriction has been firmly set in place and is regularly reinforced by the voice of authority in its efforts to create a national identity, the mental socialization process makes eating restricted items distasteful and even disgusting.[136] Just one example suffices here. The basis for the listing of pork as an excluded food has been debated and often points to identity or ideology issues involving the "othering" of enemy groups.[137] While it is not possible to completely dismiss these arguments, it is also quite likely that pigs were simply not considered of great value to the ancient Israelites, since their only product was meat, while other animals—like sheep, goats, and cows—provided multiple benefits.[138]

Final Thoughts

In many ways, law is shaped by and simultaneously shapes society. Sometimes it is simply a matter of maintaining order or protecting property, but there is always in the background a hint of how it upholds cultural identity. Not every law will appear in every community, since environmental and demographic conditions vary. Still, those that ban murder, theft, and fraud are the most common in all the legal collections in the Near East. In most cases, they touch on the senses in some way. By examining these touch points, their origin and usefulness can be better understood.

5

Religious Practice
Sacred Place and Sacred Performance

IN MANY WAYS, the images and descriptions of the gods and specific religious worship and ritual practices have their origin and power in the world of the senses. What we know about ancient Israelite and ancient Near Eastern religious practice comes to us from the texts that they produced. In many cases, the description of a particular ritual, its purpose, and in some cases its origin are reflective of the role played by religious officiants and the intent to both instruct and energize the people. The sheer repetition of orchestrated rituals as part of major events, such as a New Year's festival, provided a sense of comfort that proper forms had been observed and life within the domain of the god(s) would remain on a relatively even keel. Rituals also played a part in reaffirming the authority of kings, high priests, and other elite figures, but for the individual worshipper, they reinforced a sense of identity and community as they served as either a passive viewer or an active participant. While ritual texts such as Leviticus 1–7 draw on the authority of the past, they also illustrate societal change when the Solomonic temple was destroyed and then replaced by a much less grandiose structure in the postexilic period.[1] Thus, in the discussion below of religious practice, some attention will be given to the social context of the biblical materials amid the analysis of sensory aspects of these practices.

Before the biblical text was written, however, came personal experience through the senses. The majesty associated with the storm as its bursts of lightning and thundering sounds filled the sky, the heat of the sun as it shined its brilliance on the heads of workers in a field, and the smell of the rain or of the flowers on a hillside were all indications to the ancients of the presence of the gods and their power at work.[2] The descriptions of their power include both the gods and the elemental monsters like Humbaba and the Bull of Heaven in the Gilgamesh epic displaying superhuman abilities that are accompanied by smoke rushing from their nostrils and fire from their mouths.[3] It was their experience of the bountiful and destructive aspects of nature—of forces beyond their ability to totally understand—and the desire to obtain the goodwill of powers greater than their own that formed the early basis for the belief in a god or gods.

Since these deities represented forces beyond human control, they generated fear as well as the promise of protection or prosperity. The sense of awe that bred respect and a desire to curry favor or to propitiate them was also aimed at forestalling disastrous events like storms from wreaking havoc in their lives. Possibly the dedication of anchors in the temple of Baal at the seaport city of Ugarit is an indication of both the hope and the expectation of smooth sailing by the merchant fleets that sailed from that city.[4] At the same time, lived religious practices from ritual performance to quiet meditation involved individual and group measures designed to focus on certain visual images, sounds, and smells to make these experiences more meaningful.[5]

One of the evolving aspects of the Israelites' understanding of their god was the removal of a visible image of the deity. The other cultures that surrounded them fashioned images of their gods, but with the command not to do so, the Israelites had to seek out other sensory associations for YHWH. Among the most important of them was the voice. When that commanding, even terrifying voice spoke to them collectively or to individuals like Moses or Elijah, there was no humanlike form to go with it. That, in turn, became the basis for the rejection of idols and the demand that the people should not fall into that practice associated with their neighbors.[6]

Idols are a major topic in the Bible and one that crosses over the senses, from seeing them to the fabrication of them to the "care and feeding" that they require daily.[7] Both Habakkuk and Second Isaiah are quite pointed in their descriptions of idols as worthless, human creations that have no real power and only sap the energies and disappoint the expectations of their worshippers.[8] The Psalms are filled with comparisons between the impotence of sacred images and the actual works of YHWH.[9] And in particular, the argument is made that these idols have no true sensory aspect to them at all, with mouths that cannot speak, noses that cannot smell, and eyes that cannot see.[10]

In focusing on the sensory aspects of religious practice, it will be necessary to discuss both individual devotions and rituals and those that involved the entire community. Just as the farmer prayed for good weather that would lead to a bountiful harvest, the city dweller prayed and made thank offerings to YHWH with the hope of a profitable business or a year without invaders threatening the city. As a community, villagers and urbanites celebrated major festivals with ritual processions, sacrifices, and commemorations. Individual families marked the birth of male children with the rite of circumcision, and the entire population of the nation was expected to honor the restrictions of the law during Sabbath. While some may have been more observant than others, which is a major issue discussed in the prophetic materials, the identity of the nation was bound up in the stipulations of the covenant with YHWH and the law.

Sight

The first places of worship mentioned in the biblical narrative appear to be simple altars built at sites associated with the ancestors at Shechem, Bethel, Hebron, and Beer-sheba.[11] Later references to high places, or *bāmôt*, portray them as roofed structures located in villages and small cities throughout Canaan, with chambers to house local priests and to store vestments and items associated with sacrificial ritual.[12] While not extravagantly large, they served the needs of individual households and small communities before an official priestly class was fully organized. Eventually, more monumental structures were designed to supersede the importance of local shrines not only by their size but by their inclusion of additional cultic items such as incense altars, standing stones (*massebôt*) such as those in the Arad temple, and Asherah poles to represent the gods of that place.[13] It is not surprising to find that they were architecturally similar in design. Although there are no archaeological remains of the Jerusalem temple, there are three Levantine Iron Age II temples known to have similar architectural footprints based on the descriptions in the biblical account: Hazor, Tell Ta'yinat (thirty-one miles west of Aleppo, Syria), and Tell Ain Dara (forty miles northwest of Aleppo).[14]

By design, temples attempted to awe visitors to the cities where they were built. Access would be restricted to the faithful who were judged to be in a pure state, and they housed the priesthood and served as places where the presence of a deity was said to reside.[15] In every case, the monumental architecture and elaborate furnishing of these temple complexes were visual demonstrations of wealth, authority, and the power of both the central government and the priestly community to create physical representations of their god's majesty and their own political influence.[16] The temple complex continued to evolve as the city, the king, and the temple became more important. Chambers and gates were added over time connecting the temple to the royal palace and serving as a visual backdrop to major events and speeches.[17] For example, Jeremiah's staging of his prophetic address in the temple gate, in what stands for the people of Jerusalem as a "central sacred space," gives him and his words greater authority, since they are publicly attached to that space.[18]

The intrinsic purpose of a temple was for the people to attempt to come in closer contact with the divine and to express thanks for blessings received or make petitions in cases in which environmental or political disasters threatened the people. The identification of sacred space where these structures were to be located often was associated with a theophany such as Moses's burning bush experience or the official transference of a religious object into a temple.[19] Once it had been established that a particular site was indeed sacred ground, ritual practice became a part of the activities associated with that site. It also transformed the site into a pilgrimage destination for the people of the surrounding region.

A prime example is the sacralization of the threshing floor of Araunah following a theophany that ends a plague. David marks this divine event by purchasing the site and a team of oxen and their threshing slide and then constructing an altar upon which he sacrifices the oxen. With that as the foundation for its transformation into sacred space, it is advantageous in the next generation for the Jerusalem temple to be constructed here by Solomon.[20] Although local high places and shrines continued to be used for worship in both the northern and southern kingdoms of Israel, the fall of the northern kingdom and the pressures placed on Judah by the Assyrian and Babylonian Empires magnified Jerusalem as the last bastion of official YHWH worship. It is possible that King Josiah at the end of Judah's monarchic history saw an advantage to establishing the Jerusalem temple as the exclusive site for YHWH worship, but tying his efforts to the language in Deuteronomy is somewhat uncertain.[21] The point to be made here is that whenever worship was transferred from local sites to a temple complex, the power of the priestly community was magnified, and the ritual performances that they directed became more elaborate visual spectacles.

Religious ritual is by its nature visual and very often communal. To be sure, individual worshippers like Samuel's mother, Hannah, could engage in prayer or private devotional acts,[22] but because many religious practices were designed as social functions, they achieved their greatest impact in public display. The construction of sacrificial altars by Noah and Abram introduced the worship of YHWH and provided a visual example for later generations of how to venerate and thank the deity. That sometimes led to disputes such as the concern over the construction of an altar in the Transjordanian territory occupied by the tribes of Reuben, Gad, and Manasseh. Despite the threat of a civil war among the tribes, ultimately the altar was accepted by both parties as a "witness" to YHWH's covenant with all the people.[23] Of course, as the nation evolved and a priestly community became more active as religious practitioners, supplanting the elders and heads of households in the village culture, these local altars (later referred to as high places, or bāmôt) were suppressed and replaced by the temple in Jerusalem, where much more elaborate public displays could occur.[24]

The daily role of the priesthood also evolved as temple complexes became larger, and the duties of the priests came to include a wide variety of tasks. Some of these duties were public, and some were restricted to the inner precincts of the temple. For instance, it became the duty of the priests and high priests in the Jerusalem temple to light the menorah each day.[25] There were also lesser servitors who functioned as doorkeepers, cleaners, and servants for the higher-ranking priests.[26] They may well have been the most publicly visible of the temple personnel, although the vestments of the priests, especially the very distinctive garments worn by the high priest, did single them out to the people.[27]

Religious processions are another case in point. They were a form of visual spectacle and were sometimes staged in demonstrations of the power of the Divine Warrior—as in the story of Joshua's capture of Jericho[28]—or as part of the reenactment of YHWH's entrance into the city of Jerusalem and welcome into the temple. The latter example comes from Psalm 68:24–25 (25–26), and although the prohibition of parading images of the deity would be prohibited in ancient Israel, the procession does contain singers and musicians to provide a tempo and accompaniment for the other participants.[29]

The mix of politics and religion also emerges when examining the procession in the story that depicts how David transports the ark of the covenant to Jerusalem. It provides several precedents for proper religious practice, most poignantly in the death of the Levite Uzzah for inappropriately touching the ark,[30] and demonstrates both the entertainment value and the long-lasting political effects of a public event. It also serves as the precursor for Solomon's accession narrative that includes a procession with the newly proclaimed king riding on David's mule into the city accompanied by the blowing of trumpets and shouts of acclimation. That is then piggybacked with the narrative of Solomon's transport of the ark into the newly constructed temple in Jerusalem.[31] It is also possible to link these processional events with Zechariah's apocalyptic vision of a king of peace and with the narrative of Jesus's triumphal entry in Mark's and Luke's Gospels.[32] Among those features of the archetypal story that seem to have the greatest impact are the use of instruments, the inclusion of dance, and the ultimate destination of the procession where sacrificial rites will occur.[33]

At its heart is the scene in which David transports a sacred object that represents the presence of YHWH into Jerusalem. Of course, he is not going to do it in the dark of night when no one would be present to see it. For it to have maximum impact, a public show is necessary and very desirable. Thus, he leads a procession into the city with Levites carrying the ark. He clothes himself only in a priestly linen garment around his waist, thereby highlighting this holy duty and temporarily downgrading his normal political role as king.[34] Even in what some like Michal might see as a shameful display, David is able to capitalize on his position as the anointed king and representative of YHWH to the nation.[35] He dances unashamedly before the people in celebration, as Jerusalem is officially transformed into both the royal capital and the dwelling place for YHWH.[36]

In the earlier phase of their journey to Jerusalem, a much larger group of instruments are mentioned proclaiming their joy and calling

on all along the route to see the ark.[37] Once they reach the city, trumpets/
shofars are sounded, announcing their arrival. Trumpets are part of
other processions that included the ark and may have been the traditional means of sounding a fanfare indicating the presence of YHWH.[38]
Their shouts attract a crowd of people who are then treated to the sight
of burnt offerings and offerings of well-being, a general blessing by
David, and the distribution of food, including bread, meat, and cakes
of raisins.[39] In this way, David's political desire to unify the tribes and a
centralized religious site are wedded. The scene ends with David's role as
king being certified by the people. Thereafter, when the story is told, it
is the procession that stands at the heart of these events, since it can be
reenacted as an integral part of the people's history and a cherished tie
to their relationship with YHWH.[40]

Thereafter, during both major and minor celebrations, festal processions effectively melded the sacred space around temple precincts
with the mundane space that surrounded it. As they wound their way
through the streets of Jerusalem with ring dances, they mapped a
pathway that carried celebrants to the temple, where sacrificial offerings
would take place and a feast of thanksgiving would occur.[41] They were
welcomed into a publicly expressed, communal celebration of harvest
seasons, New Years, and other major calendrical occasions and thereby
encouraged in their belief in the power of the deity and the importance
of the temple in their lives.[42]

Yet another visual feature of religious practice is the set of vestments
worn by priests, especially the high priest. These garments served as a
visual extension of their person that sent a social message to their col-
leagues and everyone who saw them in public or in the commission of
their priestly duties.[43] Each piece of their vestments provided a visible
distinction for the priesthood, a uniform with elaborate and colorful
embroidery that was also a badge of their obligation to exemplify in
their person the concepts of holiness and purity. The ordination ceremony in which the priest was anointed and clothed in these garments
became a visual spectacle before the people that thereafter marked
that person with the authority to carry out priestly duties.[44] There are
detailed descriptions of the manufacture of the separate items that made
up the set of vestments worn by priests and by the high priest as well as
the specific occasions/ceremonies in which they were to be worn.[45] Most
importantly, the garments that they wore while performing their sacred

duties were to be made of linen, a material, as Ezekiel notes, that would not cause them to sweat.[46]

Because their public ordination and investiture set priests aside as a distinctive group within Israelite society, they also had specific restrictions placed upon them to maintain their ritual purity and aura of holiness.[47] That, for instance, formed the basis for the priestly ordinances that restricted them from contact with the dead, restricted their marriage choices, and forbade them from tearing their vestments as a ritual of mourning.[48] Perhaps that is why Ezekiel's street theater performance in which he, a priest, plays like a child in the dust of the street would be both shocking to his audience and a signal that what he says and does goes beyond normal practice.[49] A further sign of the importance of the priest's person as a symbol of purity is found in Zechariah's postexilic vision of the high priest Joshua. He is first portrayed as wearing "filthy clothing," which is stripped from his person and then replaced with "clean" apparel. The transformation not only restores his ability to carry out his priestly duties but more importantly represents the removal of his and Jerusalem's guilt, defilement, and unworthiness. Both have been purified and now bear the outward trappings of that condition.[50]

Sound

One of the most pervasive sounds associated with religious worship was prayer. Spoken prayer functioned in most cases as a combination of verbal plea, petition, pledge, and praise. In the biblical text, public communal prayers such as those in Psalms appear in poetry, while prayers spoken by individuals are in prose.[51] A prayer could be spoken by either gender or as an independent devotional statement separate from the usual ties to the household. For example, even though the childless Hannah has been reassured by her husband, Elkanah, of her value to him, she takes a step without direct solicitation of priestly mediation, voicing a vow that would have an impact on her husband and household.[52] Her prayer is spoken silently, but the assumption is that it could be heard by YHWH, and that is in turn demonstrated when she becomes pregnant. Her votary oath to dedicate the child as a Nazirite in service to the deity at the shrine at Shiloh follows a pattern found in Leviticus.[53] Hannah's subsequent song of praise parallels the structure found in Psalms of a lament that first cries out in distress and concludes with an acknowledgment of the power of the divine and a hymn of thanksgiving.[54] Prayer could be the most personal as well as the collective expression of a devotee's interaction with the deity and did not require the temple setting, since in many cases a prayer reflected a "life setting," including illness, that would prevent the worshipper from going to the temple.[55] It voiced the innermost feelings of a person and the voice of the people when they cried out in either their suffering or their joy.[56]

In terms of communal prayer, several instances could be defined as a form of acknowledgment of the power and authority of the deity. It was collective recognition of the divine energy that filled the world and empowered every creature.[57] It also demanded of worshippers that they proclaimed the "greatness" and the specific acts that exemplified the deeds of YHWH. By praising the deity, a form of verbal sacrifice was made, but it was also designed to energize the community and make them one with creation in their hymn to the creator.[58]

Once prayer had become formalized in writing, it also could serve as a creed to be spoken, read, and displayed. A case in point is the Shema: "Hear O Israel, the Lord is our God, the Lord alone."[59] This prayer was to be inculcated into every Israelite's consciousness, recited to children, and constantly in one's thoughts. In addition, a performance was commanded during morning prayers that included the tefillin, or phylacteries, small boxes bound around the arm and across the forehead that contained a parchment with verses from the Torah. To meet the command to "write on the doorposts," a tradition developed in which a tube, the *mezuzah*, containing the verse was to be affixed to the doorpost of each house, displaying that household's commitment to the one God.[60] These latter injunctions most likely fit a late period in Israelite history, but they demonstrate how spoken prayer can be expanded into visual modes as well.[61]

A spoken prayer could also take the form of a chant or incantation designed to greet the deity, draw the god's attention to a specific need, or prevent harm to the worshipper when entering sacred space. The latter case appears to be the purpose for the threefold chant "This is the temple of the Lord" spoken by persons who intended to cross the threshold of the gate of the Jerusalem temple. It may also be a reiteration of the belief in the invulnerability of Jerusalem because of the presence of YHWH in that place.[62] The purpose and rhythm of the chant are comparable to the

Šuilla rubric in Akkadian incantation texts that instructed the worshipper or penitent to speak their message three times.[63]

Passing from profane to sacred space implied crossing the liminal zone of the threshold or doorway, and this was a step that had to be taken carefully and with whatever precautions were available.[64] Note the Philistine priests' precaution not to step on the threshold of the temple of Dagon in Ashdod and the prophetic admonition about leaping over the threshold.[65] With that in mind, Jeremiah publicly denounces this threefold formula as "deceptive," since it can have no protective value for those who continue to violate the covenant.

While much of prophetic speeches and the penitential psalms are filled with the consequences of Israel's failure to obey the voice of YHWH, that voice is seldom heard and then only by prophets like Moses, Elijah, and Isaiah. More often, the voice emanates from a fiery theophany or above the mercy seat of the ark of the covenant without a physical appearance of the deity.[66] The voice is also characterized in terms of a mighty wind driving the waves or rushing like a whirlwind down a mountainside, the roar of thunder in the sky, or the crashing of the sea.[67] These naturalistic sounds may be a residue of Israel's associations with their neighbors' religions that viewed the natural world as filled with gods and thus associated them with the majestic sounds of power manifested in the heat of the sun, the rush of the waves on a shoreline, or the cacophony of a storm. In the biblical text, these images are often equated with YHWH's control over the realms of nature, understanding and using its power, and being fully in command of its destructive and beneficial properties.[68]

Once the Jerusalem temple is constructed and inaugurated by King Solomon, entire groups of priests are organized into choir guilds and orchestras to provide music at every major celebration. The Psalms describe their joyous melodies as they sing the Lord's praise and play on their tambourines, ten-stringed harps, and lyres.[69] It is likely that similar guilds of musicians and singers were organized to serve in the Bethel temple after the division of the kingdom.[70]

Among the Jerusalem choir masters and music directors appointed to lead the singing were Asaph, Heman, and Jeduthun, each of whom commanded a performing group.[71] The music, which included antiphonal choirs, functioned as a showcase for particular celebrations such as the Sabbath day or the commemoration of the coronation of a king.[72]

In some cases, the music that they composed and performed functioned as a mnemonic of the history of the nation as well as a means of glorifying YHWH in song.[73] Festal processions celebrating the new moon, full moon, and other calendrical events also included the sounds of trumpets (shofars), lutes, harps, tambourines, pipes, and clashing cymbals.[74] Pilgrims in the Persian period (550–325 BCE) who were coming to Jerusalem to worship during the major festivals and who were from throughout the Near Eastern world may have hastened their step by singing one or all of the Songs of Ascent to acknowledge their allegiance to YHWH while at the same time demonstrating that wherever the people lived, they, like Jerusalem, embodied "Zion."[75]

Orchestral performance also functioned as a part of the religious practices of all the Near Eastern cultures and was associated, sometimes by the use of particular instruments, with specific rituals and sacrifices.[76] Numerous Egyptian tomb paintings depict harp players performing before a god or blowing a trumpet (shofar), and artistic objects and palace reliefs from Canaan and Mesopotamia picture processions of musicians playing a variety of stringed and percussion instruments.[77] A further testimony to this musical tradition is found in the elaborate dedication ceremony for Nebuchadnezzar's massive golden statue of his god. His royal musicians played all the instruments listed in the Psalms.[78] Many of the superscriptions in the Psalms include instrumentation, but Psalm 150 pulls together a scene of praise within the temple grounds with the shofar blasting, the strings of harps and lyres being strummed, and tambourines, cymbals, and pipes being sounded as the priest danced in harmony with the music.[79]

Smell

It seems clear that the sense of smell was just as important to the ancient Israelites as the senses of sight and hearing. They were certainly aware of foul odors tied to decay and rot. They could savor the sweet smell of spices as well as the sharp aromas associated with a worker's active or passive vocations, and they could distinguish a person's relative health, wealth, or poverty through their sense of smell.[80] In fact, the use of incense was undoubtedly tied to membership in the priestly class, marking them as associated with the work of and the presence of the deity.[81] It is also likely that members of the priestly community could also be identified by their body odor, which reflected their diet, which came from their portion of the sacrificial meat and was thus higher in protein than that of many of the other Israelites.[82]

Given the emphasis on the connection between sacrifice and a "pleasing" olfactory reaction by YHWH in many biblical texts, it is not surprising that incense had a wide use as a fumigant in personal residences as well as part of cultic worship. It was also used as part of various other rites, including burials.[83] Its aroma, like that of acceptable sacrifices, was designed to communicate a "pleasing odor" that evoked the blessing of the deity.[84] The importance of that aroma is included in YHWH's curse on a disobedient nation that includes laying their cities to waste and a refusal to "smell your pleasing odors."[85] That helps explain why a private mixture of various aromatic ingredients was reserved for the exclusive use of the temple personnel.[86] Specialized pottery vessels were created to hold and dispense the incense mixture and oil, and incense shovels scooped it onto the altar for burning. Throughout the ritual, it was the responsibility of the priests to ensure that all the proper steps were taken to prevent YHWH's displeasure, and should anyone else usurp that role, it would be considered a further provocation of the deity.[87]

Ultimately, incense became a distinctive feature of the smells associated with the sacred precincts and those who worked therein.[88] However, physical evidence of the use of very costly substances like frankincense, stacte, onycha, and galbanum either in the Jerusalem temple or on domestic altars has been lacking. It is likely that the incense altars were cleaned regularly, and many were destroyed. One exception is the incense altars found in the excavation of Tel Arad in the 1960s. The small shrine incorporated into this southern Judahite fort was only used for about fifty years during the eighth century BCE. It was then completely interred either to prevent it from being desecrated by the Assyrian invaders or perhaps as part of Hezekiah's reform that required the centralization of official worship rites in Jerusalem, while all other local high places and shrines were decommissioned.[89]

The residue that had been collected from these two Arad altars during excavation was submitted for chemical analysis. Among the results was an indication that incense fragrances were ignited by animal fat in the case of frankincense and animal dung in the case of cannabis. That would be made necessary by the lack of other fuels. What this suggests is that Arad, like Beer-sheba, was associated with the South

Arabian incense trade during the period when Judah was subject to Assyrian hegemony and that the fort at Arad was able to make use of these aromatic substances in their cultic activities. It also demonstrates that the inhaling of a psychoactive material (cannabis) was employed to induce a mind-altering ecstasy during these ceremonies.[90]

Smell was also associated with illness. Sores or wounds could mortify and emit a foul smell.[91] For example, Job's breath becomes foul because of his many maladies, and even his family finds him too disgusting to be around.[92] Their reluctance to approach him may be due to concern over infection or the transmission of impurity.[93] That is apparently the case when the house of a leper appears to have become infected by them in much the same way as the noxious vapors of its inhabitant. At that point, a priest would be required to inspect it, both by eye and by nose. That, in turn, might result in drastic steps, including demolishing the house.[94]

Touch

Since touch has been defined in this volume as any of the motor functions of the body, it is appropriate to take note of a variety of ritual acts that were associated with worship or purification.[95] Among these was fasting, which was often accompanied by other ritual acts such as mourning when it was appropriate to tear one's clothing or wear sackcloth while adorned with ashes.[96] Like any other form of spiritual denial, fasting could serve as a form of religious atonement or preparation for a life-changing event, or it could be employed to help focus the mind on things other than the body's needs.[97] However, fasting could also contribute to the manifestation of a food disorder or a badge of pride to demonstrate to others one's extreme piety, neither of which was a positive outcome. It then became simply a public display associated with insincere fasting that is condemned in the Prophets and the Gospels.[98]

The hands and arms were often used in religious ceremonies or acts of worship. In some cases, religious rites included the elevation of the hands with palms turned forward to "greet" the deity or to draw the deity's attention to the worshippers as the ceremony progressed.[99] The Israelites were warned, however, that YHWH would not take note of their gesture or their entreaties if their sacrifices and their worship were hollow and meaningless.[100]

There is also a sense in some of the Psalms that in the absence of the temple or it being too far away from the worshipper, lifting one's hands toward the Lord's sanctuary served this same purpose of greeting YHWH and bonding with the blessings emanating from the deity.[101] The equivalency of this gesture to the burning of incense or to the odor emitted by a sacrificial offering evoked right behavior and a plea to preserve the worshipper from evil speech or action.[102] It may also have certified home worship practices not as equivalent to those in the temple but in harmony with them.[103] The postexilic covenant renewal ceremony conducted by Ezra includes a public gathering in which he "blesses the Lord, the Great God," and the people respond with the affirmation "Amen, Amen" as they lift up their hands before bowing to the ground to worship.[104] During the regular sacrificial process, the priest was expected to elevate his hands to showcase the item being offered, displaying it to the body of worshippers and to the deity.[105] Once the ceremony had been successfully completed, uplifted hands then functioned as a way to pronounce a blessing on the people.[106]

There were also instances in which waving the hands was associated with curing the sick. For instance, when the Syrian general Na'aman seeks out the Israelite prophet Elisha to cure his skin disease, he becomes angry with the prophet when he does not appear before him in person or call on YHWH or wave his hands over the skin eruptions on the sufferer's body. Instead, Na'aman is instructed by Elisha's servant Gehazi to go wash in the Jordan River seven times. Although angry at what he considers an unorthodox instruction, Na'aman eventually is convinced to take this step and is cured.[107] It is the touch of the river—already associated with sacred space since the miraculous crossing by both Elijah and Elisha—that is the transformative element in this case, reinforcing Elisha's authority as a prophet.[108]

As noted above and in previous chapters, the physical sensation of movement that was expressed in dance, whether spontaneous or part of ritual performance, was a familiar part of the celebrations in both the village and city cultures. From David's dancing before the ark as it was carried into Jerusalem at the inception of his kingship to the celebratory dances of women welcoming a victorious army and its leaders back to their midst, dance functioned as a joyous and very natural aspect of life and religious expression in times of celebration.[109] That same joy was expressed in rituals associated with the temple in Jerusalem that include music and dance.[110]

Since ritual purity was a necessity for priests to engage in religious activities, it was important that they did not come in physical contact with objects such as a corpse or persons (lepers) who were defined as unclean. Of course, nonpriests had a similar concern regarding becoming ritually unclean, but their occupations did not depend on that state of being. There was the further concern over indirect contact. If a person touched a dead body, they were by that contact made unclean and potentially could contaminate others.[111] Plus, if they subsequently touched any kind of food, it was then made unclean.[112] However, there was some disagreement over whether a person, a priest, or his clothing could transmit ritual purity to another person or object. Lamentations (dating to the destruction of Jerusalem in 586 BCE) and the postexilic prophet Haggai both agree that only impurity could be transmitted by indirect touch, while the exilic prophet Ezekiel cautions priests to remove their vestments before leaving the temple to prevent the transmission of their holiness to nonpriests.[113] The difference in interpretation may hinge on a more negative attitude toward the priestly class by those who associated them with the fall of Jerusalem and the inability of the postexilic community to complete the restoration of the temple.

While indirect touch did have the potential to transmit impurity and thus was to be avoided, the Ezekiel passage suggests a tradition in which ritual purity could be transmitted through the touch of a garment invested with purity. An interesting application of the power of indirect touch thus occurs in the story of the woman with a persistent hemorrhage in the Synoptic Gospels.[114] She only touches Jesus's robe, not his person, and yet she is healed by this indirect contact. Although, because of her bleeding, she would be in an impure state and thus need to be avoided, there is no sense that Jesus is contaminated, even temporarily, by her impurity.[115] In fact, like in the interpretation in Ezekiel 44:19 regarding priestly garments, it seems that Jesus's garment has been infused with his holiness—something implied when other persons had attempted to touch his robe[116]—and thus could transmit inadvertently to her through touch a new, ritually pure state as well as a restoration to health.[117]

The divine rationale for ritual purity among the Israelites is explicitly stated in the Holiness Code in Leviticus: "You shall be holy, for I am holy."[118] The various categories or conditions that resulted in an impure state (death, blood, semen, and scale disease) had as their common feature their association with death.[119] One means of maintaining ritual purity and a continuance of life for priests as well as all Israelites was through ritual bathing in a *miqweh*.[120] These ritual baths have been excavated in several first-century CE towns and villages, including Sepphoris and Jericho, as well as near the Temple Mount in Jerusalem.[121] While only priests were required to maintain a state of physical perfection, impurity for all others could result from physical contact via genital discharge, a corpse, the clothing or furniture defiled by a woman experiencing her menstrual period, a woman who had given birth, or venereal disease, among other causes.[122] Any of these forms of defilement would prevent a person from entering the sacred precincts of the temple, and thus the easy proximity of ritual baths near the Temple Mount would be a necessity. One exception to this rule involved persons who had touched a corpse but were still enjoined by YHWH to keep the Passover feast.[123]

Taste

Food associated with rituals such as the Passover meal contained symbolic meaning as well as distinctive tastes tied to emotions and the re-creation of the story. Food thus became a system of communication that spoke to each successive generation and served as a mnemonic that emphasized the importance of the story during the performance of the ritual.[124] It was the memory associated with previous practice that added power and provided new significance to a ritual meal. In that way, the Last Supper, which at its foundation was a faithful reenactment of the original Passover meal, became the basis for the development of a reshaped communal meal as it evolved into the Eucharist during the early Christian era.[125]

Another example is found in Ezekiel's vision of a restored temple, which also contains a Passover celebration, and its commemoration on the first month ensures that the temple will be in its purest state for the festival.[126] The elements of the meal serve as a memorial tying the past, the present, and the future together for the celebrants as they taste each successive portion of the feast. In the same way, the "bitter herbs" symbolize and bring once again to mind the bitterness experienced by their ancestors while celebrating the moment of liberation made possible by their god.[127]

Even eschatological meals such as the one described in Isaiah's "Little Apocalypse" provide insight into ritual meals associated with religious celebrations. Patterned after feasts tied to the reenactment of major events such as YHWH's entrance into Jerusalem when David brings the ark into that city, the celebrants enjoy a rich meal that consists of aged wines and the marrow from the bones of sacrificial animals.[128] The banqueters on the holy mountain are carried to gustatory exuberance as their eyes examine and their taste buds savor the unusual opportunity provided by such a menu, joyously detecting and relishing each course of rich food.[129]

Tastes that might ordinarily be avoided also played a part in the social drama of religious ritual. The contrast of sweet and bitter that symbolized the best and worst natures of a marriage may have been the foundation of the Sotah ritual and functioned as a reversal in the couple's relationship. It began when the suspicious husband brought his wife to the priest. He would also bring along a barley offering but would not pour olive oil or add frankincense as if it was the normal *minhah* offering, which was one celebration designed to produce a "pleasing odor" for the deity.[130] In this case, however, it served as an "offering of remembrance," perhaps signifying how previous memories of a good marriage had been eroded by the husband's suspicions. The priest then concocted a potion from holy water and dust from the floor of the tabernacle, into which he dissolved the ink from the curse he wrote out on parchment.[131] He would dishevel and uncover the woman's hair as if she was in mourning and then require her to hold the "offering of jealousy" in her hand while an execration oath was pronounced. The expectation was that after she consumed the potion, she would either remain sound of body and thus innocent of the charge of infidelity or experience the force of the curse, damaging her uterus to the extent that she would become infertile.[132] The bitterness that she had tasted was the result of both what was contained in the cup and the enforcement of shame heaped upon her by her husband, who in the end bore no iniquity for forcing the issue simply based on his own jealousy.[133]

Final Thoughts

Much religious practice and ritual was based on the experiences of the senses and was effectually keyed to memory. To see, to hear, to touch, to smell, to taste triggered the mind, allowing meaning to be enhanced and remembrance to add greater significance to action. It was in ritual performance that the authority of the priest was made manifest, and the worshipper was brought once again into a communal relationship with the deity and with all other worshippers. In fact, it was essential to the efficacy of the religious ritual to engage the senses and to make the connection between the realm of the divine and all creation.[134]

Conclusion

A FEW REFLECTIONS are necessary to add an exclamation point to the value of sensory analysis as another tool for the study of the ancient Israelites. In the chapters contained in this volume, I have attempted to tie events, persons, and places to their sensory characteristics. Sometimes that included technical information on the climate (wind patterns, rainfall, and temperature), demographics, and physiological aspects of how the nervous system, the ear, the eye, and the taste buds communicate information to the body. It has also been possible to demonstrate how well sensory analysis partners with archaeological research and various social science methods such as memory studies and spatiality theory. In every case, the intent has been to tie this data to specific examples from the biblical or ancient Near Eastern texts. It is the sensory responses of these ancient peoples that are being explored with the aim of providing yet another window into the text. And the hope is that through the introduction of this analytical tool, the modern reader can better understand and even empathize with both the people and their world.

It may seem the most natural thing to consider the role that the senses play in everyday life; they can very easily become submerged into the background of a narrative. The audience may be gripped by the words or actions of the principal characters but may not consider the influences of a scorching breeze, an uneven path that makes walking difficult, the sound of animals grazing, or the smells emanating from a nearby dwelling. All these sensations are present whether or not they are explicitly mentioned by the storyteller, and they add a sensual foundation that only requires a bit of imagination and a realization that the characters are not operating in a soundproof booth or a cultural vacuum.

It is the sensitivity to the physical and social environment that brings a story alive and allows both the ancient and present-day audience to better experience the emic impressions of the time and place being portrayed. The rhythm of life in a small village had its own pace governed by the seasons and the constant need to care for fields of grain, vineyards, and domestic animals. Every one of the senses must be brought into play to become attuned to that world. Their lives, while simple by modern standards, found identity and pleasure in familiar sights and sounds. For them, there was joy in the birth of a new child and in the celebrations associated with a good harvest. Their expectation, like that of farmers in any time or place, was that life consisted of hard work and eventual reward. Despite the heat of the sun burning their skin, the tasks at hand had to be completed. That included many sensory experiences such as having their muscles strained and their nostrils choked with dust while the physical bustle of activity of a harvest culminated in bringing the stalks of grain to the threshing floor to be processed.[1]

Unwalled villages had few defenses against invading armies or even raiding bands. That must have raised the level of anxiety when word was received of these groups on the move.[2] The sight of an approaching stranger brought with it the social obligations that an unexpected visit entails.[3] Even with a heightened threat level, life went on, and it would be hard to imagine a village without the smell of bread baking, the whirling of the spindle, and the thump of a loom as cloth was woven. The sweet taste of honey gathered from the comb brought a smile to the face. The feel of the first rain of the season on the face brought with it the promise of fields that could be plowed and planted, with a new harvest anticipated.

Ramping up the size of the population housed in and around the walls of a town also required an acknowledgment of the magnified individual and group activities that brought that place to life. Within the walls, the narrow streets zigzagged through the town and opened into the public square or a temple complex that would be filled with people going about their daily activities and with children at play.[4] In those districts where various industries were housed, potters worked away on their muddy wheels producing the vessels needed by every household.[5] Tanners created leather products while filling the air with the nocuous odors of the finishing process. Wagons rattled their way into the town bringing agricultural goods to feed the city dwellers, and traders set up their booths around the city gate, loudly hawking their wares to all passersby.[6] And the sights of the town would also include a greater mixture of persons, some from other countries, wearing different clothing styles. The more cosmopolitan flair would be reflected in a faster pace of life, a larger variety of trade goods, and a more exotic mixture of smells from imported incense and spices.

On the sensory scale, warfare created a host of visual, oral, and tactic experiences for its participants on both sides. Larger settlements were often a target for invading armies, and much of the history of ancient Israel is marked by regular military campaigns, the besieging of cities, and the pain and devastation of those caught in the middle of these conflicts.[7] Every war or local skirmish resulted in personal loss for its victims, including enslavement, maiming, and death. However, war was also a visual spectacle and a political arena for the powerful who used it for their political purposes and glorified themselves on monumental steles and in palace reliefs.[8]

As one of the most pervasive and destructive activities of human interaction, physical conflict, including its raised emotions and the sensory overload during a battle, can be studied from its inception to its grisly conclusion in the biblical texts. From the boots or sandals of a host of soldiers on the march to their arrangement in ranks prior to a battle to the anticipatory rattle of their weapons being drawn and their horses shivering to rush into the conflict, warfare filled the mind with images and sounds.[9] To ignore these sensory cues is to leave the narrative a two-dimensional, hollow account.

Like warfare, legal activity was also a familiar accompaniment to life in human communities both large and small. The regulation of what a society deemed proper behavior maintained the human compact and prevented conflicts from getting out of hand. Because law in ancient Israel was often a process of consensus rather than dependence on legal precedent and because it was judged to be given to the people by YHWH, it had both a mundane and a sacred character. That may help explain why the voice of a witness and the use of a communal space like the city gate so often form a part of the sensory landscape. Obviously, there were some basic legal principles that were designed to prevent theft, murder, and fraud. However, the concept of societal purity also was a factor that moved some legal issues, such as adultery or homicide, into the realm of the priest and a determination of guilt, innocence, or restoration of purity by YHWH.[10]

The communal character of many of these legal proceedings—which drew on the community to be present, hear the words of the witnesses, and occasionally participate in a communal form of punishment (stoning)—made it clear to the people that they had to all affirm what was considered honorable and shameful within their settlement. Trust was essential, and it could only be assured when potential violations were discussed and acted upon in public. After all, ancient Israel was an oral and aural society that continually retold its story so that every succeeding generation shared their common values.

In a similar way, the role of the priests in ancient Israel was to serve as the religious professionals in their society. While some of their duties could only be conducted within the precincts of the temple complex, there were many occasions when public spectacle was at the heart of their ritual performances. It was important that the person(s) who brought their sacrifice to the temple could witness that the priests took the proper steps necessary for their animals or grain to be accepted by the deity. If someone had become ritually impure because of deforming disease or contact with the dead, it was essential for the priest to examine them, consider the legal and physical regulations, and provide a solution for that person and the community.

Festivals tied to the agricultural year, major celebrations like the Passover, local events keyed to the Sabbath, and the new moon all provided a welcome relief from work and an opportunity to express the joy of the people with what their god had provided. Of course, there were also opportunities for personal devotions and prayers as expressed in the Psalms, but ancient Israel was a communal society, and it best expressed its religious beliefs through group activities like processions that included song and dance and a variety of musical instruments. The sensory elements of worship were heightened using a special blend of incense, the smell of sacrifices being burned on the altar, and the special vestments worn by the priests that allowed them to stand out and represent the piety of the nation.

By examining each of these aspects of life in ancient Israel, in both the rural and urban settings, this volume has attempted to provide a representative sample of how these ancient people could be better understood within their social context. It is important that every aspect of their existence has been examined, from the archaeological remains to the literary record that has come down to us from the ancient Near East. Sensory analysis in accompaniment with other methods helps make this possible and should be considered an essential tool by those who wish to dig deeper into the world of the Bible.

Appendix

Decalogue

The Decalogue is first spoken directly to Moses and the people at Mount Sinai/Horeb, the only occasion when direct speech is aimed at the full assembly of the people.[1] The laws are then inscribed on stone tablets, creating a visual image based on the original oral communication. Thereafter, the tablets can be held up, read, and described to the people, but like the other stories that celebrate YHWH's actions and gifts, they are initially meant to be spoken and heard. It is only when they are compiled into a written narrative that they can then be seen and studied.

Commandment	Sensory category	Justification
No other gods before YHWH (Exod 20:2–3; 34:14; Deut 5:7)	Sound and touch	No worship by voice or activity of other gods
Idols prohibited (Exod 20:4–6; 34:17; Deut 5:8–10; 27:15)	Sight, sound, and touch	Seeing an idol, worshipping an idol with the voice, and creating an idol
Oath taking (Exod 20:7; Deut 5:11)	Sound	Speaking an oath using YHWH's name
Sabbath (Exod 20:8–11; 34:2; Deut 5:12–15)	Touch	Work involves physical activity
Honor parents (Exod 20:12; Deut 5:16; 27:16; Lev 20:9)	Sound and touch	Hearing the voice of the parents, expressing obedience, and carrying out tasks to honor and take care of parents
Murder (Exod 20:13; Deut 5:17)	Touch	Physical attack leading to death
Adultery (Exod 20:14; Deut 5:18)	Touch	Inappropriate physical contact
Theft (Exod 20:15; Deut 5:19; Lev 19:11, 13)	Touch	Taking property
False witness (Exod 20:16; Deut 5:20; Lev 19:12)	Sound	Speaking untruths or perjured testimony
Coveting (Exod 20:17; Deut 5:21)	Sound and touch	Expressing desires and taking action to deprive a neighbor of his household's property

Covenant Code

Generally considered the oldest of the legal collections in the Hebrew Bible, the Covenant Code reflects life during the settlement period (1200–900 BCE) and focuses on situations that are most appropriate to village and small city life. There is no formal judiciary, only an occasional assembly of the village elders, and there are no direct references to a king or priesthood.[2]

Legal statement	Sensory category	Comments
Debt slavery: male (Exod 21:2–6; Deut 15:12–17)	Sound and touch	Voices "love for master and wife" with intent to remain in slavery; taken to doorpost and awl driven through the earlobe—note that Deuteronomy also allows this for female slaves (compare Exod 21:7–11)
Death by violence (Exod 21:12–14)	Touch	Unintentional death by striking allows culprit to flee (see refuge cities—Num 35:10–15, 22–28; Deut 4:21–43; 19:4–7); intentional murder—can remove culprit from sanctuary in temple at the altar (see Joab–1 Kgs 2:28–34)
Striking father or mother (Exod 21:15): execution	Touch	Failure to honor parents (compare Code of Hammurabi 195)
Kidnapping (Exod 21:16; Deut 24:7): execution	Touch	Theft
Cursing father or mother (Exod 21:17)	Sound	Failure to honor parents
Injury liability (Exod 21:18–19)	Touch	Fighting resulting in nonlethal result: pay costs of recovery
Striking slave (Exod 21:20–21)	Touch	Beating slave results in punishment for the owner if the slave dies of injuries
Miscarriage (Exod 21:22–25)	Touch	Fight results in miscarriage to be paid with fine unless further harm to mother: lex talionis

Legal statement	Sensory category	Comments
Loss of eye or tooth by slave (Exod 21:26–27)	Touch	Owner striking slave who loses eye or tooth: slave goes free
Goring ox liability (Exod 21:28–32)	Touch	Various levels of liability for injuries caused by goring ox depending on its history and death of its victims: ox stoned
Uncovered pit results in dead ox or donkey (Exod 21:33–34)	Touch and sight	Liability for uncovered pit: compensation for dead animals
Goring ox kills another ox (Exod 21:35–36)	Touch	Depending on the history of goring: variable compensation
Theft of ox or sheep (Exod 22:1–4)	Touch and sight	Varying fines for theft and discovery of stolen animals
Time factor in burglary (Exod 22:2)	Touch and sight	Death of burglar only punished if death occurs after sunrise
Unauthorized grazing (Exod 22:5)	Touch and sight	Restitution for loss of field or vineyard produce
Arson (Exod 22:6)	Touch and sight	Restitution for loss of grain
Theft of money or goods given in trust (Exod 22:7–8)	Touch	Thief fined or determination by divination of responsibility
Disputed ownership (Exod 22:9)	Sound and sight	Divination determines disputed ownership of property
Loss of animals kept in trust (Exod 22:10–13)	Touch and sight	Depending on whether the loss was seen or proof of theft or mangling is available: fine
Oversight of hired animal (Exod 22:14–15)	Sight and touch	Fine for injury to hired animal depends on whether owner was present
Seduction of virgin (Exod 22:16–17)	Touch	Intercourse with virgin: forced marriage or payment of bride-price
Bestiality (Exod 22:19)	Touch	Bestiality: death
Sacrifice to other gods (Exod 22:20)	Sound and touch	Assuming ritual of sacrifice includes voice and action

Legal statement	Sensory category	Comments
Abuse of resident alien, widow, or orphan (Exod 22:21–24; 23:9)	Sound and touch	Abuse and cry of the oppressed answered by YHWH
Cloak taken in pledge (Exod 22:26–27)	Touch	Need cloak for protection against the night chill
Revile God or curse leader (Exod 22:28)	Sound	Cursing God or recognized leaders
No mangled meat (Exod 22:31)	Touch and taste	Prohibit eating meat managed by animals
False witness and impartiality (Exod 23:1–3)	Sound	Speaking falsely, favoring the majority or the poor forbidden
Return lost animals (Exod 23:4)	Sight and touch	Return enemy's property
Set free burdened animal (Exod 23:5)	Sight and touch	Relieve overburdened animal even if it belongs to an enemy
False charge or bribe prohibited (Exod 23:6–8)	Sound and touch	No speaking false charge or taking bribe to pervert justice
Sabbatical year, fallow fields, and food for poor (Exod 23:10–11)	Touch and taste	Fallow fields provide food for the poor and animals
Sabbath rest (Exod 23:12; 35:2–3; Num 15:32–36)	Touch	Rest equates to inactivity; kindle no fire on Sabbath: violator stoned
Invoke other gods (Exod 23:13)	Sound	Call on other gods prohibited
Annual festivals (Exod 23:14–19a; 34:18–20, 22–26a)	Touch, taste, and sight	Bring firstfruits, "choicest" for offerings, and eat unleavened bread
No boiling kid in mother's milk (Exod 23:19b; 34:26b; Deut 14:21b)	Touch and taste	Mixing milk and meat prohibited

Deuteronomic Code

Once the ancient Israelites had evolved into a more complex society (ca. 900–600 BCE), with its elite and priestly hierarchy based in cities, especially Jerusalem, the tone of its legal pronouncements also became more city oriented. There is an assumption in the Deuteronomic Code, which dates to the late monarchic or early exilic period (600–500 BCE), of the role of an organized priesthood and a more formal judicial process involving judges.[3] There is also an increasing concern with ritual purity and moralizing the purpose of the laws that will become full blown in the Priestly and Holiness Codes. There are also some modifications of laws that first appear in the Covenant Code, but these changes occur under the pressure of new social situations that require expansion or revision.

Legal statement	Sensory category	Comments
Shema (Deut 6:4–9; 10:12–22)	Sound and touch	Fear YHWH; speak, teach, write, bind words
No laceration or shaving forelocks for the dead (Deut 14:1)	Touch and sight	Prohibition of practice by non-Israelites
Dietary laws (Deut 14:3–21)	Touch and taste	Clean and unclean foods
Debt slavery (Deut 15:12–17)	Touch	Drive an awl through the earlobe at the doorpost (compare Exod 21:2–6)
Eat portion of sacrifice (Deut 15:19–23; compare 17:1)	Taste, touch, and sight	Sacrifices must be unworked and without defect such as blindness—can eat it even if it has defect but not the blood
Judges reject bribes (Deut 16:18–20)	Sight	Impartiality of justice must be dispensed—bribes blind the eye
Worship of other gods (Deut 17:2–7)	Sound and touch	Accusations of idolatry confirmed by testimony of two witnesses: stoning at gates
Divination and child sacrifice (Deut 18:9–14)	Touch and sound	Forbidden practices of other religions include various forms of divination, speaking spells by shamans, and child sacrifice

Legal statement	Sensory category	Comments
Three cities of refuge (Deut 19:1–13)	Touch	Refuge cities spaced to allow unintended killer to flee to safety; avenger of blood is "hot," but avoid shedding innocent blood; note exception for murderer
Property marker (Deut 19:14)	Touch	No moving of property markers—theft of allotted property
Two witnesses required (Deut 19:15)	Sound	Conviction requires the spoken testimony of two witnesses
Malicious witness (Deut 19:16–19)	Sound and touch	Malicious witness / false witness faces YHWH, judges, and priests and receives same punishment as the convicted would
Rules of warfare (Deut 20:2–9; 24:5)	Sound	Priests exhort troops about the aid of the Divine Warrior and officials exempt troops with specific needs
Corpse discovered: heifer ritual to purify (Deut 21:1–9)	Sight, sound, and touch	To expiate guilt of "innocent blood" after body is found: ritual sacrifice and oath
POW bride (Deut 21:10–14)	Sight and touch	Seeing a female captive and wishing to marry her requires a ritual of transformation and mourning—"inspection of clothes and fingernails"
Primogeniture (Deut 21:15–17)	Sound	Right of inheritance for firstborn upheld by father acknowledging him
Rebellious son (Deut 21:18–21)	Sound and touch	Failure to honor parents, heed their words: son taken to gate where testimony is given, and he is stoned
Hanged man (Deut 21:22–23)	Sight and touch	Hanged man taken down before night and buried
Neighbor's property (Deut 22:1–3)	Sight and touch	Return lost animal or property when found

Legal statement	Sensory category	Comments
Fallen animal (Deut 22:4; compare Exod 23:5)	Sight and touch	Help up fallen donkey or ox
Cross-dressing (Deut 22:5)	Sight and touch	Prohibit cross-dressing; inappropriate mixing or gender appearance
Use of natural resources (Deut 22:6–7; see Lev 22:28)	Sight and touch	Take the eggs, not the mother bird
Building code (Deut 22:8)	Touch	Include safety rail to prevent falls and bloodguilt
Inappropriate mixes (Deut 22:9–11)	Sight and touch	Do not mix seed in vineyard, plow with ox and donkey, wear clothes of wool and linen
Tassels (Deut 22:12; Num 15:38–39)	Sight and touch	Sew tassels on four corners of your garment: memory aid
False charge against wife (Deut 22:13–21)	Sight, sound, and touch	Bloody sheet presented as proof of virginity and testimony to elders; failure to produce sheet: stoning
Adultery (Deut 22:22; Lev 20:10)	Sight and touch	Adultery: death of both
Rape and adultery (Deut 22:23–27)	Sight, touch, and sound	Rape of engaged virgin—punishment depends on whether her cry for help would be heard (town or countryside)
Rape of virgin (Deut 22:28–29)	Sight and touch	Theft of father's rights: fine and forced marriage
Ritual impurity, emissions (Deut 23:9–14)	Sight and touch	Nocturnal emissions and human waste must be kept out of the camp
Vows (Deut 23:21–23)	Sound	Vows spoken and heard by witnesses must be fulfilled
Shared produce (Deut 23:24–25)	Sight, taste, and touch	Permissible to eat grapes or grain from neighbor's field but not harvest them

Legal statement	Sensory category	Comments
Garment taken in pledge (Deut 24:12–13, 17; Exod 22:26–27)	Touch	Return garment at night for protection against the cold—no taking widow's garment
Gleaning (Deut 24:19–21; Lev 19:9–10)	Sight and touch	Allow widow, orphan, and alien to glean
Flogging (Deut 25:1–3)	Sound, touch, and sight	Judges decide dispute; flogging; forty lashes allowed
Levirate obligation (Deut 25:5–10)	Sound, sight, and touch	Spurned widow speaks to elders at the gate; remove his sandal, spit in his face, declare unwillingness to "build up brother's house"
Woman intervenes in fight (Deut 25:11–12)	Touch	Hand cut off for grasping genitals during fight
False balances (Deut 25:13–16; Lev 19:35–36)	Sight and touch	Prohibit two sets of weights or balances = theft
Mislead the blind (Deut 27:18)	Sight, sound, and touch	Curse on anyone who misleads the blind on the road

Priestly and Holiness Codes

Much of the legal material in the Priestly and Holiness Codes relates to the social context of the postexilic period (500–400 BCE).[4] The Priestly materials and the Holiness Code are found in Exodus 25–31; 35–40; Leviticus 1–27; and Numbers 1–10. The laws in Leviticus 17–26 compose a distinct collection dealing with issues of ritual purity and strict obedience to the law, recognizing in that way the holiness of YHWH. Many of these laws relate to cultic and ritual behavior, and they highlight the role of the priestly community. More attention will be given to them in the chapter on religious practice.

Numbers

Unclean and leprous persons exclude from camp (Num 5:2–3)	Touch and sight	Removing impurity from camp
Test of adulteress wife (Num 5:12–31)	Touch, taste, sound, and sight	Trial by ordeal, consume mixture, see distended uterus, take oath
Nazirite vow (Num 6:2–21)	Touch, taste, and sound	Speak vow and accept restrictions in diet and touch (hair, corpse)
Offerings—"pleasing odor" (Num 15:2–16)	Touch and smell	Prescription for offerings
Portion of food donated as offering (Num 15:18–20)	Taste and touch	Eat bread but give some back to YHWH
Fringes (Num 15:37–39)	Sight and touch	Attach fringes to garments as a memory aid on sight
Daughters of Zelophehad inheritance coda (Num 27:1–12; 36:6–9)	Sound	Petition to inherit father's inheritance; marriage restricted to clans without father's tribe
Vows by women (Num 30:1–16)	Sound	Vow is binding unless a father or husband expresses disapproval, and it is nullified

Leviticus

Incest (Lev 18:6–18)	Touch	Various sexual prohibitions based on sexual rights of the household
Illicit sexual relations (Lev 18:19–23; 20:13, 18)	Touch	No intercourse during menstruation, no male-on-male sex, no kinswoman
Revile deaf or stumbling block before blind (Lev 19:14)	Sound and touch	Mistreatment of those with disabilities (see Job 29:15)
Cutting hair or beard (Lev 19:27)	Sight and touch	No round off hair or edges of beard
Gash in mourning / tattoos (Lev 19:28)	Sight and touch	No gashes for the dead or tattoos
Blasphemy (Lev 24:10–23)	Sound	All within earshot must participate in stoning culprit

Notes

Introduction

1 David Howes, "Resounding Sensory Profiles: Sensory Studies Methodologies," in *Sounding Sensory Profiles in the Ancient Near East*, ed. Annette Schellenberg and Thomas Krüger (Atlanta: SBL, 2019), 48.

2 David Le Breton, *Sensing the World: An Anthropology of the Senses* (London: Bloomsbury, 2017), 1–6.

3 First John 1:1, 3; Dorothy Lee, "The Gospel of John and the Five Senses," *JBL* 129, no. 1 (2010): 126.

4 He had been warned about her coming by YHWH, but it is the way he handles the encounter that adds to his authority and to his message for Jeroboam (1 Kgs 14:1–6).

5 This detail about a daily atmospheric occurrence is an indicator that the author or editor of the story had experienced this "evening breeze" as it wafted across the land of Canaan from the Mediterranean Sea (Gen 3:8).

Chapter 1: Village Life

1 The term *emic* represents the "insider" perspective of those who lived in a particular time and place. An *etic*, or "outsider," perspective represents the uninitiated view of anyone not part of the original community that produced the story in the Bible.

2 Victor H. Matthews, *The History of Bronze and Iron Age Israel* (New York: Oxford University Press, 2019), 64–80.

3 Marko Lamberg, Minna Mäkinen, and Merja Uotila, "A Rural Living Sphere," in *Physical and Cultural Space in Pre-industrial Europe: Methodological Approaches*

to Spatiality, ed. Marko Lamberg, Marko Hakanen, and Janne Haikari (Lund: Nordic Academic, 2011), 289–290.

4 Ellen Robbins, "The Pleiades, the Flood, and the Jewish New Year," in *Ki Baruch Hu: Ancient Near Eastern, Biblical, and Judaic Studies in Honor of Baruch A. Levine*, ed. Robert Chazan, William W. Hallo, and Lawrence H. Schiffman (Winona Lake, IN: Eisenbrauns, 1999), 333, notes that when the Pleiades in the constellation Taurus sets during the day, that marks the beginning of the dry season, and correspondingly, when it rises during the day, that marks the beginning of the rainy season. See Amos 5:8.

5 References to each of the items described here in order include Ps 8:3 and Amos 8:5; Joel 2:10; Prov 25:23; Job 1:19; Gen 15:11; and Judg 14:5.

6 Gen 38:14–15.

7 See Exod 3:3 and Josh 9:4–5.

8 Victor H. Matthews and Don C. Benjamin, *Old Testament Parallels: Laws and Stories from the Ancient Near East*, 4th ed. (Mahwah, NJ: Paulist, 2016), 165–166 (hereafter cited as OTP-4).

9 See Lev 26:16 and Gen 27:1.

10 First Kgs 14:4–6.

11 Lachish Letter 4 mentions that a signal fire at Azekah had gone out, indicating the village had fallen to invaders (Matthews and Benjamin, *OTP-4*, 217).

12 First Sam 17:1.

13 Gen 26:12–33; 34:8–10.

14 Ruth 4:1–3.

15 Douglas R. Clark, "Bricks, Sweat and Tears: The Human Investment in Constructing a 'Four-Room' House," *NEA* 66, nos. 1–2 (2003): 36.

16 Avraham Faust, *The Archaeology of Israelite Society in Iron Age II* (Winona Lake, IN: Eisenbrauns, 2012), 223. See Lev 12:2 and 18:19.

17 Avraham Faust, "The Four Room House: Embodying Iron Age Israelite Society," *NEA* 66, nos. 1–2 (2003): 26.

18 Second Kgs 4:10.

19 Lawrence E. Stager, "The Archaeology of the Family in Ancient Israel," *BASOR* 260 (1985): 17.

20 Hos 13:3.

21 Clark, "Bricks," 40.

22 John D. Currid, "The Deforestation of the Foothills of Palestine," *PEQ* 116 (1984): 1–11.

23 See Gen 12:6; 35:8; and 1 Sam 14:2.

24 Nathan MacDonald, *What Did the Ancient Israelites Eat? Diet in Biblical Times* (Grand Rapids, MI: Eerdmans, 2008), 91–93.

25 Jennie R. Ebeling, *Women's Lives in Biblical Times* (London: T&T Clark, 2010), 33–36; MacDonald, *Diet in Biblical Times*, 26–27. See 2 Sam 17:28.

26 Oded Borowski, *Daily Life in Biblical Times* (Atlanta: SBL, 2003), 29. See Deut 12:10.

27 Oded Borowski, *Agriculture in Iron Age Israel* (Winona Lake, IN: Eisenbrauns, 1987), 15–18. See Isa 5:1–7.

28 Colin Renfrew and Paul Bahn, *Archaeology: Theories, Methods and Practice* (London: Thames & Hudson, 2004), 207.

29 See Prov 24:30–31 for a caution to those who are too lazy to maintain their terraces and fields.

30 For these activities, see Isa 5:1–2 and Jer 23:29; 1 Kgs 4:25 and Isa 36:16; and Isa 28:24–25.

31 Jacob Ben-Joseph, "The Climate in Eretz Israel during Biblical Times," *HS* 26, no. 2 (1985): 226–229.

32 Deut 33:28; Hos 14:5.

33 Job 14:11.

34 See Gen 24:13, 43; and 29:2–3.

35 Exod 2:16.

36 Faust, *Archaeology of Israelite Society*, 165; Job 24:11.

37 Judg 6:11.

38 For activities on the threshing floor, see Num 18:27; Deut 15:14; Job 5:26; 2 Sam 24:22; Isa 41:15, 16; Ps 1:4; Hos 13:3; and Amos 9:9.

39 Sir 26:7.

40 Deut 16:14–15; 26:12–13.

41 Victor H. Matthews, "Physical Space, Imagined Space, and 'Lived Space' in Ancient Israel," *BTB* 33, no. 1 (2003): 13. See Ruth 3:3–6.

42 Judg 4:4–5.

43 Gen 35:16–19.

44 Fat persons are characterized as complacent idolaters (Deut 31:20) or comedic characters, like King Eglon of Moab (Judg 3:17). Of course, those who had "grown fat" would be considered prosperous (Deut 31:20; Neh 9:25; Job 15:27).

45 Texts highlighting these emotions include Mal 1:13; Job 4:14–15; 16:4, 16; Pss 22:7; 47:1 (2); 64:8; Lam 2:15–16; Gen 17:17; 21:9; 29:11; Ezra 3:13; and Eccl 10:19.

46 Texts dealing with articles of clothing include Exod 3:5; Josh 9:5; 2 Sam 15:30; Mic 1:8; Gen 38:14; Jdt 10:3; Judg 5:30; and Job 38:14.

47 Exod 22:22; Ruth 2:2.

48 Exod 28:42.

49 Bird and other animal sounds are found in 1 Sam 15:14 and Song 2:12. Traditional wisdom (Prov 26:2) incorporates these sounds: "Like a sparrow in its flitting, like a swallow in its flying, an undeserved curse goes nowhere."

50 Gen 27:22; 1 Sam 26:17.

51 Judg 12:5–6.

52 Job 33:15–19.

53 Judg 5:11; 1 Sam 18:6.

54 Exod 2:6.

55 Ezek 33:3; 2 Sam 5:24; 1 Sam 27:8–9; 30:1–3. Sounds associated with warfare will be dealt with in a later chapter.

56 Assaf Yasur-Landau, "Behavioral Patterns in Transition: Eleventh-Century B.C.E. Innovation in Domestic Textile Production," in *Exploring the Longue Durée: Essays in Honor of Lawrence E. Stager*, ed. J. David Schloen (Winona Lake, IN: Eisenbrauns, 2009), 508.

57 Jennie R. Ebeling, "Engendering the Israelite Harvests," *NEA* 79, no. 3 (2016): 186–194.

58 Gen 18:6; 1 Sam 28:24.

59 Carol L. Meyers, "Having Their Space and Eating There Too: Bread Production and Female Power in Ancient Israelite Households," *Nashim: A Journal of Jewish Women's Studies and Gender Issues* 5 (2002): 21. See Eccl 12:3–4 and Isa 47:2.

60 Prov 25:19.

61 For these processes, see 1 Sam 28:24; Lev 2:42; 2 Sam 13:8; Num 6:19; and Ebeling, *Women's Lives*, 50.

62 See Judg 9:53.

63 See Judg 4:21. A reversal motif places a woman into the role of a man as the defender of the household. Another example is found in the story of Abigail in 1 Sam 25:18–38.

64 Lynn Huggins-Cooper, *Spinning and Weaving* (Yorkshire: Pen & Sword History, 2019), 6.

65 Yasur-Landau, "Behavioral Patterns in Transition," 508.

66 Carol L. Meyers, "Material Remains and Social Relations: Women's Culture in Agrarian Households of the Iron Age," in *Symbiosis, Symbolism, and the Power of the Past: Canaan, Ancient Israel, and Their Neighbors from the Late Bronze Age through Roman Palaestina*, ed. William G. Dever and Seymour Gitin (Winona Lake, IN: Eisenbrauns, 2003), 435–436.

67 See Job 7:6; Isa 19:9; and Prov 31:19.

68 Judg 16:14; Scott B. Noegel, "Evil Looms: Delilah—Weaver of Wicked Wiles," *CBQ* 13, no. 2 (1993): 198.

69 For narrative evidence of these sounds, see Sir 38:29; Isa 44:12–13; Deut 19:5; and Wis 13:11.

70 Passages dealing with each aspect of herding include Lev 27:32; Pss 23:4; 78:70–71; Gen 30:38; 37:20; 1 Chr 4:39–40; Job 24:2; 1 Sam 24:3; Mic 2:12; and Jer 23:3.

71 Ezek 34:14.

72 Sounds and sights keyed to these outside activities are mentioned in Deut 32:11; Isa 5:2; 31:5; Job 4:10; 37:4–10; Amos 3:8; Jer 25:30; 1 Sam 15:14; and Ps 147:16–17.

73 Texts dealing with shearing include Gen 31:19; 38:13; 1 Sam 25:2, 4, 11; and Isa 53:7.

74 Second Sam 13:23–29; Jeffrey C. Geoghegan, "Israelite Sheepshearing and David's Rise to Power," *Bib* 87, no. 1 (2006): 56–57.

75 Deut 11:11; Ps 65:10 (11); Isa 28:24; David C. Hopkins, "'All Sorts of Field Work': Agricultural Labor in Ancient Palestine," in *To Break Every Yoke: Essays in Honor of Marvin L. Chaney*, ed. Robert B. Coote and Norman K. Gottwald (Sheffield: Sheffield Phoenix, 2007), 152.

76 Narratives describing plowing are found in 1 Sam 13:20; Job 39:10; Hos 10:11b; and Judg 3:31. For a description of the terms used for plowing and opening the furrows, see John F. Healey, "Ancient Agriculture and the Old Testament (with Special Reference to Isaiah XXVIII 23–29)," in *Prophets, Worship and Theodicy: Studies in Prophetism, Biblical Theology, and Structural and Rhetorical Analysis, and on the Place of Music in Worship*, OTS 23 (Leiden: Brill, 1984), 114–115.

77 See Ps 91:12 and Matt 4:6.

78 See Eccl 11:1–7, which also enjoins the farmer to watch the clouds and the direction of the winds, since wet ground means they cannot harvest the fields, and high winds disrupt sowing.

79 For sounds associated with sowing, see Pss 65:10 (11), 13; 126:5–6; and Isa 30:23.

80 For this farming hazard, see Mark 4:4 and Luke 8:5.

81 For other examples of chancy surfaces, see Matt 13:4–8 and 2 Esd 8:41.

82 For sounds and perils endangering the harvest, see Hos 10:8; 2 Chr 6:28; Amos 4:9; Joel 1:4; 2:25; and Jer 46:23.

83 Borowski, *Agriculture*, 60.

84 Borowski, 61. See Deut 16:9 and Joel 3:13.

85 Texts describing the work and the strain on the harvesters are Isa 16:10; 17:5; 18:4; Prov 26:1; Ruth 2:9; Deut 16:9; Jer 50:16; and Joel 3:13.

86 Texts describing the work on the threshing floor include Num 18:27; Deut 15:14; Hos 10:11; and Isa 41:15.

87 Texts describing the sounds and tasks of processing grain include Pss 1:4; 83:13; Isa 41:16; Hos 13:3; Ruth 3:2, 7; Jer 15:7; Job 21:18; Sir 26:7; and 1 Sam 23:1.

88 John Currid and Avi Navon, "Iron Age Pits and the Lahav (Tell Halif) Grain Storage Project," *BASOR* 273 (1989): 72–76.

89 The sounds and aspects of the harvest are found in Isa 5:6; 17:6; Prov 27:18; and Deut 24:20. See Borowski, *Agriculture*, 115.

90 The treading of the grapes and associated sounds are found in Amos 9:13; Isa 63:3; Joel 3:13; Jer 25:30; and Deut 31:19.

91 See Exod 27:20. The blind Samson does this work in Judg 16:21. See also Philip J. King and Lawrence E. Stager, *Life in Biblical Israel* (Louisville, KY: Westminster John Knox, 2001), 96.

92 Judg 9:9; Ebeling, "Engendering the Israelite Harvests," 194.

93 Passages describing the sounds of celebration include Ps 89:15; Isa 16:9; Judg 21:19, 21; Job 21:11–12; Eccl 10:19; and 1 Sam 1:3.

94 Many of the Psalms are laments reflecting the emotions of those with illness (Pss 6; 38) or who have experienced a loss (Ps 94) or who are weeping (Ps 30:5).

95 Isa 26:17; Gen 37:34.

96 See Gen 35:16–18 and 1 Sam 4:19–22.

97 Sounds associated with personal tragedies are given in Num 12:12; Job 3:16; 16:16; 30:31; and Zech 12:10.

98 Her despair would be heightened in this region, which is known for its howling winds (Deut 32:10).

99 The sounds of weeping are found in Eccl 3:4; Luke 6:21; Gen 21:16; 29:11; and 1 Sam 30:3–4.

100 Joyous singing and dancing are referenced by Laban in Gen 31:27. See also Exod 15:20 (the crossing of the Red Sea); Judg 11:34; 1 Sam 18:6; and Ps 47:1 (2).

101 Gestures of approval and disapproval appear in Job 16:9; 27:23; Pss 22:7; 64:8; Ezek 6:11; 25:6; Nah 3:19; and Zeph 2:15.

102 Judg 5:11.

103 Second Sam 19:35 (36).

104 Job 1:17.

105 See Victor H. Matthews, "Hospitality and Hostility in Genesis 19 and Judges 19," *BTB* 22, no. 1 (1992): 3–11; and Gen 18:1–15. Note that Abraham's offer of "a little bread" turns into "three measures of choice flour" made into cakes, a slaughtered calf from the herd, and "curds and milk." Their amused laughter is found in Gen 17:17 and 18:12.

106 Mark S. R. Jenner, "Follow Your Nose? Smell, Smelling, and Their Histories," *AHR* 116, no. 2 (2011): 339.

107 Exod 19:10; 29:4; Lev 13:34; Num 8:7; Deut 23:10–11.

108 Ian D. Ritchie, "The Nose Knows: Bodily Knowing in Isaiah 11.3," *JSOT* 87, no. 25 (2000): 65.

109 Num 11:5; Song 7:8.

110 See "The Sufferer and the Soul," lines 90–95, in Matthews and Benjamin, *OTP-4*, 242.

111 David Howes, "Olfaction and Transition: An Essay on the Ritual Use of Smell," *Canadian Review of Sociology and Anthropology* 24, no. 3 (1987): 399–401.

112 Ruth 3:3.

113 Matthews and Benjamin, *OTP-4*, 321–324.

114 Gen 27:27.

115 See Song 4:11 and Hos 14:6.

116 Deut 21:10–13; Don C. Benjamin, *The Social World of Deuteronomy: A New Feminist Commentary* (Eugene, OR: Cascade, 2015), 134–135.

117 Gen 41:42.

118 Matthews and Benjamin, *OTP-4*, 146.

119 First Kgs 14:10.

120 See Deut 23:13 (14) and Isa 25:10. Note Isaac taking his evening walk in the fields in Gen 24:63.

121 Ezek 4:12, 15.

122 Saul's team of oxen in 1 Sam 11:5–7 is a representation of his wealth. That may also be the case with Elisha's team of oxen in 1 Kgs 19:19–21, since he demonstrates his intention to shift to a new occupation by slaughtering the animals and sharing the boiled meat with the people of his village.

123 Jer 2:24. See J. A. Thompson, *The Book of Jeremiah* (Grand Rapids, MI: Eerdmans, 1980), 178.

124 Gen 37:14–16; Luke 2:8.

125 Jer 16:4. See the casualties of Sisera's army referred to in Ps 83:10.

126 Second Kgs 9:37; Jer 8:2.

127 Meyers, "Having Their Space," 23–28.

128 Gen 25:29.

129 Michael M. Holman, "Did the Ancient Israelites Drink Beer?," *BAR* 36, no. 5 (2010): 51–54.

130 Cynthia Shafer-Elliott, *Food in Ancient Judah: Domestic Cooking in the Time of the Hebrew Bible* (Abingdon, UK: Routledge, 2014), 21–22.

131 Chris L. Whittle et al., "Human Breath Odors and Their Use in Diagnosis," *Annals of the New York Academy of Sciences* 1098, no. 1 (2007): 252–266.

132 Constance Classen, *Worlds of Sense: Exploring the Senses in History and across Cultures* (London: Routledge, 1993), 79.

133 First Sam 25:11.

134 Gen 8:21; Exod 29:18; 1 Sam 2:13.

135 Exod 12:8–9.

136 Isa 22:13.

137 Anne Katrine de Hemmer Gudme, "A Pleasing Odour for Yahweh: The Smell of Sacrifices on Mount Gerizim and in the Hebrew Bible," *Body and Religion* 2, no. 1 (2018): 14.

138 Gen 27:31; Exod 24:6.

139 Ps 38:5. Honey could also serve as a disinfectant and sealant for wounds.

140 John J. Pilch, *Healing in the New Testament: Insights from Medical and Mediterranean Anthropology* (Minneapolis: Fortress, 2000), 39–54.

141 Isa 1:6.

142 Lev 13:20; Job 18:13.

143 Lev 13:47–49.

144 See Isaiah's prescription of a poultice of mashed figs for King Hezekiah's infected boil in 2 Kgs 20:7.

145 See the gang of four lepers in 2 Kgs 7:3–4.

146 David Stacey, "Seasonal Industries at Qumran," *BAIAS* 26 (2008): 13.

147 Laura B. Mazow, "The Root of the Problem: On the Relationship between Wool Processing and Lanoline Production," *Journal of Mediterranean Archaeology* 27, no. 1 (2014): 35–36.

148 Gen 27:27.

149 First Sam 12:17–18.

150 Job 14:9.

151 Villages could seldom support a Levite. See Micah's hiring of a Levite as a private priest for his household in Judg 17:7–13.

152 See Gen 8:21a and Exod 29:18—contra Lev 26:31.

153 Sarah Malena, "Spice Roots in the Song of Songs," in *Milk and Honey: Essays on Ancient Israel and the Bible in Appreciation of the Judaic Studies Program at the University of California, San Diego*, ed. Sarah Malena and David Miano (Winona Lake, IN: Eisenbrauns, 2007), 166–167.

154 Lee, "Gospel of John," 116.

155 M. G. F. Martin, "Sight and Touch," in *The Senses: Classical and Contemporary Philosophical Perspectives*, ed. Fiona Macpherson (Oxford: Oxford University Press, 2011), 205–206.

156 See Isa 59:10. Note Isa 42:16a, where the blind are guided on paths "they have not known."

157 For these gestures of affection, see Gen 21:18; 26:8; and 29:11, 13.

158 Gestures associated with touch include the oath ritual in Gen 24:2, 9; Israel's blessing of Joseph's sons in Gen 48:13–20; and David's mourning ritual in 2 Sam 1:11.

159 Gen 18:1; 1 Sam 11:9. Jacob reminds Laban that he has worked diligently in both hot and cold weather in Gen 31:40.

160 See the plea of the day laborer in "Yavneh Yam Letter," in Matthews and Benjamin, *OTP-4*, 395.

161 Deut 28:22. Note the temporary comfort from the heat brought by a cloud's shadow in Ps 25:5.

162 For cold temperatures, see Job 37:9–10 and Prov 25:25.

163 See the value of sensation in cooking in Ps 58:9 and Ruth 2:2, 7.

164 See Deut 25:4 and Isa 1:3.

165 See Gen 34:25 for the pain associated with circumcising adult males.

166 The movement of a fetus is found in Gen 25:22 and Luke 1:41. For the pain of childbirth, see Gen 3:16; 1 Sam 4:19; 1 Chr 4:9; Isa 66:7; Jer 6:24; 50:43; John 16:20–21; and 1 Thess 5:3.

167 For instances describing pain, see Pss 38:5; 48:6; Isa 1:6; Job 30:17; Deut 28:27; and Prov 26:21.

168 A list of spices can be found in Song 4:13–14. See Malena, "Spice Roots," 167.

169 Lytton J. Musselman, *A Dictionary of Bible Plants* (Cambridge: Cambridge University Press, 2012), 26–27.

170 Shafer-Elliott, *Food in Ancient Judah*, 26. The style and capacity of cooking pots and changes in cooking techniques help archaeologists distinguish between village and urban settings and preferences.

171 Margie Burton, "Biomolecules, Bedouin, and the Bible: Reconstructing Ancient Foodways in Israel's Northern Negev," in Malena and Miano, *Milk and Honey*, 216–217, 224.

172 Burton, 230; MacDonald, *Diet in Biblical Times*, 32.

173 The tastes of foods are mentioned in Gen 27:4; Jer 31:29; Exod 12:8; Num 5:18; and Ruth 2:14. See MacDonald, *Diet in Biblical Times*, 23; and Musselman, *Dictionary of Bible Plants*, 28–29.

174 Luke 11:42; Matt 23:23; Isa 28:25–27.

175 For honey, see Ps 19:10 (11); Prov 24:13; 1 Sam 14:27–29; Exod 16:31; and Num 11:7–8.

176 For references to figs, which must be eaten as soon as they ripen, see Isa 28:4; Amos 8:21; and 1 Sam 30:12.

177 Job 6:6.

178 Num 11:5.

179 Yi-Fu Tuan, *Space and Place: The Perspective of Experience* (Minneapolis: University of Minnesota Press, 1977), 10.

180 The smell of the mandrake's flower and its fruit, which has an apple-like fragrance, would be distinctive. See Gen 30:14.

181 Second Kgs 4:39–40.

182 See Exod 15:23–25 and 2 Kgs 2:19–22.

Chapter 2: Urban Life and the Senses

1 Fiona Macpherson, "Individuating the Senses," in Macpherson, *Senses*, 9, distinguishes between the "distal stimulus," associated with perceiving an object, and the "proximal stimulus," the quality of an object that stimulates the senses.

2 Timothy M. Willis, *The Elders of the City: A Study of the Elders-Laws in Deuteronomy* (Atlanta: SBL, 2001), 14–19.

3 See the description of city walls and defenses in C. H. J. de Geus, *Towns in Ancient Israel and in the Southern Levant* (Leuven, Belgium: Peeters, 2003), 10–13.

4 Ronny Reich, "A Note on the Population Size of Jerusalem in the Second Temple Period," *RB* 121, no. 2 (2014): 299–301.

5 Amnon Ben-Tor, *Hazor: Canaanite Metropolis, Israelite City* (Jerusalem: Israel Exploration Society, 2016), 133–141.

6 Egon H. E. Lass, "Flotation Procedures in the Southern Levant: A Summary of 20 Years of Work, Part II," *Strata* 29 (2011): 103.

7 Jeffrey R. Zorn, "Estimating the Population Size of Ancient Settlements: Methods, Problems, Solutions, and a Case Study," *BASOR* 295 (1994): 31–48.

8 David Ussishkin, *Megiddo-Armageddon: The Story of the Canaanite and Israelite City* (Jerusalem: Israel Exploration Society, 2018), 387.

9 See Jer 37:21 for reference to the "baker's street" and Jer 18:2–3 for the "potter's house."

10 A closer examination of the priestly community, religious practice, and the role of the temple will be provided in chapter 5, "Religious Practice."

11 See Christopher A. Rollston, "Scribal Education in Ancient Israel: The Old Hebrew Epigraphic Evidence," *BASOR* 344 (1998): 47–68. Rollston, through his evaluation of inscriptional evidence, advocates for the existence of a scribal education that trained individuals in a meticulous style of writing distinctive to an old Hebrew script identifiably different from that produced in the Aramaic script from Phoenicia.

12 Keith Whitelam, "The Symbols of Power: Aspects of Royal Propaganda in the United Monarchy," *BA* 49 (1986): 166–173.

13 Jodi Magness, *Stone and Dung, Oil and Spit: Jewish Daily Life in the Time of Jesus* (Grand Rapids, MI: Eerdmans, 2011), 130–133.

14 See Amos 2:7 and 5:12 for abuses of power that affect the poor and those without influence.

15 Gen 19:1.

16 See mentions of wealthy merchants in Isa 23:8 and Ezek 27:12–25.

17 See how YHWH serves as the shade that protects one from the heat of the sun in Ps 121:5. See Zech 8:4 for the vision of a restored Zion that allows the old to be at rest in safety.

18 Josh 2:15.

19 A description of casemate walls and their uses is found in Yigal Shiloh, "The Casemate Wall, the Four Room House, and Early Planning in the Israelite City," *BASOR* 268 (1987): 3–15.

20 A sign of the sensual value of city walls is voiced by the Mesopotamian hero Gilgamesh, who boasts about the ramparts and well-laid brickwork of his city of Uruk (James B. Pritchard, ed., *Ancient Near Eastern Texts Relating to the Old Testament*, 3rd ed. [Princeton, NJ: Princeton University Press, 1969], 97 [hereafter cited as *ANET*]).

21 See Rahab's bundles of flax in Josh 2:6.

22 Second Kgs 4:8–10. See 1 Sam 9:25, where Saul is also accommodated temporarily with a bed on the roof of a house.

23 Magen Broshi, "The Population of Iron Age Palestine," in *Biblical Archaeology Today, 1990*, ed. Avraham Biran and Joseph Aviram (Jerusalem: Israel Exploration Society, 1993), 14–17, estimates that the population of Canaan shrunk from 140,000 in 1600 BCE to 60,000–70,000 in 1200 BCE as the Egyptian hegemony over the region deteriorated. However, by 1000 BCE, the population had been restored to 150,000, then to over 400,000 by 734 BCE, with 350,000 inhabitants in the kingdom of Israel and 110,000 in Judah.

24 See Ps 60:2; Amos 1:1; and Jeffrey R. Chadwick and Aren M. Maeir, "Judahite
    Gath in the Eighth Century B.C.E.: Finds in Area F from the Earthquake to the
    Assyrians," *NEA* 81, no. 1 (2018): 48–50.

25 Avraham Faust, "Residential Patterns in the Ancient Israelite City," *Levant* 35
    (2003): 131.

26 Faust, 132–133.

27 See the food shortages caused during a siege of Samaria in 2 Kgs 6:24–30.

28 See Ezek 16:55.

29 See mentions of the "highway to the fuller's field" in Isa 7:3 and 36:2.

30 See the delegation sent to David by Hiram of Tyre with cedar trees, carpenters,
    and masons in 2 Sam 5:11.

31 See Gen 19:1 for Lot's stance in the gateway of Sodom. Other examples are
    found in Deut 21:19; 22:15; and Prov 31:23.

32 Willis, *Elders of the City*, 33–42.

33 The euphemism for *old age* is *gray headed*, and it appears in Gen 44:29; Deut
    32:25; 1 Kgs 2:6; and several more places.

34 See the reference to the widow's son's illness that left him almost unable to breathe
    in 1 Kgs 17:17. See also Ben Sira's lament that some long-lasting illnesses even
    baffle the physician in Sir 10:10.

35 The legislation regarding the examination and treatment of "lepers" is found in
    Lev 13–14. An example of their continued interaction with the general popula-
    tion of a city is found in 2 Kgs 7:3–9.

36 See the restrictions placed on those who are "blind or lame, disfigured or deformed"
    in Lev 21:18.

37 Lev 19:14; Deut 27:18.

38 Acts 3:2.

39 Exod 4:11 is YHWH's response to Moses that God "makes" the deaf and the
    blind while declaring these are not punishments but instead physical realities.
    See Sarah J. Melcher, "Genesis and Exodus," in *The Bible and Disability: A Com-
    mentary*, ed. Sarah J. Melcher, Mikeal C. Parsons, and Amos Yong (Waco, TX:
    Baylor University Press, 2017), 48–50.

40 Luke 14:21.

41 2 Sam 9:13; Prov 26:7.

42 Job 29:15.

43 For wedding celebrations, see Matt 22:10; John 2:1; and Tob 9:2–5.

44 See Isa 5:22 for a mocking tone condemning those who are champions at drink-
    ing wine. Nicole L. Tilford, "When People Have Gods: Sensory Mimicry and
    Divine Agency in the Book of Job," *HBAI* 5, no. 1 (2016): 46, notes how violent
    emotions are tied to faster breathing and the emission of hot air.

45 Job 15:12; Ps 39:3.

46 Job 16:16. Ps 69:3 indicates that a further symptom of extended crying is a
    parched throat.

47 Job 12:25; Ps 107:27; Prov 23:29; Isa 29:9.

48 Isa 28:8; Jer 25:27.

49 Lam 4:5 refers to "those who are nurtured in purple," a very expensive dye. See
    Alicia J. Batten, "Clothing and Adornment," *BTB* 40, no. 3 (2010): 148–159,

for a discussion of clothing as a social tool to mark an individual's status and specific identity.

50 See 2 Sam 18:11; 20:8; and 2 Kgs 1:8.

51 Exod 28:33–34 and 39:24–26 describe the elaborately decorated hem of the priestly robe, and 1 Sam 15:27 singles out Saul's hem as distinctive to the person of the king and to his rule of the kingdom.

52 Judg 5:30.

53 Ezek 27:24.

54 The condemnation of fancy, braided hairstyles in 1 Pet 3:3 is an indication of a fairly common practice.

55 See Isa 54:11–12 and 1 Tim 2:9.

56 Isa 3:18–22.

57 Ezek 16:10–14.

58 See Hos 2:13. Compare similar language in Ezek 23:1–21, the prophet's litany of religious and political crimes committed by Oholah (= Samaria) and Oholibah (= Jerusalem).

59 See Gen 24:30.

60 See Isa 61:10.

61 See Prov 1:9; and Amir Golani, "Revealed by Their Jewelry: Ethnic Identity of Israelites during the Iron Age in the Southern Levant," in *Beyond Ornamentation: Jewelry as an Aspect of Material Culture in the Ancient Near East*, ed. Amir Golani and Zuzanna Wygnańska (Warsaw: University of Warsaw Press, 2014), 269–296.

62 Seth S. Horowitz, *The Universal Sense: How Hearing Shapes the Mind* (New York: Bloomsbury, 2012), 13–16.

63 Second Sam 18:24–27.

64 See Deut 22:23–24. Compare the claim of Potiphar's wife in Gen 39:15–18, although that involves accusing a slave.

65 In Jeremiah's oracle against Babylon, note the silencing of the clamor of that great city at its destruction by YHWH (Jer 51:55).

66 For references to the use of a walking staff, see Zech 8:4 and Mark 6:8.

67 In a picture of restored peace for Jerusalem, Zech 8:5 describes the children at play. Note Job's despairing reference to the carefree dancing and singing children of the wicked accompanied by the merry sound of instruments (21:11–12).

68 Kristine H. Garroway, *Growing Up in Ancient Israel: Children in Material Culture and Biblical Texts* (Atlanta: SBL, 2018), 202–222.

69 In the description of the ideal wife in Prov 31:10–31, she seeks out the best wool and flax to weave, works diligently with her spindle and loom, and ultimately judges that her "merchandise is profitable."

70 Sir 26:29–27:8.

71 Prov 2:16; 6:24; and 7:5 describe the enticing "smooth words" of the adulteress, who compels the fool to enter her snare (7:21–23).

72 See Prov 26:3.

73 See Jer 5:8, which compares lustful horses to Israelites desiring their neighbors' wives.

74 See 2 Kgs 4:7; Neh 13:15–16; and Amos 8:5.

75 Ben Sira (Sir 40:28–30), however, admonishes against "the life of the beggar" when there is the opportunity to be a contributing member of society.

76 Ps 37:25.

77 Victor H. Matthews, "The Art of Lying at King David's Court," *BTB* 47, no. 2 (2017): 80–86.

78 The scene is described in 2 Sam 17:1–14, and Ahithophel's suicide after his advice is not taken occurs in 17:23.

79 See John J. Mearheimer, *Why Leaders Lie: The Truth about Lying in International Politics* (New York: Oxford University Press, 2011), 6–31, for an analysis of political speech.

80 Jer 18:3; Sir 38:29.

81 See 2 Kgs 12:11–12. Ps 60:2 discusses the need to make repairs to the city's defenses after an earthquake.

82 Avraham Biran, *Biblical Dan* (Jerusalem: Israel Exploration Society, 1994), 147–154. See Isa 44:12 for a blacksmith at work at his forge.

83 See Isa 38:14, in which Hezekiah compares his groaning to the clamor of swallows and cranes.

84 Wis 17:19.

85 For Moses's use of Mount Sinai as a speaking platform, see Exod 24 and 34:29–34, and for the Sermon on the Mount, see Matt 5:1–7:29. Note Joshua's similar use of Mount Gerizim at Shechem for a public address (Josh 24:1–28).

86 The scene played out in 2 Kgs 9:30–37 contains a public claim and public challenge of authority and results in Jezebel's death at the hands of several eunuchs who act on Jehu's words.

87 See the acoustic tests applied to the ruins of Shiloh and Shechem in B. Cobbey Crisler, "The Acoustics and Crowd Capacity of Natural Theaters in Palestine," *BA* 39, no. 4 (1976): 128–141.

88 See Jeremiah's Temple Sermon (Jer 7:2 and 26:2) and his trial in the New Gate of the Temple (26:10), Absalom in Jerusalem's gate area (2 Sam 15:2), and Hezekiah in "the square at the gate of the city" (2 Chr 32:6).

89 The common criteria for a fortified city were walls, gates, and bars (Deut 3:5; 1 Sam 23:7; 2 Chr 8:5).

90 Of course, that did not always end well, as Gaal discovers when trying to defend Shechem against Abimelech in Judg 9:34–41. See also David seating himself in the gate in 2 Sam 19:8.

91 See the execution of idolaters in Deut 17:2–5. See also the case of the "rebellious son" in Deut 21:18–21.

92 Biran, *Biblical Dan*, 239–243. Note how Job obtains public recognition when he chooses to take his seat in the square near the gate of his city, and when "the ear" hears him and "the eye" sees him, they commend him for his statements (Job 29:7–11).

93 See Isa 59:14. Amos 5:10–15 also decries a society that hates those who "reprove in the gate" and fail to establish justice.

94 This example of cognitive dissonance is played out as a public spectacle in 1 Kgs 22:1–40.

95 Jer 19; compare Exod 32:19. Execration rituals involved a publicly stated curse and concluded with the smashing of an object (sometimes a figurine) that either

contained the name of the place or people being cursed or functioned as a surrogate. See Michael S. Donahou, *A Comparison of the Egyptian Execration Ritual to Exodus 32:19 and Jeremiah 19* (Piscataway, NJ: Gorgias, 2010), 128–130, 191–198.

96 The news so startles Eli that he falls over backward from his seat and breaks his neck (1 Sam 4:12–17).

97 For a description of the various percussion instruments used by the ancient Israelites, see John A. Smith, *Music in Religious Cults of the Ancient Near East* (London: Routledge, 2021), 112–113.

98 The scene in 2 Sam 6 shows the power of public display to raise the voices of approval for a new king.

99 Prov 11:12–13 contrasts the foolish statements of the person who belittles others and the gossip with those wise enough to remain silent. Compare Eccl 3:7, with its admonition that there is a time to be silent and a time to speak, and Ps 69:12, which negatively depicts "those who sit in the gate" gossiping about the pious acts of the righteous.

100 Lev 10:3.

101 Baruch A. Levine, "Silence, Sound, and the Phenomenology of Mourning in Biblical Israel," *JANES* 22 (1993): 91.

102 First Kgs 19:11–13 indicates Elijah hears the "sheer silence" and interprets it, rather than the sounds of the wind and earthquake that precede it, as evidence of a true theophany.

103 Isa 56:10.

104 Constance Classen, David Howes, and Anthony Synnott, *Aroma: The Cultural History of Smell* (London: Routledge, 1994), 17–18, quote Sophocles's description of fifth-century BCE Thebes, saying the city is "heavy with a mingled burden of sounds and smells, of groans and hymns and incense."

105 Cornelius Houtman, "On the Function of the Holy Incense (Exodus XXX 34–8) and the Sacred Anointing Oil (Exodus XXX 22–33)," *VT* 42, no. 4 (1992): 459, notes that every person has a personal odor and points to Gen 27:27; Ps 45:8 (9); and Hos 14:7 as examples.

106 Diane Ackerman, *A Natural History of the Senses* (New York: Random House, 1990), 5.

107 Kjeld Nielsen, "Ancient Aromas: Good and Bad," *BRev* 7, no. 3 (1991): 28.

108 Ezek 44:18.

109 See Jer 29:17 for figs long past their expiration date. For the condition of the streets, see Edward Neufeld, "Hygiene Conditions in Ancient Israel (Iron Age)," *BA* 34, no. 2 (1971): 45.

110 Both the psalmist (Pss 18:42; 69:2, 14) and the prophets refer to the mire in the streets (Isa 10:6; Mic 7:10). See also 2 Sam 22:43.

111 Joshua Schwartz, "Dogs, 'Water' and Wall," *SJOT* 14, no. 1 (2000): 104; 1 Sam 25:22.

112 See Isa 22:13.

113 See the curse of Jeroboam's household, comparing its fiery demise to dung burned "until it is all gone," in 1 Kgs 14:10. Ezek 4:12–15 describes the prophet's and priest's disgust at eating food cooked over an "unclean" fire fueled by human dung. On this, see Daniel I. Block, *The Book of Ezekiel, Chapters 1–24* (Grand Rapids, MI: Eerdmans, 1997), 186–187.

114 Neufeld, "Hygiene Conditions," 46–48, 57.

115 Prov 27:9 indicates that "perfume and incense make the heart glad" and presumably the air more fragrant. See Seung Ho Bang and Oded Borowski, "Local Production of a Small Rectangular Limestone Incense Altar at Tell Halif, Israel: Iconographic Considerations," *BASOR* 377 (2017): 49–67.

116 Andrew J. Koh, Andrea M. Berlin, and Sharon C. Herbert, "Phoenician Cedar Oil from Amphoriskoi at Tel Kedesh: Implications concerning Its Production, Use, and Export during the Hellenistic Age," *BASOR* 385 (2020): 110.

117 See Lev 17:6 and Num 18:17 for a description of how animal fat was transformed into smoke, producing a pleasing odor for God.

118 See Gen 8:21; Exod 29:18; Lev 1:9; and Num 15:3.

119 See Exod 30:34–38; and Gudme, "Pleasing Odour for Yahweh," 7–24.

120 For the refining of silver and gold, see Ps 12:6 and Prov 17:3, and the vapor and smoke from a furnace are referenced in Sir 22:24. Prov 10:26 describes smoke as an irritant to the eyes.

121 Thus, Simon the Tanner, who provides Peter with a place to stay in Joppa, has a house "by the seashore" (Acts 10:6, 32).

122 King and Stager, *Life in Biblical Israel*, 161–162.

123 Isa 50:2 refers to the smell of a fish kill when the waters of a river dry up. See also mentions of the stench of the dead fish in Exod 7:18 and frogs in Exod 8:14.

124 Excavated latrines like those in Deut 23:13 (14) work in open country but not in a city.

125 See Jodi Magness, "What's the Poop on Ancient Toilets and Toilet Habits?," *NEA* 75, no. 2 (2012): 80–87.

126 Jane M. Cahill et al., "It Had to Happen: Scientists Examine Remains of Ancient Bathroom," *BAR* 17, no. 3 (1991): 64–69.

127 MacDonald, *Diet in Biblical Times*, 38. See Neh 13:15–16.

128 MacDonald, 79, discusses Amos's condemnation of the wealthy and their overindulgence (Amos 6:4–6).

129 See 2 Sam 13:8 and Jer 37:21. Note also that not every baker was as careful as they should have been, supplying Hosea (7:8) with an image of "a cake not turned" and undoubtedly raising the stink of its burnt surface.

130 Prov 27:9.

131 See Deut 12:27; 33:10; 1 Sam 2:28; and 1 Kgs 12:33.

132 Mark M. Smith, *Sensing the Past: Seeing, Hearing, Smelling, Tasting, and Touching in History* (Berkeley: University of California Press, 2007), 60–61.

133 See Isa 1:23; 5:23; Amos 2:6–7; and 5:12.

134 Classen, Howes, and Synnott, *Aroma*, 126–127.

135 Dominika A. Kurek-Chomycz, "The Fragrance of Her Perfume: The Significance of Sense Imagery in John's Account of the Anointing in Bethany," *NovT* 52, no. 4 (2010): 339, points out that the anointing of Jesus's feet with nard was considered an extravagance rather than an everyday practice and associates the act with a transitionary step leading to the passion.

136 See Isa 3:20; and Jenner, "Follow Your Nose?," 341.

137 The compliments contained in the Song of Songs include the statement that a person's breath has the scent of apples (Song 7:8) and that their body and clothing produce a wave of fragrance from scented oils (1:3) and mandrake (7:13).

138 Prov 7:17.
139 See Song 1:12–14 and 4:10–14 for descriptions of the uses of nard, myrrh, henna blossoms, and spices. A fuller analysis is found in Malena, "Spice Roots," 165–184.
140 Lise Manniche, *Sacred Luxuries: Fragrance, Aromatherapy, and Cosmetics in Ancient Egypt* (Ithaca, NY: Cornell University Press, 1999), 63.
141 See Athalya Brenner, "Aromatics and Perfumes in the Song of Songs," *JSOT* 25, no. 8 (1983): 75–81.
142 Le Breton, *Sensing the World*, 171.
143 See Ps 38:5 for wounds that fester and produce foul odors. See also Mark 5:25–29 for the hemorrhaging woman.
144 See Whittle et al., "Human Breath Odors," 252–266. Job 19:17 includes Job's lament that his "breath had become repulsive to his wife."
145 See the statutes in Lev 12 and 15 for ritual cleansing and bathing. Bathsheba's bathing herself following her menstrual period (2 Sam 11:2–4) follows a pattern also found in Near Eastern texts. See Marten Stol, *Women in the Ancient Near East* (Boston: Walter de Gruyter, 2016), 438–441. Interestingly, Ezekiel (23:40–42) condemns Oholibah (= Jerusalem) for preparing herself by bathing and adorning herself with jewelry and other finery to honor her "lovers" (= foreign rulers and gods).
146 Le Breton, *Sensing the World*, 190–193. See the longing of infants for their mothers' milk as a metaphor in 1 Pet 2:2–3.
147 Tuan, *Space and Place*, 10, 12.
148 Alex Purves, "Introduction: What and Where Is Touch?," in *Touch and the Ancient Senses*, ed. Alex Purves (London: Routledge, 2018), 2.
149 See 2 Sam 19:35 (36) for Barzillai's symptoms of aging. See also 1 Kgs 1:1 and Eccl 4:11 for the inability to warm the body.
150 See Lev 13:30–37 and 21:20 for the examination of an itching disease and a blemish in the eye. Deut 28:27 describes a variety of physical afflictions, including boils, ulcers, and an incurable itch.
151 Macpherson, "Individuating the Senses," 11.
152 Mark Paterson, *The Senses of Touch: Haptics, Affects and Technologies* (Oxford: Berg, 2007), 20–21.
153 For references to runners, see 2 Sam 18:24–27; Prov 4:12; Isa 40:31; and Jer 51:31. For the competitiveness and joy that accompany runners' determination to win a race, see Ps 19:5 and 1 Cor 9:24–25.
154 See 1 Kgs 9:27; Isa 33:23; and Jonah 1:7. See also the descriptions of Paul's voyages in Acts.
155 See the plague of darkness in Exod 10:21. Yael Avrahami, *The Senses of Scripture: Sensory Perception in the Hebrew Bible* (New York: T&T Clark, 2012), 107, correlates that expansion of feeling in darkness to the blind's enhanced sense of touch.
156 Judg 16:23–30.
157 See Deut 28:29. Note how the phrase "Like the blind we grope along the wall" becomes a common metaphor in Isa 59:10; Lam 4:14; and Zeph 1:17.
158 Consider the time and skill required to create the colored yarn and threads used to produce the priestly vestments in Exod 28:38 and 39:1–3 and the intricate

needlework necessary in making the various curtains in the tabernacle in Exod 26:31 and 27:16.

159   Prov 31:13.

160   See Jer 6:23 and Ezek 21:11.

161   See Jael's use of a mallet and a tent peg to dispatch Sisera in Judg 5:26. See also the careful craftsmen who sawed blocks of stone to measure in building the Jerusalem temple in 1 Kgs 7:9.

162   See the use of a grinding stone in Isa 47:2 and Matt 24:41. For kneading bread, see 2 Sam 13:8.

163   See Luke 12:55. For the "east wind," see Isa 27:8. Like many sensual experiences, the touch of wind or the feeling of heat scorching the skin (Hos 13:5; Rev 16:8–9) and the sight of dried-up fields during a drought (Deut 28:22) all contribute to a store of memories that reemerge when an experience reoccurs.

164   Neufeld, "Hygiene Conditions," 53.

165   Judg 16:9.

166   See the happy scene in Eccl 9:7–8, which combines the enjoyment of food with the opportunity to wear formal (white) garments and have oil poured on the head.

167   See Exod 4:27–31 for the incident with Zipporah and Moses. See also Exod 12:7 for the apotropaic use of lamb's blood on the doorposts.

168   See 2 Sam 13:11–14 and 13:23–29.

169   The combination of Saul's grasping the hem and Samuel's use of the event is found in 1 Sam 15:26–29.

170   See 1 Kgs 11:29–31.

171   Esth 1:5–8.

172   Second Sam 13:27–28.

173   Job 12:11 notes that the "ear test[s] words as the tongue taste[s] food." In the case of the "sons of the prophet" who prepare a stew and then discover when they taste it that "there is death in the pot," they save themselves by being able to discern the danger (2 Kgs 4:39–40).

174   Nicola Perullo, *Taste as Experience: The Philosophy and Aesthetics of Food* (New York: Columbia University Press, 2016), 54.

175   Edmund T. Rolls, "The Texture and Taste of Food in the Brain," *Journal of Texture Studies* 51, no. 1 (2020): 23–44.

176   Prov 27:7.

177   John 2:7–10.

178   F. Nigel Hepper, *Baker Encyclopedia of Bible Plants* (Grand Rapids, MI: Baker, 1992), 101.

179   Prov 9:1–6. See also Ps 75:8 and Isa 1:22.

180   See Judg 16:25; 1 Sam 25:36; and Eccl 9:7.

181   Song 7:9.

182   Second Macc 15:38–39.

183   Prov 23:31–35. For an exploration of the theme of intoxication, see Cary E. Walsh, "Under the Influence: Trust and Risk in Biblical Family Drinking," *JSOT* 90, no. 25 (2000): 13–29.

184   See Song 4:14 and Rev 18:13.

185   Job 6:6. See MacDonald, *Diet in Biblical Times*, 40.

186 Exod 12:8. See Musselman, *Dictionary of Bible Plants*, 28–29, 39–40.
187 Yannis Hamilakis, "Archaeologies of the Senses," in *The Oxford Handbook of the Archaeology of Ritual and Religion*, ed. Timothy Insoll (New York: Oxford University Press, 2011), 208–209.
188 See Prov 24:13–14; Pss 19:7–10; and 119:103. When Ezekiel consumes the proffered scroll from YHWH, he commends it as tasting as sweet as honey (Ezek 3:3; compare Rev 10:10).
189 For the bitter taste of beer, see Isa 24:9. For spiced wine made with pomegranates, see Song 8:2. Pomegranate wine is also mentioned in Egyptian love poetry. See Barbara H. Fowler, *Love Lyrics of Ancient Egypt* (Chapel Hill: University of North Carolina Press, 1994), 26, 49.
190 See the provisions that Abigail takes to David in 2 Sam 25:18. See also the offerings that include oil, wine, pomegranates, and figs taken to the Levites in Tob 1:7.
191 Jer 31:29; Ezek 18:2.
192 See Prov 10:26 for an allegory between the taste of vinegar and a dissatisfied employer.
193 Ruth 2:14; Prov 25:20.
194 See Job 20:14–16 and Lam 3:15.
195 See Hos 10:4 for false statements growing as a weed among the furrows in the fields.
196 See Musselman, *Dictionary of Bible Plants*, 62–63; and Matt 27:34.

Chapter 3: Sensory Aspects of Warfare

1 See 1 Sam 30:1–20 for the depiction of this raid and David's subsequent retaliation.
2 The hero is Ehud in Judg 3, and it is Samson in Judg 13–16.
3 Judg 9:34–44.
4 See the military coups by Zimri in 1 Kgs 16:15–18 and Jehu in 2 Kgs 9.
5 For depictions of ancient warriors, their weapons, and battle scenes, see Yigael Yadin, *The Art of Warfare in Biblical Lands in the Light of Archaeological Discovery* (London: Weidenfeld & Nicolson, 1963).
6 Victor H. Matthews, "Introduction," in *Writing and Reading War: Rhetoric, Gender, and Ethics in Biblical and Modern Contexts*, ed. Brad E. Kelle and Frank R. Ames (Atlanta: SBL, 2008), 1–2.
7 Isaiah (in 2:4) and Micah (in 4:3) both express sentiments indicating that they had intimate experiences of war based on the activities of the Assyrian invaders.
8 Charlie Trimm, "God's Staff and Moses' Hand(s): The Battle against the Amalekites as a Turning Point in the Role of the Divine Warrior," *JSOT* 44, no. 1 (2019): 199–200.
9 For the use of this model, see Victor H. Matthews, "Spatial and Sensory Aspects of Battle in Biblical and Ancient Near Eastern Texts," *BTB* 49, no. 2 (2019): 82–87.
10 The identification of a village as a settlement with "no walls" and the classification of its houses as being in "open country" are included in the law of Jubilees (Lev 25:31).

11 See Lot's flight to Zoar in Gen 19:20–22. See also reference to flight to the mountains in Ps 11:1.

12 See Isa 10:28–32 and Jer 4:5–6. Since the villages that Isaiah lists here are only two or three miles from Jerusalem, the people probably fled to the capital city. See Joseph Blenkinsopp, *Isaiah 1–39* (New York: Doubleday, 2000): 260–261, for the itinerary of the Assyrian forces.

13 Egyptian and Mesopotamian records and monuments document these events and depict prisoners being taken away with only a few possessions. See Izak Cornelius, "The Image of Assyria: An Iconographic Approach by Way of a Study of Selected Material on the Theme of 'Power and Propaganda' in the Neo-Assyrian Palace Reliefs," *OTE* 2, no. 1 (1989): 41–60.

14 Mic 1:8–15.

15 See Num 21:25–30, in which the invading Israelites in Transjordan capture the cities and villages of King Sihon and settle themselves in the villages of the Amorites and Heshbon, with the defeated men forced to flee while their women are taken as captives. For the Danites' exploits in taking Laish, see Judg 18:27–30.

16 See 2 Sam 18:24–26; 2 Kgs 9:17; and Isa 62:6.

17 See the role and responsibility of the sentinel in Ezek 33:1–6.

18 See 2 Sam 18:24–27.

19 For mentions of hilltop signals, see Isa 13:2; 18:3; and 30:17. The Lachish letters dating to the invasion of Judah by the Babylonian forces of Nebuchadnezzar in 587 BCE include a chilling mention of the signal fire at Azekah having gone out. See Matthews and Benjamin, *OTP-4*, 217.

20 See 2 Kgs 18:26–27 for the plea by King Hezekiah's advisers that the Assyrian Rabshakeh address them in the diplomatic language of Aramaic so that the general populace of Jerusalem during the 701 BCE siege would not become demoralized.

21 See these events in Isa 7.

22 See the defenses for Jerusalem created by Uzziah in 2 Chr 26:10, 15, including machines designed to shoot arrows and cast large stones.

23 See Volkmar Fritz, *The City in Ancient Israel* (Sheffield: Sheffield Academic, 1995), 103–108, for a description of the defenses of the city of Lachish and the Assyrian depictions of the siege that captured it in 701 BCE.

24 See Jer 32:24 and 33:4. The siegeworks, along with ramps and battering rams, raised around Jerusalem by the Babylonian army of Nebuchadnezzar are described in Ezekiel's theatrical performance in Ezek 4:2. Ezek 26:7–9 provides a description of the forces brought against Tyre by the Babylonians.

25 Ruth Jacoby, "The Representation and Identification of Cities on Assyrian Reliefs," *IEJ* 41, nos. 1–3 (1991): 126–130.

26 See Jeremiah's admonition to the people of Jerusalem to "Sharpen the arrows! Fill the quivers!" in Jer 51:11. Note the preparations for war in Jdt 4:5, including securing hilltops and fortifying villages.

27 See Victor H. Matthews, "Taking Calculated Risks: The Story of the Cannibal Mothers (2 Kgs 6:24–7:20)," *BTB* 43, no. 1 (2013): 4–13, for a graphic example of how the social norms become strained.

28 See the description of starving people in Lam 2:19–20, including a reference to cannibalism. Ezek 7:19 describes a city in which there is no longer food available at any price.

29 See Judg 9:34–36.

30 For a biblical example, see 2 Sam 10:8.

31 See Judg 20:19–35.

32 *ANET*, 236–237. On the reliability of Egyptian monumental inscriptions for historical reconstructions of events, see William J. Murnane, "Rhetorical History? The Beginning of Thutmose III's First Campaign in Western Asia," *JARCE* 26 (1989): 183–189.

33 For this reversal of fortunes using the gate as a refuge, see Judg 9:40; 2 Sam 11:23; and Ezek 21:15.

34 Second Sam 23:8–39. See 1 Sam 8:11 for the prophet's argument against a king in which the tribes would have to give up their sons, conscripted as charioteers, cavalry, and infantry in the army. See Charlie Trimm, *Fighting for the King and the Gods: A Survey of Warfare in the Ancient Near East* (Atlanta: SBL, 2017), 97–129, for the various methods used by nations and empires in the ancient Near East for collecting troops for military expeditions.

35 Rehoboam assembles troops in 1 Kgs 12:21, and Ahab does the same in 1 Kgs 20:15.

36 Judg 3:27; 6:34.

37 For the devastation caused by an army on the march, see Josh 8:20–21; Judg 20:40; Isa 14:31; and Jer 5:17.

38 Judg 4–5.

39 For the use of scouts, see 1 Sam 26:4.

40 See Exod 14:26–31. See also Erasmus Gass, "The Deborah-Barak Composition (Jdg 4–5): Some Topographical Reflections," *PEQ* 149, no. 4 (2017): 326–335.

41 For the dread brought on by darkness, see Wis 17:5–6.

42 Judg 7:19–22.

43 William W. Hallo and K. Lawson Younger, eds., *The Context of Scripture* (Leiden: Brill, 1997), 2.2A:8–11 (hereafter cited as *COS*).

44 Although the prophet is attributing the role of a guide or scout to YHWH, Isa 42:16 suggests these tasks.

45 Robert T. Tally Jr., *Spatiality* (London: Routledge, 2013), 2.

46 See Ben Sira's admonition to remain weary on a smooth path in Sir 32:21. Note Jeroboam's strategy of laying an ambush to try to catch Abijah's troops from Judah in a vise between two contingents of his army in 2 Chr 13:13–20. The Divine Warrior's intervention foiled this effort.

47 See the Annals of Shalmaneser III, which describe burning cities and cutting down orchards (*COS* 2.113C:267). See similar activities in Jer 7:20.

48 *COS* 2.119:302.

49 Isa 1:7.

50 See Gideon's battle with the combined forces of the Midianites and Amalekites in the Valley of Jezreel in Judg 6:33–35. See also the site of Saul's final battle against the Philistines who were encamped at Aphek while the Israelites staged themselves "by the fountain that is in Jezreel" in 1 Sam 29:1.

51 An abbreviated account appears in 2 Kgs 23:29, and a later, more embellished version is in 2 Chr 35:20–24.

52 *COS* 2.2A:8–11.

53 See 1 Sam 17:1–3; and John A. Beck, "David and Goliath, a Story of Place: The Narrative-Geographical Shaping of 1 Samuel 17," *WTJ* 68, no. 2 (2006): 324–326.

54 See Moshe Garsiel, "The Valley of Elah Battle and the Duel of David with Goliath: Between History and Artistic Theological Historiography," in *Homeland and Exile: Biblical and Ancient Near Eastern Studies in Honour of Bustenay Oded,* ed. Gershon Galil, Mark Geller, and Alan R. Millard (Leiden: Brill, 2009), 393–395.

55 On the use of space in 1 Kgs 22, see Victor H. Matthews, *More Than Meets the Ear* (Grand Rapids, MI: Eerdmans, 2008), 114–129.

56 See Paul E. Dion, "The Horned Prophet (1 Kings XXII 11)," *VT* 49, no. 2 (1999): 259–260, for this prophetic prop.

57 For an analysis of the dialogue between Ahab and Micaiah, see Keith Bodner, "The Locutions of 1 Kings 22:28: A New Proposal," *JBL* 122, no. 3 (2003): 533–546.

58 Second Sam 18:9–10.

59 For this break in protocol, see Saul M. Olyan, "Honor, Shame, and Covenant Relations in Ancient Israel and Its Environment," *JBL* 115, no. 2 (1996): 208–211.

60 Second Sam 18–19:8.

61 See 1 Sam 17:4–11. It is reminiscent of single combat challenges in Homer's *Iliad*, in which Trojan and Greek heroes square off between the armies. See Neal Bierling, *Giving Goliath His Due: New Archaeological Light on the Philistines* (Grand Rapids, MI: Baker Academic, 1992), 147–148.

62 See the account in 2 Sam 2:12–17. See also F. Charles Fensham, "The Battle between the Men of Joab and Abner as a Possible Ordeal by Battle?," *VT* 20, no. 3 (1970): 356–357; and Garsiel, "Valley of Elah Battle," 404–409.

63 See the analysis of their respective weapons in Garsiel, "Valley of Elah Battle," 399–404.

64 Note the use of this image in Caravaggio's early seventeenth-century painting of the scene. Madadh Richey, "Goliath among the Giants: Monster Decapitation and Capital Display in 1 Samuel 17 and Beyond," *JSOT* 45, no. 3 (2021): 336–356, argues that David's beheading of the giant Goliath is comparable to Gilgamesh taking Humbaba's head and Perseus decapitating Medusa. In that way, the story goes beyond taking a human head and propels David into the role of a monster slayer, hero, and worthy monarch.

65 See 1 Sam 21:1–9; and Stanley J. Isser, *The Sword of Goliath: David in Heroic Literature* (Atlanta: SBL, 2003), 35–37.

66 Song 6:4 suggests that the very sight of the banners of enemy nations is overwhelming.

67 Jer 4:5–6 describes using a standard as a signal to retreat into fortified cities, while Jer 4:21 refers to conflict underway with the sound of trumpets and the sight of standards on display.

68 Abimelech divides his forces into three companies (Judg 9:43), and Saul uses the same tactic when attacking the Ammonites to relieve the siege of Jabesh-Gilead (1 Sam 11:11).

69 Isa 31:9.

70 Irene Winter, "Royal Rhetoric and Development of Historical Narrative," *Studies in Visual Communication* 7, no. 2 (1981): 2–38.

71 See John A. Emerton, "The Value of the Moabite Stone as an Historical Source," *VT* 52, no. 4 (2002): 488–489. For similar rhetoric describing the role of the Divine Warrior, see Josh 8:1–2, 18, 24–27; Judg 2:14; and 1 Sam 23:4.

72 See Alice Mandell and Jeremy D. Smoak, "Reading beyond Literacy, Writing beyond Epigraphy: Multimodality and the Monumental Inscriptions at Ekron and Tel Dan," *Maarav* 22, nos. 1–2 (2018): 82–86.

73 Nah 3:2–3; Ramesses III's Medinet Habu inscription describes how enemy troops are "netted, beached, surrounded, put to death and stacked head to foot in piles" (see Matthews and Benjamin, *OTP-4*, 164).

74 See Ezek 37:1–2 for such an abandoned battle site. A similar scene with mountains filled with skulls and birds making their nests in them is found in Ninurta-kudurrī-Uṣur's Annals #2 (*COS* 2.115B:280).

75 See Päivi Maaranen, "Landscapes of Power," in Lamberg, Hakanen, and Haikari, *Physical and Cultural Space*, 241, who contends that power is connected to landscapes and the ways that people experience these spaces over time.

76 For biblical references to these sounds, see Judg 5:22; Job 39:23; and Jer 47:3.

77 See the Philistines' initial fright when they hear the Israelites shout about the coming of the ark of the covenant and the turnaround when they are warned against becoming slaves of the Hebrews in 1 Sam 4:5–10.

78 The events are detailed in 2 Kgs 7:6, but like in the case in 1 Sam 7:7–11, the enemy force's panic is caused by the intervention of the Divine Warrior, who in this latter case causes a "thundering voice" to be heard.

79 See Ezek 23:24 for an army traveling with chariots and wagons.

80 Mark M. Smith, "Producing Sense, Consuming Sense, Making Sense: Perils and Prospects for Sensory History," *Journal of Social History* 40, no. 4 (2007): 852.

81 Alain Corbin, "A History and Anthropology of the Senses," in *Time, Desire and Horror: Towards a History of the Senses* (Cambridge: Polity, 1995), 183.

82 See Jehoshaphat and Ahab going into battle and the Aramaean captains all in chariots with bowmen in 1 Kgs 22:31–35.

83 See Job 39:25 for the shouting of commands.

84 See 2 Kgs 24:16 for the Babylonian army incorporating troops from conquered nations. See also Sargon II's Annals for a similar practice by the Assyrians (*COS* 2.118A:293).

85 Sarah Pink, *Doing Sensory Ethnography* (London: Sage, 2009), 76.

86 Second Chr 20:21. See Smith, *Music in Religious Cults*, 64.

87 See the Israelites' order of march outlined in Num 10:12–25.

88 For a description of camp building, see Davide Nadali, "Esarhaddon's Glazed Bricks from Nimrud: The Egyptian Campaign Depicted," *Iraq* 68 (2006): 109–119. See also the depictions in Yadin, *Art of Warfare*, 236–237. Regimental encampments for the Israelite tribes are detailed in Num 1:52 and 2:2.

89 See Ps 80:6 for reference to enemies laughing at the Israelites' inability to withstand them.
90 For the exploits of these "Mighty Men," see 2 Sam 23:8–39.
91 See Josh 1:10–11 and 3:2–4 for officers circulating through the Israelite encampment giving orders and warning the people to strictly obey them.
92 See Deut 20:1–9 and 1 Sam 13:9.
93 Second Sam 5:24; 1 Chr 14:15.
94 See Goliath's taunting of Saul's army and instances of challenges in 2 Sam 21:20–21 and 23:9. For a discussion of these practices, see Susan Niditch, *War in the Hebrew Bible: A Study of the Ethics of Violence* (New York: Oxford University Press, 1993), 92–94.
95 See how intimidating that sound could be in Isa 21:15. See also the anticipatory effect created by swords "drawn for slaughter" in Ezek 21:28.
96 For the deadly sight and sound of flights of arrows, see Isa 5:28; Hab 3:11; and 2 Mac 10:30.
97 See Judg 20:16 and 1 Mac 9:11 for references to slingers as a distinct contingent of an army.
98 See Jer 6:23 and 50:42 for this metaphor. Trumpets signal an attack in Judg 7:19–20 and 2 Chr 13:12, and a battle cry is found in Job 39:25 and Zeph 1:16.
99 For trumpets used as signaling devices, see Judg 7:18–22; Sir 26:27; 2 Sam 2:28; 18:16; and 20:22.
100 Smith, "Producing Sense," 851–852.
101 For a comparison of massive armies to locust swarms, see the account of Ramesses II's Battle of Qadesh in *COS* 2.5A:32–38; compare Judg 6:5 and Joel 1:4–7.
102 For this metaphor, see Sennacherib's Bavian Rock Inscription in *COS* 2.119E:305.
103 For this wider conflict, see 1 Sam 14:22–23; 17:52; and 2 Sam 18:8.
104 See 2 Chr 13:15; Job 39:25; 41:29; and Zeph 1:14–16.
105 See Job 24:12 and Ezek 30:24 for these pitiful cries of the wounded and dying.
106 For the use of spears, see 2 Sam 2:23 and 23:21. For sword thrusts, see Judg 3:21–22 and 2 Sam 20:9.
107 Corbin, "History and Anthropology," 186–187.
108 For these sounds, see Ezek 21:21–22; 26:9–11; and 1 Macc 5:30.
109 For the listing of these mighty warriors, see 1 Chr 12:1–15.
110 See Judg 5:22; 2 Kgs 7:6; Isa 5:28; and Nah 3:3.
111 For these images, see Pss 7:13; 76:3; and Hab 3:11.
112 For examples of divine retribution, see 2 Kgs 21:13–15; Jer 15:5–9; and Lam 2:2–9.
113 See Deut 1:41; Job 39:23; and Jer 47:3.
114 See Jer 51:11 and Ezek 21:9–11 for this practice.
115 See Job 39:19–25 and Jer 8:6, 16.
116 See 2 Kgs 15:16; Mordechai Cogan, "'Ripping Open Pregnant Women' in Light of an Assyrian Analogue," *JAOS* 103, no. 4 (1983): 755–757; and Peter Dubovsky, "Ripping Open Pregnant Arab Women: Reliefs in Room L of Ashurbanipal's North Palace," *Or* 78, no. 3 (2009): 415–416.
117 See these gestures and loud expressions of mockery in Lam 1:7 and 2:15–16.

118 See the removal of King Adoni-bezek's thumbs and big toes in Judg 1:6. For a discussion of the Assyrian postconflict treatment of prisoners, see Erika Bleibtreu, "Grisly Assyrian Record of Torture and Death," *BAR* 17, no. 1 (1991): 53–61, 75.

119 Thus Ninurta-kudurrī-Uṣur, the Neo-Babylonian governor of Suḫu, proudly points out his prisoners by proclaiming he "removed the hands and lower lips of eighty of their troops and let them go free to spread the news of my glory" (Suḫu Annals #2; *COS* 2.115B:280).

120 See T. M. Lemos, "Shame and Mutilation of Enemies in the Hebrew Bible," *JBL* 125, no. 2 (2006): 227–228. See how Adoni-bezek has his thumbs and big toes removed after being defeated by the men of Judah and Simeon in Judg 1:5–6.

121 Note the display of Saul's dismembered body before the walls of Beth-shean in 1 Sam 31:8–10.

122 Compare similar celebrations in Exod 15:20 and Ps 68:25. For this spectacle, see the reception that Jephthah receives in Judg 11:34.

123 While this scene in 1 Sam 18:6 celebrates David's generalship, it provides the narrative impetus for Saul's jealousy and the break between them.

124 See Isa 14:31 for the personification of gates wailing at the fall of a city, Jer 4:29 for frightened city dwellers fleeing, and Jer 4:8 for others putting on sackcloth to mourn their loss.

125 See Num 20:14–21 for the forced detour when the Edomites do not let the Israelites cross their territory.

126 His speech appears in both 2 Kgs 18:13–37 and Isa 36.

127 Mordechai Cogan and Hayim Tadmor, *II Kings* (New York: Doubleday, 1988), 242n7, cite Nimrud Letter ND 2632, which describes Assyrian officials standing before the Marduk Gate of Babylon calling on the people to refrain from rebellion.

128 Josephus, *J.W.* 2.16:362–401. See Ehud Ben Zvi, "Who Wrote the Speech of Rabshakeh and When?," *JBL* 109, no. 1 (1990): 80.

129 See Victor H. Matthews, "Messengers and the Transmission of Information in the Mari Kingdom," in *Go to the Land I Will Show You: Studies in Honor of Dwight W. Young*, ed. Victor H. Matthews and Joseph Coleson (Winona Lake, IN: Eisenbrauns, 1996), 267–274.

130 Compare the debate between Ahithophel and Hushai in 2 Sam 17:1–14 when Absalom asks for their advice following David's flight from Jerusalem.

131 See these events in 2 Sam 10. On the breaking of political treaties and the shame imposed on David's men, see Lemos, "Shame and Mutilation," 225–241; and Olyan, "Honor, Shame, and Covenant Relations," 201–218.

132 See David's sweaty condition after a battle in 4 Macc 3:8.

133 While Ps 38:5 is referring to a human's festering wound, the medical principle and the smell are the same.

134 See the injunction to do just that in Deut 23:13 (14).

135 Amos 4:10. It is possible that there is a similar case of an army in distress in Joel 2:20.

136 A common metaphor used for this reaction is "to melt in fear." See Josh 2:9, 24; 2 Sam 17:10; Isa 8:6; and 14:31.

137 See Job 39:25. Tilford, "When People Have Gods," 46, notes that violent emotions produce heightened breathing patterns.

138 See Job 29:20 and Jer 8:6, 16.
139 Job 39:19–25. See Deborah O. Cantrell, *The Horsemen of Israel: Horses and Chariotry in Monarchic Israel (Ninth–Eighth Centuries B.C.E.)* (Winona Lake, IN: Eisenbrauns, 2011), 13–15.
140 *COS* 2.119E:305. See David Howes, "Can These Dry Bones Live? An Anthropological Approach to the History of the Senses," *Journal of American History* 95, no. 2 (2008): 442–451, for a sensory analysis of ancient smells.
141 See Judg 3:21–22. A similar scene appears in 2 Sam 3:27, in which Joab kills Abner with a knife to the belly.
142 See 2 Sam 20:10, where Joab assassinates Amasa with a sword thrust to the abdomen, leaving his dying victim to wallow in his own blood.
143 For a few examples, see Josh 10:37; 1 Sam 15:8; and 2 Sam 15:14.
144 See Ps 83:9–10; Isa 34:2; Jer 9:22; 25:33; and Amos 4:10.
145 See Deut 32:42; and Smith, "Producing Sense," 849.
146 Ackerman, *Natural History of the Senses*, 67–68.
147 The pleasant feel of a fire is found in Isa 44:16. For references to sharpened weapons, see Jer 51:11 and Ezek 21:9–10. Note the metaphors that equate a sharp tongue with a sharp razor (Ps 52:2) and sharp swords (Pss 57:4; 64:3).
148 See Eccl 10:10. One of the most often used phrases in descriptions of a battle involves striking with the edge of the sword (see Josh 6:21; 10:28; 1 Sam 15:8; and 2 Sam 15:14). That reflects the more common style of cutting rather than thrusting with a sword.
149 First Sam 17:40. See Judg 20:16 and 1 Chr 12:2 for the dexterity and accuracy achieved by slingers.
150 For the consequences of long marches, see Deut 8:4.
151 Paterson, *Senses of Touch*, 20–21.
152 Alert warriors do not stumble (2 Sam 22:37; Isa 5:27), while other, less agile ones are subject to stumbling (Jer 46:12). Combining darkness and a slippery path is disastrous (Jer 23:12).
153 Isa 41:17.
154 Jos 10:24.
155 See 2 Sam 22:39–40 and 1 Kgs 5:3. This latter passage adds the element of divine assistance in victory.
156 See Abigail's action in 1 Sam 25:24. See also the admonition to kings to serve YHWH with fear and kiss his feet in Ps 2:10–11.
157 First Kgs 2:5.
158 Second Sam 11:8.
159 Job 15:26.
160 See 2 Sam 22:35 and 2 Chr 14:8.
161 See Hos 7:15 and 1 Mac 4:7 for references to military training. See also Ps 18:32–41 for the equipping and physical attributes of a warrior, with the help of the Divine Warrior, for battle.
162 See 1 Kgs 22:34; 2 Kgs 8:28–29; and 1 Mac 1:18.
163 See Jer 14:17 for the crushing blow that wounds an opponent.
164 For the binding and treatment of wounds, see Job 5:18; Ezek 30:21; and Luke 10:34. See Ps 38:5 for the onset of gangrene in a wound. Isa 1:6 describes the treatments of various injuries.

165 Ignace J. Gelb, "Prisoners of War in Early Mesopotamia," *JNES* 32, nos. 1–2 (1973): 70–98.

166 See Joshua Jeffers, "Fifth-Campaign Reliefs in Sennacherib's 'Palace without Rival' at Nineveh," *Iraq* 73 (2011): 87–116; and Vanessa Davies, "The Treatment of Foreigners in Seti's Battle Reliefs," *JEA* 98 (2012): 73–85.

167 Isa 20:2–6.

168 Pearl Elman, "Deuteronomy 21:10–14: The Beautiful Captive Woman," *Women in Judaism* 1, no. 1 (1997), http://wjudaism.library.utoronto.ca/index.php/wjudaism.

169 For this sign of surrender, see Ps 72:9 and Isa 49:23. In 3 Macc 5:48, the dust raised by elephants approximates the cloud of dust raised by an army on the march.

170 John Marriott and Karen Radner, "Sustaining the Assyrian Army among Friends and Enemies in 714 BCE," *JCS* 67 (2015): 128–129.

171 Judg 6:4–11.

172 First Sam 14:24–27.

173 Compare Jephthah's unwise oath in Judg 11:30–31 and Achan's violation in Josh 7:1. See P. Kyle McCarter, *1 Samuel* (New York: Doubleday, 1980), 250–251; and Marsha C. White, "Saul and Jonathan in 1 Samuel 1 and 14," in *Saul in Story and Tradition*, ed. Carl S. Ehrlich (Tübingen: Mohr Siebeck, 2006), 129–133.

174 Avrahami, *Senses of Scripture*, 99, contrasts Jonathan's revived strength with the faintness of Saul's troops.

175 First Sam 14:31–33; Deut 12:23–27; Lev 19:26.

176 First Sam 14:34–35. See Tony W. Cartledge, *1 and 2 Samuel* (Macon, GA: Smyth & Helwys, 2001), 184–185.

177 Matthews and Benjamin, *OTP-4*, 205.

Chapter 4: Law and the Senses

1 Edward Ullendorff, "Thought Categories in the Hebrew Bible," in *Studies in Rationalism, Judaism and Universalism in Memory of Leon Roth*, ed. Raphael Loewe (London: Routledge & Kegan Paul, 1966), 287.

2 The diorite stela containing a copy of Hammurabi's Code includes an image of the god Shamash commissioning the king to create the set of laws. The prologue to the laws declares that the gods Anum and Enlil chose Hammurabi to "cause justice to prevail in the land" (*ANET*, 163–164).

3 On the discussion of the use of these legal collections, see Anne Fitzpatrick-McKinley, *The Transformation of Torah from Scribal Advice to Law* (Sheffield: Sheffield Academic, 1999), 81–112.

4 Raymond Westbrook, "Cuneiform Law Codes and the Origins of Legislation," *ZA* 79, no. 2 (1989): 201–222; Bruce Wells, *The Laws of Testimony in the Pentateuchal Codes* (Wiesbaden, Germany: Harrassowitz, 2004), 11–15.

5 Peter Haas, "'Die He Shall Surely Die': The Structure of Homicide in Biblical Law," *Semeia* 45 (1989): 75.

6 Exod 20:4–6; Deut 4:1–40; Isa 44:17; Hab 2:18.

7 For a repetition of this sensory polemic against idols, see Ps 115:5–7; Sir 30:19; and Wis 15:15. Avrahami, *Senses of Scripture*, 63, 68, sees the polemic against

idols in Deut 4:28 as a way of comparing them to YHWH, who has these senses and is therefore "a sign of his power and authority."

8 Avrahami, *Senses of Scripture*, 274–275, notes that there was no conscious hierarchy of the senses in ancient Israel. However, she does point to sight as a primary tool for the acquisition of knowledge, which was later passed on or presented orally.

9 Deut 25:5–10. For the relation between this passage and the prohibition in Lev 20:21, see Benjamin Kilchör, "Levirate Marriage in Deuteronomy 25:5–10 and Its Precursors in Leviticus and Numbers: A Test Case for the Relationship between P/H and D," *CBQ* 77, no. 3 (2015): 429–440.

10 Gen 38:6–10; Ruth 4:1–12.

11 See Ayelet Seidler, "The Law of Levirate and Forced Marriage—Widow vs. Levir in Deuteronomy 25.5–10," *JSOT* 42, no. 4 (2018): 435–456.

12 Exod 23:4–5; Deut 22:1–4.

13 Exod 20:15; 22:1 (21:37).

14 Exod 22:16–17; Deut 22:28–29. The corresponding law in the Code of Hammurabi (CH) 130 (Matthews and Benjamin, *OTP-4*, 116) sentences the rapist to death and exonerates the young woman.

15 Morrow, *Introduction to Biblical Law*, 243. See how Tamar, lacking witnesses, goes into mourning after being raped by her brother Amnon in 2 Sam 13:10–19.

16 See Exod 20:14 and Lev 20:10. The corresponding law to Deut 22:23–27 in CH 129 (Matthews and Benjamin, *OTP-4*, 116) also includes being caught in adultery, but the act is treated as a civil offense that could be pardoned by the husband. See Anthony Phillips, "Another Look at Adultery," *JSOT* 20, no. 6 (1981): 3–25.

17 See Carolyn Pressler, *The View of Women Found in the Deuteronomic Family Laws* (Berlin: Walter de Gruyter, 1993), 31–35.

18 Cheryl B. Anderson, *Women, Ideology, and Violence: Critical Theory and the Construction of Gender in the Book of the Covenant and the Deuteronomic Law* (London: T&T Clark, 2004), 89–91.

19 Exod 22:1–4 seems to be arranged illogically and is reordered in the NRSV. The fine imposed is equal to twice the value of the animals. See Thomas B. Dozeman, *Exodus* (Grand Rapids, MI: Eerdmans, 2009), 539.

20 See Bernard S. Jackson, *Theft in Early Jewish Law* (Oxford: Clarendon, 1972), 41–48.

21 See Exod 22:2–3 (22:1 in Hebrew). Jackson, *Theft in Early Jewish Law*, 49, makes a philological case for this form of thievery being exclusively tied to breaking into a sheepfold. CH 21 (Matthews and Benjamin, *OTP-4*, 114), which does relate to housebreaking, makes no distinction about time and simply condemns the burglar to being walled up in the hole he has dug in the wall.

22 Deut 21:1–9. See Henry McKeating, "Development of the Law on Homicide in Ancient Israel," *VT* 25, no. 1 (1975): 63–64, on the pollution of the land through bloodshed.

23 For comparison with other Near Eastern rituals, see Jeffrey H. Tigay, *The JPS Torah Commentary: Deuteronomy* (Philadelphia: Jewish Publication Society, 1996), 192n9, 381, and the excursus on Deut 21:1–9, 472–476. See also Benjamin, *Social World of Deuteronomy*, 133–134.

24 Since the killing of the heifer is not done by priests and is not performed on an altar, it cannot be classified as a sacrifice. See David P. Wright, "Deuteronomy 21.1–9 as a Rite of Elimination," *CBQ* 49, no. 3 (1987): 390–393; and Calum M. Carmichael, "A Common Element in Five Supposedly Disparate Laws," *VT* 29, no. 2 (1979): 131–133.

25 Joseph Blenkinsopp, "Deuteronomy and the Politics of Post-mortem Existence," *VT* 45, no. 1 (1995): 4.

26 Wright, "Deuteronomy 21.1–9," 394–395.

27 Deut 21:22–23.

28 See Deut 23:9–14 for the caution against displaying improprieties. See also the discussion in Carmichael, "Five Supposedly Disparate Laws," 138–139.

29 Deut 21:18–21.

30 Exod 20:12. Near Eastern Wisdom literature from both Assyria and Egypt includes this maxim to honor one's parents. See "Teachings of Ahiqar" and "Teachings of Ankhsheshonq," in Matthews and Benjamin, *OTP-4*, 341, 344.

31 See Joseph Fleishman, "Legal Innovation in Deuteronomy XXI 18–20," *VT* 53, no. 3 (2003): 324–327, on this antisocial behavior.

32 See Exod 38:8 for another mention of these women, who are required to relinquish their Egyptian copper mirrors for use in fabricating the basin of bronze used for cultic purposes. On these two passages, see Edward L. Greenstein, "Recovering 'the Women Who Served at the Entrance,'" in *Studies in Historical Geography and Biblical Historiography: Presented to Zecharia Kallai*, ed. Gershon Galil and Moshe Weinfeld (Leiden: Brill, 2000), 169–173.

33 See McCarter, *1 Samuel*, 91–93.

34 On the crimes and fate of Eli's sons, see 1 Sam 2:22–25, 27–34; and 4:10–11. See also John T. Willis, "Anti-elide Narrative Tradition from a Prophetic Circle at the Ramah Sanctuary," *JBL* 90, no. 3 (1971): 288–308.

35 See how the covenant statement evolves from Gen 12:1–3 to 15:7–16 to 17:1–22.

36 Exod 19:4–6. See Carol L. Meyers, *Exodus* (Cambridge: Cambridge University Press, 2005), 144–151.

37 See Lev 26:14–20; Deut 8:11–20; and 28:15–68. Brian M. Britt, "Curses Left and Right: Hate Speech and Biblical Tradition," *JAAR* 78, no. 3 (2010): 636, notes that the threat of the curse is as powerful as its being spoken.

38 Lev 24:10–23; Dylan R. Johnson, *Sovereign Authority and the Elaboration of Law in the Bible and the Ancient Near East* (Tübingen: Mohr Siebeck, 2020), 72–74.

39 See Jer 11:2–5; Ezek 16:59–63; and Victor H. Matthews, *The Hebrew Prophets and Their Social World* (Grand Rapids, MI: Baker Academic, 2012), 19.

40 Exod 24:3; Mal 4:4.

41 Exod 20:3–7.

42 The episode occurs in Num 25:1–9, and the call to remember what they have seen is in Deut 4:3–4.

43 Ezek 22:1–12.

44 See Num 14:20–23 and Josh 5:6 for the condemnation of the disobedient Israelites fated by YHWH to die in the wilderness rather than enter the promised land. That warning is repeated numerous times: Deut 4:26; 8:19–20; and 30:15–20.

45 Votive statements relating to the dedication of property to the shrine (Lev 27:1–13) will be discussed in chapter 5, "Religious Practice."

46 First Sam 1:10–11. Hector Avalos, *Illness and Health Care in the Ancient Near East: The Role of Greece, Mesopotamia, and Israel* (Atlanta: Scholars Press, 1995), 336, sees the shrine at Shiloh as the appropriate place where a person with a health-care concern could petition YHWH.

47 See Ruth Fidler, "A Wife's Vow—the Husband's Woe? The Case of Hannah and Elkanah (1 Samuel 1.21, 23)," *ZAW* 118, no. 3 (2006): 385–386; and Jacques Berlinerblau, *The Vow and the Popular Religious Groups of Ancient Israel: A Philological and Sociological Inquiry* (Sheffield: Sheffield Academic, 1996), 77–80.

48 See Francesco Cocco, *Women in the Wilderness: The "Female Legislation" of the Book of Numbers (Num 5,11–31; 27,1–11; 30,2–17)* (Tübingen: Mohr Siebeck, 2020), 168–170, for a discussion of the conditional vow in Near Eastern literature.

49 Although *ḥerem* (holy war) is not mentioned here, this case is like the attack on Jericho in Josh 6:12–21, when its people and property are devoted to YHWH for giving them the victory.

50 See Jephthah's vow in Judg 11:30–31. See also the consequences when he sees that his daughter is the first to come celebrate his victory in Judg 11:34–36. The vow taken by the Israelites as they prepare to attack the city of Arad is in Num 21:2–3.

51 See Deut 23:21–23 and Eccl 5:2–4. The instance from Wisdom literature warns to never speak rashly without thinking.

52 First Sam 1:21.

53 Num 30:1–15. See Jacques Berlinerblau, "The Israelite Vow: Distress or Daily Life?," *Bib* 72, no. 4 (1991): 549–555.

54 See Nahman Avigad, "Two Phoenician Votive Seals," *IEJ* 16, no. 4 (1966): 243–251.

55 See Jer 7:8–9; Hos 4:1–2; Amos 2:6–8; 5:11–12; and 8:4–6.

56 Second Sam 12:1–15. Compare Elijah's confrontation of Ahab and the king's abject response in 1 Kgs 21:17–29.

57 Amos 4:1–4.

58 An echo of the legal protections is found in Zech 7:10. See Harold V. Washington, *Injustice Made Legal: Deuteronomic Law and the Plight of Widows, Strangers, and Orphans in Ancient Israel* (Grand Rapids, MI: Eerdmans, 2002), 31–37.

59 Exod 22:21–24; 23:9. See Deut 10:18 and Ps 68:5 for YHWH's role as the ultimate protector of the weak and poor.

60 Deut 24:19–21; Lev 19:9–10.

61 See Ronald Simkins, "The Widow and Orphan in the Political Economy of Ancient Israel," *Journal of Religion and Society* 10 (2014): 22–24.

62 See the restatement of this legal injunction in Jer 34:14. See Bernard S. Jackson, "The Prophet and the Law in Early Judaism and the New Testament," *Jewish Law Association Studies* 7 (1994): 71, on the fluid nature of legal custom and its eventual inviolate wording.

63 Exod 21:2–6; Deut 15:12–17; Lev 25:39–43. See Adrian Schenker, "The Biblical Legislation on the Release of Slaves: The Road from Exodus to Leviticus," *JSOT* 78, no. 23 (1998): 23–41.

64 Bernard S. Jackson, *Wisdom Laws: A Study of the Mishpatim of Exodus 21:1–22:16* (New York: Oxford University Press, 2006), 113–114, also suggests "Elohim" here refers to the "household gods."

65 See Calum M. Carmichael, "The Three Laws on the Release of Slaves (Ex 21, 2–11; Dtn 15,12–18; Lev 25,39–46)," *ZAW* 112, no. 4 (2000): 513–515, on the relation to the household gods and Elohim in this law in Exod 21:6. See Victor Hurowitz, "'His Master Shall Pierce His Ear with an Awl' (Exodus 21:6)—Marking Slaves in the Bible in Light of Akkadian Sources," *American Academy for Jewish Research* 58 (1992): 54–77, for various measures used in Mesopotamian literature and law to mark and thus restrict the movements of slaves.

66 The Decalogue and legal codes provide the foundation: Exod 20:16; Deut 5:20; and Lev 19:12.

67 Exod 23:1–3. Gossiping is depicted as a social ill in Ps 69:12; Prov 20:19; Ezek 36:3; Sir 28:13; and 1 Tim 5:13.

68 Num 35:30. This same standard of evidentiary conviction is found in Hammurabi's Code, nos. 1–4 (Matthews and Benjamin, *OTP-4*, 112–113).

69 See Tigay, *Deuteronomy*, 184.

70 Deut 17:6; 19:15–21. See the discussion in Bernard M. Levinson, *Deuteronomy and the Hermeneutics of Legal Innovation* (New York: Oxford University Press, 1997), 120–123.

71 See Pss 27:12 and 35:11. Prov 6:16–19 includes false witness among the things that YHWH hates.

72 First Kgs 21:8–14; the follow-up episode in 2 Kgs 9:21–23. See Calum M. Carmichael, "Biblical Laws of Talion," *HAR* 9 (1985): 108–111.

73 First Kgs 21:17–29; 2 Kgs 9–10.

74 Deut 22:13–21.

75 See the discussion of this passage and the issues raised about its adherence to the law of false accusation and the principle of lex talionis in Bruce Wells, "Sex, Lies, and Virginal Rape: The Slandered Bride and False Accusation in Deuteronomy," *JBL* 124, no. 1 (2005): 41–72.

76 On the aspects of marriage contracts and their judicial consequences, see T. M. Lemos, *Marriage Gifts and Social Change in Ancient Palestine* (Cambridge: Cambridge University Press, 2010), 36–41. See also Tikva Frymer-Kensky, "Virginity in the Bible," in *Gender and Law in the Hebrew Bible and the Ancient Near East*, ed. Victor H. Matthews, Bernard M. Levinson, and Tikva Frymer-Kensky (Sheffield: Sheffield Academic, 1998), 93–95.

77 Num 5:11–31. See Cocco, *Women in the Wilderness*, 109–114.

78 See the discussion of the destructive effects of jealousy and distrust in Richard S. Briggs, "Reading the *Sotah* Text (Numbers 5:11–31): Holiness and a Hermeneutic Fit for Suspicion," *BibInt* 17, no. 3 (2009): 312–316.

79 Num 5:24, 27.

80 Num 5:29–31. See Johanna Stiebert, "Divinely Sanctioned Violence against Women: Biblical Marriage and the Example of the *Sotah* of Numbers 5," *Bible and Critical Theory* 15, no. 2 (2019): 83–108.

81 See Exod 23:8; Deut 10:17; 16:19; and 27:25.

82 See Job 6:22; Isa 1:23; 5:23; and Amos 5:12.

83 See Amos 2:7; 5:11; and 8:4.

84 Classen, Howes, and Synnott, *Aroma*, 3–6.

85 Deut 23:12–14.

86 Isa 34:3 describes the smell of unburied corpses. See John 11:39, in which Martha warns Jesus that her brother, Lazarus, has been in his tomb for four days and there will be a stench when the tomb is opened.

87 Second Kgs 9:37; Ps 83:10; Jer 9:22. For the connection between smell and memory, see Steve van Toller and George Dodd, eds., *Perfumery: The Psychology and Biology of Fragrance* (London: Chapman & Hall, 1988), 123.

88 Exod 22:6. Note Samson's commission of arson as a form of revenge in Judg 15:4–5.

89 Lev 13–15.

90 Ackerman, *Natural History of the Senses*, 80–82. See a drunkard's lack of sensation in Prov 23:35.

91 While most of these laws are found in the Priestly and Holiness Codes, there are instances in the Deuteronomic Code regarding animals judged to be clean and unclean (Deut 14:3–21).

92 Exod 22:10–13.

93 Exod 22:14–15.

94 Exod 22:26–27; Deut 24:12–13.

95 Amos 2:8. See Jeremy M. Hutton, "Amos 1:3–2:8 and the International Economy of Iron Age II Israel," *HTR* 107, no. 1 (2014): 110–112.

96 Yavneh Yam inscription in Matthews and Benjamin, *OTP-4*, 394–395.

97 Matthews and Benjamin, 245–253. See F. W. Dobbs-Allsopp, "The Genre of the Meṣad Ḥashavyahu Ostracon," *BASOR* 295 (1994): 49–55.

98 Exod 21:16 is very brief, while Deut 24:7 expands the categories of the crime. See Louis Stulman, "Encroachment in Deuteronomy: An Analysis of the Social World of the D Code," *JBL* 109, no. 4 (1990): 626.

99 See Stulman, 616–620, for an outline of capital crimes. See also Myrto Theocharous, "Stealing Souls: Human Trafficking and Deuteronomy 24:7," in *For Our Good Always: Studies on the Message and Influence of Deuteronomy in Honor of Daniel I. Block*, ed. Jason S. DeRochie, Jason Gile, and Kenneth J. Turner (Winona Lake, IN: Eisenbrauns, 2013), 499–508.

100 See Yael Shemesh, "Rape Is Rape Is Rape: The Story of Dinah and Shechem (Genesis 34)," *ZAW* 119, no. 1 (2007): 2–21.

101 See Robert P. Carroll, "Removing an Ancient Landmark: Reading the Bible as Cultural Production," in *Borders, Boundaries and the Bible*, ed. Martin O'Kane (London: Sheffield Academic, 2002), 6–14.

102 Deut 19:14; 27:17; Prov 23:10. The Egyptian "Teachings of Amen-em-ope" contains similar statements, including a response by the gods to this injustice. See Matthews and Benjamin, *OTP-4*, 328.

103 Deut 27:18; Lev 19:14. See Baruch A. Levine, *JPS Torah Commentary: Leviticus* (Philadelphia: Jewish Publication Society, 1989), 128. Avalos, *Illness and Health Care*, 390–391, suggests that these provisions are "minimal" and actually reflect a society that prefers to "unburden overpopulated cities of the most burdensome social classes."

104 Exod 20:15; 21:15; Matthews and Benjamin, *OTP-4*, 118.

Notes   163

105 Exod 20:13; 21:12–14. See Haas, "Structure of Homicide," 76–77.
106 Jacob Milgrom, *JPS Torah Commentary: Numbers* (Philadelphia: Jewish Publication Society, 1990), 292, notes the chiastic structure of this passage framing intentional and unintentional actions.
107 Num 35:16–21 discusses intentional murder, and Num 35:22–23 lists two examples of unintentional acts that prove to be mortal.
108 Deut 19:4–5.
109 Pamela Barmash, "Blood Feud and State Control: Differing Legal Institutions for the Remedy of Homicide during the Second and First Millennia B.C.E.," *JNES* 63, no. 3 (2004): 185.
110 Exod 21:12–14; Num 35:6–15, 22–34; Deut 19:1–13. See the application in Josh 20:1–9. See also A. Graeme Auld, "Cities of Refuge in Israelite Tradition," *JSOT* 10, no. 4 (1978): 26–40.
111 See Exod 21:14; and Jeffrey Stackert, "Why Does Deuteronomy Legislate Cities of Refuge? Asylum in the Covenant Collection (Exodus 21:12–14) and Deuteronomy (19:1–13)," *JBL* 125, no. 1 (2006): 47.
112 Adonijah's gesture is in 1 Kgs 1:50–53. Joab's failed attempt at asylum is in 1 Kgs 2:28–35.
113 Deut 21:15–17. See Frederick E. Greenspahn, "Primogeniture in Ancient Israel," in *"Go to the Land I Will Show You": Studies in Honor of Dwight W. Young*, ed. Victor H. Matthews and Joseph Coleson (Winona Lake, IN: Eisenbrauns, 1996), 76.
114 Gen 48:13–20.
115 Gen 24:2–9.
116 Gen 47:29–31. Note that the dying Joseph asks his brothers to swear to return his body to Canaan, but there is no reference in this case to the use of the thigh as part of the oath taking (Gen 50:24–26).
117 Gen 31:41–42, 51–54. See Meir Malul, "More on *Paḥad Yiṣḥāq* (Genesis 31:42,53) and the Oath by the Thigh," *VT* 35, no. 2 (1985): 192–200.
118 Richard A. Freund, "Individual vs. Collective Responsibility: From the Ancient Near East and the Bible to the Greco-Roman World," *SJOT* 11, no. 2 (1997): 279–281.
119 Deut 22:8.
120 Exod 21:33–34.
121 Exod 21:28–36; Laws of Eshnunna 53–55 and CH 250–252 in Martha T. Roth, *Law Collections from Mesopotamia and Asia Minor* (Atlanta: Scholars Press, 1995), 67, 128.
122 See J. J. Finkelstein, *The Ox That Gored* (Philadelphia: American Philosophical Society, 1981), 20; and Meir Malul, *The Comparative Method in Ancient Near Eastern and Biblical Legal Studies* (Kevelaer, Germany: Butzon & Bercker, 1990), 151–152.
123 Martha T. Roth, "Errant Oxen or the Goring Ox Redux," in *Literature as Politics, Politics as Literature: Essays on the Ancient Near East in Honor of Peter Machinist*, ed. David S. Vanderhooft and Abraham Winitzer (Winona Lake, IN: Eisenbrauns, 2013), 400–401.
124 Exod 21:18–19.
125 Exod 21:22–25. Several other Near Eastern laws deal with this circumstance, but they are predicated on intentional rather than inadvertent harm to the

mother and fetus. See Sophie LaFont, "Ancient Near Eastern Laws: Continuity and Pluralism," in *Theory and Method in Biblical and Cuneiform Law: Revision, Interpolation and Development*, ed. Bernard M. Levinson (Sheffield: Sheffield Academic, 1994), 108–114.

126 Exod 21:20–21; 26–27. On the proper use of natural resources, see Deut 22:6–7.

127 Deut 25:11–12.

128 Matthews and Benjamin, *OTP-4*, 127.

129 See the review of various interpretations in Marc Cortez, "The Law on Violent Intervention: Deuteronomy 25:11–12 Revisited," *JSOT* 30, no. 4 (2006): 431–447.

130 Smith, "Producing Sense," 85–87.

131 Deut 23:24–25.

132 Deut 24:19–21; Lev 19:9–10.

133 Exod 22:31.

134 Exod 23:19b; 34:26b; Deut 14:21b. See J. Webb Mealy, "You Shall Not Boil a Kid in Its Mother's Milk (Exod. 23:19b; Exod. 34:26b; Deut. 14:21b): A Figure of Speech?," *BibInt* 20, nos. 1–2 (2012): 67–72, for the way in which the original meaning of this phrase may have transformed over time.

135 See the analysis in Alan Cooper, "Once Again Seething a Kid in Its Mother's Milk," *JSIJ* 10 (2012): 109–143.

136 On the social character of taste, see Ackerman, *Natural History of the Senses*, 128–130. See the various restricted items in Deut 14:3–21.

137 See Max D. Price, *Evolution of a Taboo: Pigs and People in the Ancient Near East* (New York: Oxford University Press, 2020), 128–130.

138 See Lidar Sapir-Hen, "Food, Pork Consumption, and Identity in Ancient Israel," *NEA* 82, no. 1 (2019): 52–59; and Marvin Harris, "The Abominable Pig," in *Community, Identity, and Ideology*, ed. Charles Carter (Winona Lake, IN: Eisenbrauns, 1996), 135–151.

Chapter 5: Religious Practice

1 See the discussion of rituals and ritual texts in Yitzhaq Feder, "Pentateuchal and Ancient Near Eastern Ritual," in Baden and Stackert, *Handbook of the Pentateuch*, 421–442.

2 Second Sam 22:9–16; Ps 18:8, 15. See Theron Young, "Psalm 18 and 2 Samuel 22: Two Versions of the Same Song," in *Seeking Out the Wisdom of the Ancients: Essays Offered to Honor Michael V. Fox on the Occasion of His Sixty-Fifth Birthday*, ed. Ronald L. Troxel, Kelvin G. Friebel, and Dennis R. Magary (Winona Lake, IN: Eisenbrauns, 2005), 53–69.

3 Exod 15:8. Matthews and Benjamin, *OTP-4*, 295, note that the messengers of the sea god Yamm "shout with tongues of fire." See comparisons with Ugaritic epic literature in Frank M. Cross, *Canaanite Myth and Hebrew Epic* (Cambridge, MA: Harvard University Press, 1973), 156–163.

4 See the description of the various manifestations and powers of the Canaanite god Baal in Karel van der Toorn, Bob Becking, and Pieter W. van der Horst, eds., *Dictionary of Deities and Demons in the Bible*, 2nd ed. (Leiden: Brill, 1999), 132–135.

5 Meredith B. McGuire, "Individual Sensory Experiences, Socialized Senses, and Everyday Lived Religion in Practice," *Social Compass* 63 (2016): 154.

6 Hector Avalos, "Introducing Sensory Criticism in Biblical Studies: Audiocentricity and Visiocentricity," in *This Abled Body: Rethinking Disabilities in Biblical Studies*, ed. Hector Avalos, Sarah Melcher, and Jeremy Schipper, Semeia Studies 55 (Atlanta: SBL, 2007), 51, uses Deut 4:12–20 to argue for audiocentrality in Deuteronomistic History. In his opinion, hearing is the privileged sense needed to perceive YHWH. Note that Elijah ultimately perceives YHWH in the "sheer silence" at Mount Horeb after being bombarded with a variety of sounds in 1 Kgs 19:11–12. Note also that when Moses enters the tent of meeting, he hears the voice of YHWH but sees no form of the deity (Num 7:89).

7 See Deut 27:15 on "casting" an idol.

8 Isa 40:19; 44:17; 45:20; 66:3; Hab 2:18.

9 Pss 31:6; 96:5; 97:7.

10 Pss 115:4–7; 135:15–17.

11 Gen 12:6–8; 13:18; 26:23–25.

12 First Sam 9:13–14; 1 Kgs 13:32; 2 Kgs 17:9. See Lisbeth S. Fried, "The High Places (*Bāmôt*) and the Reforms of Hezekiah and Josiah: An Archaeological Investigation," *JAOS* 122, no. 3 (2002): 439–441.

13 See Doron Ben-Ami, "Mysterious Standing Stones: What Do These Ubiquitous Things Mean?," *BAR* 32, no. 2 (2006): 38–45. Elizabeth Bloch-Smith, "Massebot Standing for Yhwh: The Fall of a Yhwistic Cult Symbol," in *Worship, Women, and War: Essays in Honor of Susan Niditch*, ed. John J. Collins, T. M. Lemos, and Saul M. Olyan (Providence: Brown University Press, 2015), 112, suggests that the standing stones at Arad may have been associated with either Baal or YHWH. For Asherah poles and other cult images, see 1 Kgs 15:13 and 2 Kgs 21:5–7.

14 For the description of Solomon's temple, see 1 Kgs 6–7. See the analysis of this text in Victor A. Hurowitz, "YHWH's Exalted House—Aspects of the Design and Symbolism of Solomon's Temple," in *Temple and Worship in Biblical Israel*, ed. John Day (New York: T&T Clark, 2005), 63–110. For the other Iron Age temples, see Smith, *Music in Religious Cults*, 10–12.

15 Deut 12:5–12; 1 Kgs 5:5. Although writing during the Roman period, Josephus paints a picture of the temple as the nexus of concentric circles of holiness and marvels at the craftsmanship and sumptuous decoration of this sacred space. See Annette Weissenrieder, "A Roadmap to Heaven: High-Priestly Vestments and the Jerusalem Temple in Flavius Josephus," in *Beyond Priesthood: Religious Entrepreneurs and Innovators in the Roman Empire*, ed. Richard Gordon, Georgia Petridou, and Jörg Rüpke (Berlin: Walter de Gruyter, 2017), 162–166.

16 See the architectural and political influence of Herod's temple-building methods in the construction of Podium 1 at the pre-Roman temple at Baalbek in Andreas J. M. Kropp and Daniel Lohmann, "'Master, Look at the Size of Those Stones! Look at the Size of Those Buildings!': Analogies in Construction Techniques between the Temples at Heliopolis (Baalbek) and Jerusalem," *Levant* 43 (2011): 38–50.

17 See André Lemaire, "The Evolution of the 8th Century B.C.E. Jerusalem Temple," in *The Fire Signals of Lachish: Studies in the Archaeology and History of Israel*

in the Late Bronze Age, Iron Age, and Persian Period in Honor of David Ussishkin, ed. Israel Finkelstein and Nadav Na'aman (Winona Lake, IN: Eisenbrauns, 2011), 195–202.

18 Jer 7; 26. See Steed V. Davidson, "'Every Green Tree and the Streets of Jerusalem': Counter Constructions of Gendered Sacred Space in the Book of Jeremiah," in *Constructions of Space IV: Further Developments in Examining Ancient Israel's Social Space*, ed. Mark K. George (New York: Bloomsbury, 2013), 118–119.

19 For examples of theophanies, see Gen 28:10–22; Exod 3:2–5; Judg 13:11–23; and Matt 17:1–4.

20 Second Sam 24:15–25; 1 Chr 21:18–22:1. See Yairah Amit, "Araunah's Threshing-Floor: A Lesson in Shaping Historical Memory," in *Performing Memory in Biblical Narrative and Beyond*, ed. Athalya Brenner and Frank H. Polak (Sheffield: Sheffield Phoenix, 2009), 13–23.

21 See Deut 12:5, 13–14; and Frederick E. Greenspahn, "Deuteronomy and Centralization," *VT* 64, no. 2 (2014): 227–235.

22 First Sam 1:10–11; 2:1–10.

23 Josh 22:10–34. See Elie Assis, "'For It Shall Be a Witness between Us': A Literary Reading of Josh 22," *SJOT* 18, no. 2 (2004): 208–231, for the contention that the negotiations result in a narrative that strengthens the unity of the tribes and their collective identity as Israel.

24 There is interesting reasoning in the judgment of the Transjordanian altar on the east bank of the Jordan River that reduces it from a sacrificial altar to "a witness" of YHWH's actions (Josh 22:10–34). See John S. Kloppenborg, "Joshua 22: The Priestly Editing of an Ancient Tradition," *Bib* 62, no. 3 (1981): 347–371.

25 Exod 27:21; 30:8; Lev 24:3–4; 2 Chr 13:11.

26 For these ranks of priests and temple servants, see 1 Chr 9:2; Ezra 7:24; and Ps 84:10.

27 See Exod 28:33–35 and 39:1–31, which detail the colorful embroidery that depicts pomegranates in violet, purple, and scarlet and the attachment of golden bells to the garment's hem that sounded as he walked. See also Cornelius Houtman, "On the Pomegranates and the Golden Bells of the High Priest's Mantle," *VT* 40, no. 2 (1990): 223–229.

28 Jos 6:1–21.

29 See Erich Zenger and Klaus Baltzer, *Psalms 2: A Commentary on Psalms 51–100* (Minneapolis: Fortress, 2005), 167–168. For instances in which divine images were carried in procession from place to place, see Victor H. Matthews, "Government Involvement in the Religion of the Mari Kingdom," *RA* 72, no. 2 (1978): 151–156; and Kenton L. Sparks, "*Enuma Elish* and Priestly Mimesis: Elite Emulation in Nascent Judaism," *JBL* 126, no. 4 (2007): 625–648.

30 See the two versions of this story in 2 Sam 6:6–7 and 1 Chr 13:9–10. A postexilic explanation for the difference between the versions is discussed in Gerrie Snyman, "Who Is Responsible for Uzzah's Death? Rhetoric in 1 Chronicles 13," in *Rhetoric, Scripture and Theology: Essays from the 1994 Pretoria Conference*, ed. Stanley E. Porter and Thomas H. Olbricht (Sheffield: Sheffield Academic, 1996), 203–217.

31 1 Kgs 1:32–40; 8:1–11; 2 Chr 5:2–14; possibly Ps 132:5–8. See Corrine L. Patton, "Psalm 132: A Methodological Inquiry," *CBQ* 57, no. 4 (1995): 643–654.

32 Zech 9:9; Mark 11:1–11; David R. Catchpole, "The 'Triumphal' Entry," in *Jesus and the Politics of His Day*, ed. Ernst Bammel and C. F. D. Moule (New York: Cambridge University Press, 1984), 319; Brent Kinman, *Jesus' Entry into Jerusalem: In the Context of Lukan Theology and the Politics of His Day* (Leiden: Brill, 1995), 54–56.

33 Pss 149:3; 150:3–5. See David P. Wright, "Music and Dance in 2 Samuel 6," *JBL* 121, no. 2 (2002): 201–225.

34 Second Sam 6:14–15; SuJung Shin, "A 'Vital Materiality' of the Ark in Its Relativity to the Body of David in 2 Sam 6," *Bible and Critical Theory* 16, no. 2 (2020): 11, 19–21.

35 Saul's daughter Michal attempts to shame David, but he already has obtained the support of the nation as Saul's successor in 2 Sam 6:16, 20–23.

36 See Karel van der Toorn and Cornelius Houtman, "David and the Ark," *JBL* 113, no. 2 (1994): 216, for the argument that the presence of the ark is tantamount to the presence of YHWH (see Josh 3:10).

37 Second Sam 6:5 lists lyres, harps, tambourines, castanets, and cymbals.

38 See Josh 6:4–5; 1 Sam 4:6–7; and Ps 47:6. Wright, "Music and Dance," 209–210, posits that other instruments were also part of this scene.

39 Second Sam 6:17–19.

40 See the recital in Ps 132 and the parallel with the Mesopotamian *akītu* festival, which ties Marduk to Babylon as a patron deity. Note the discussion of the traditions about the ark in Daniel E. Fleming, "David and the Ark: A Jerusalem Festival Reflected in Royal Narrative," in Vanderhooft and Winitzer, *Literature as Politics*, 75–95.

41 Pss 30:11 (12); 42:4; 118:27. See Frank-Lothar Hossfeld and Erich Zenger, *A Commentary on Psalms 101–150* (Minneapolis: Fortress, 2011), 243.

42 For a discussion of the phenomenological aspects of rituals and the ways in which they avoid becoming routines without real meaning, see Massimo Leone, "Transcendence and Transgression in Religious Processions," *Signs and Society* 2, no. 2 (2014): 314–349.

43 Nili S. Fox, "Biblical Sanctification of Dress: Tassels on Garments," in *Built by Wisdom, Established by Understanding: Essays on Biblical and Near Eastern Literature in Honor of Adele Berlin*, ed. Maxime L. Grossman (Bethesda: University Press of Maryland, 2013), 89.

44 For this very elaborate ceremony, see Lev 8.

45 For descriptions of priestly vestments, see Exod 28 and 39:1–31. For rituals requiring priestly vestments, see Lev 6:8–11, and for the commemoration of the Day of Atonement, see Lev 16.

46 Lev 6:10–11; Ezek 44:18; Jacob Milgrom, *Leviticus 1–16* (New York: Doubleday, 1991), 384.

47 For the special duties of the Levites and their exemption from the census required of other tribes, see Num 1:47–53.

48 Lev 21. See John E. Hartley, *Leviticus* (Dallas: Thomas Nelson, 1992), 351.

49 Ezek 4:1–8. For a discussion of Ezekiel's use of "sign-acts," see Block, *Ezekiel*, 170–180.

50 Zech 3. See James C. VanderKam, "Joshua the High Priest and the Interpretation of Zechariah 3," *CBQ* 53, no. 4 (1991): 553–570.

51 Adele Berlin, "Hannah and Her Prayers," *Scriptura* 87 (2004): 229.

52 Fidler, "Wife's Vow," 374–376.

53 First Sam 1:9–18; Lev 27:1–6. For the requirements of a Nazirite, see Num 6:1–21. See also Levine, *Leviticus*, 193.

54 First Sam 2:1–10; Pss 22; 116. See J. Gerald Janzen, "Prayer and/as Self-Address: The Case of Hannah," in *A God So Near: Essays on Old Testament Theology in Honor of Patrick D. Miller*, ed. Brent A. Strawn and Nancy R. Bowen (Winona Lake, IN: Eisenbrauns, 2003), 113–127.

55 See Ps 102; and Erhard Gerstenberger, "Non-temple Psalms: The Cultic Setting Revisited," in *The Oxford Handbook of the Psalms*, ed. William P. Brown (New York: Oxford University Press, 2014), 340–342.

56 See William H. Bellinger Jr., *Psalms as a Grammar for Faith: Prayer and Praise* (Waco, TX: Baylor University Press, 2019), 57–67.

57 See Pss 8; 28:8; 90:11–12; 104; and 150.

58 See Ps 148:1–4, 7–12; and Erhard Gerstenberger, "The Power of Praise in the Psalter: Human-Divine Synergies in the Ancient Near East and the Hebrew Scriptures," in *Between Israelite Religion and Old Testament Theology: Essays on Archaeology, History, and Hermeneutics*, ed. Robert D. Miller (Leuven, Belgium: Peeters, 2016), 31–48.

59 Deut 6:4–9; echoed in 11:18–20 and Prov 6:21.

60 See later developments in Franz Landsberger, "The Origin of the Decorated Mezuzah," *HUCA* 31 (1960): 149–166; and Josiah Derby, "'. . . Upon the Doorposts . . . ,'" *JBQ* 27, no. 1 (1999): 40–44.

61 For a discussion of the Shema and its place within the development of Scripture, see Nathan MacDonald, "The Date of the Shema (Deuteronomy 6:4–5)," *JBL* 136, no. 4 (2017): 765–782.

62 Michael Avioz, "A Rhetorical Analysis of Jeremiah 7:1–15," *TynBul* 57, no. 2 (2006): 182–183, ascribes these words to the false prophets and Jeremiah's efforts to dispel the people's belief in them. William L. Holladay, *A Commentary on the Book of the Prophet Jeremiah Chapters 1–25* (Philadelphia: Fortress, 1986), 242, is closer to the mark, tying them to the triple utterance rhetorical pattern found in Isa 6:3; Jer 22:29; and Ezek 21:32.

63 Jer 7:4, 8–10. See Thomas Staubli, *Werbung für die Götter: Heilsbringer aus 4000 Jahren* (Fribourg: Universitätsverlag, 2003), 49; and Christopher G. Frechette, *Mesopotamian Ritual-Prayers of "Hand-Lifting" (Akkadian Šuillas): An Investigation of Function in Light of the Idiomatic Meaning of the Rubric* (Münster: Ugarit-Verlag, 2012), 229–230.

64 See Lucia M. Tissi, "Sanctuary Doors, Vestibules, and *Adyta* in the Works of Neoplatonic Philosophers," in *Sacred Thresholds: The Door to the Sanctuary in Late Antiquity*, ed. Emilie M. van Opstall (Leiden: Brill, 2018), 142–147.

65 First Sam 5:5; Zeph 1:9.

66 Num 7:89; Deut 4:10–12.

67 First Sam 7:10; 2 Sam 22:14; Job 9:7; 37:2–5; Pss 18:13; 29:3–9; Jer 25:30–31.

68 See Job 28:23–27; and Alex Luc, "Storm and the Message of Job," *JSOT* 87, no. 25 (2000): 116–122.

69 Pss 27:6; 33:2; 92:3; 147:7; 149:3. New Christian worshippers are exhorted to sing hymns and psalms among themselves to praise God and commune

together as a counterpoint to the drunkenness at Greek banquets (Eph 5:19; Col 3:16). See Craig A. Evans, "Ephesians 5:18–19 and Religious Intoxication in the World of Paul," in *Paul's World*, ed. Stanley E. Porter (Leiden: Brill, 2008), 181–200.

70 See the condemnation of their empty performances in Amos 5:23 and 8:10.

71 First Chr 25:1–8.

72 Pss 2 and 92. See the analysis of the antiphonal character of Ps 92 in Nissim Amzallag, "Foreign Yahwistic Singers in the Jerusalem Temple? Evidence from Psalm 92," *SJOT* 31, no. 2 (2017): 218–227.

73 See 1 Chr 16:4–6 and especially Pss 78–89. See also Michael D. Goulder, "Asaph's History of Israel (Elohist Press, Bethel, 725 BCE)," *JSOT* 65, no. 20 (1995): 71–81.

74 Pss 81:1–3 (4); 150:3–5; Hossfeld and Zenger, *Psalms 101–150*, 659.

75 Pss 120–134. See Loren Crow, *The Songs of Ascents (Psalms 120–134)* (Atlanta: Scholars Press, 1996), 182–187; and Susan Gillingham, "The Zion Tradition and the Editing of the Hebrew Psalter," in Day, *Temple and Worship*, 310–312.

76 J. H. Eaton, "Music's Place in Worship," in Barton, Carroll, and Fokkelman, *Prophets, Worship and Theodicy*, 86–87.

77 Sarit Paz, *Drums, Women, and Goddesses: Drumming and Gender in Iron Age Israel* (Fribourg: Vandenhoeck & Ruprecht, 2007); see figures 2.6, 3.5, and 6.1 on pages 51, 70, and 88, respectively.

78 Dan 3:1–7. See Terence C. Mitchell, "The Music of the Old Testament Reconsidered," *PEQ* 124 (1992): 124–143; and Eaton, "Music's Place," 87–93, for a discussion of instrument types and their usages.

79 See Hossfeld and Zenger, *Psalms 101–150*, 654–664.

80 For olfactory contrasts, see the rotting fish along the Nile in Exod 7:18, the decaying corpses in Isa 34:3, the fragrance of a blossoming grapevine in Hos 14:6, and the perfumed clothing of the lover in Song 4:11. See the discussion of the sense of smell in Houtman, "Holy Incense," 458–462.

81 Kirsten Nielsen, *Incense in Ancient Israel* (Leiden: Brill, 1986), 101.

82 See Lev 7:31–35; 1 Sam 2:12–16; Classen, *Worlds of Sense*, 79; and MacDonald, *Diet in Biblical Times*, 78–79.

83 See, for example, Exod 30:1; Lev 16:12–13; Num 7:14–86; Deut 33:10; and 1 Sam 2:28. For the use of incense as part of a burial process, see 2 Chr 16:14.

84 See Noah's sacrifice following the flood in Gen 8:20–21. See also the standardized use of the phrase "pleasing odor" in Lev 1:9; 2:2, 9, 12; 6:15; Num 15:3; and 28:2, among many examples.

85 Lev 26:31. Ritchie, "Nose Knows," 60, notes that "sweet smells" that are offered by a negligent or disobedient priest provoke rather than placate the Lord. On this, see Isa 65:3 and Amos 5:21.

86 Exod 30:34–38.

87 See Ezekiel's vision of seventy elders who are inappropriately taking on the priestly role with their incense lamps in Ezek 8:11.

88 See Carol L. Meyers, "Fumes, Flames, or Fluids: Reframing the Cup-and-Bowl Question," in *Boundaries of the Ancient Near Eastern World: A Tribute to Cyrus H. Gordon*, ed. Meir Lubetski, Claire Gottlieb, and Sharon Keller (Sheffield: Sheffield Academic, 1998), 30–39.

89   First Kgs 18:4. See Fried, "High Places," 437–465. Fried concludes that the destruction of cultic sites in Judah by 701 BCE was due to the invasions by Pharaoh Sheshonq I and the Assyrian kings Tiglath-pileser III, Shalmaneser V, Sargon II, and Sennacherib. Fried, 461.

90   Eran Arie, Baruch Rosen, and Dvory Namdar, "Cannabis and Frankincense at the Judahite Shrine of Arad," *TA* 47, no. 1 (2020): 5–28.

91   Ps 38:5; Rev 16:2.

92   Job 19:17. Contrast the lover's sweet-smelling breath that is like apples in Song 7:8.

93   Houtman, "Holy Incense," 460.

94   Lev 14:34–47. Presumably, the smell of mold is pervasive.

95   See Lev 13:30–37 and 21:20 for the examination of an itching disease and a blemish in the eye. Deut 28:27 describes a variety of physical afflictions, including boils, ulcers, and an incurable itch.

96   First Kgs 21:29; Isa 58:5. For a fuller description, see H. A. Brongers, "Fasting in Israel in Biblical and Post-biblical Times," in *Instruction and Interpretation: Studies in Hebrew Language, Palestinian Archaeology and Biblical Exegesis*, ed. Hendrik A. Brongers, OTS 20 (Leiden: Brill, 1977), 1–21.

97   See Ezra 9:5; Pss 35:13; 69:10; and Joel 2:12. See also Joseph B. Tamney, "Fasting and Dieting: A Research Note," *RRelRes* 27, no. 3 (1986): 255–256.

98   See Isa 58:3–5 and Matt 6:16.

99   See Deut 32:40 and Ps 63:4. The gesture appears in Egyptian art with devotees honoring the gods with uplifted arms, and it also is in the Akkadian Šuilla rubric, which requires the hand-lifting gesture as part of the sacred rite. See Staubli, *Werbung für die Götter*, 49; and Frechette, *Mesopotamian Ritual-Prayers*, 11–15.

100 Isa 1:15; 59:2; Mic 3:4.

101 See Pss 28:2; 134:2; and Hossfeld and Zenger, *Psalms 101–150*, 488–489. Note the admonition against lifting one's eyes to idols in Ezek 18:6, 15; and 33:25.

102 Ps 141:2. See Thomas Booij, "Psalm 141: A Prayer for Discipline and Protection," *Bib* 86, no. 1 (2005): 97–106.

103 Erhard Gerstenberger, *Psalms, Part 2, and Lamentations* (Grand Rapids, MI: Eerdmans, 2001), 414.

104 Neh 8:6. See Michael W. Duggan, *The Covenant Renewal in Ezra–Nehemiah (Neh 7:72B–10:40): An Exegetical, Literary and Theological Study* (Atlanta: SBL, 2001), 88–89.

105 See Lev 7:30; and Jacob Milgrom, "The Alleged Wave-Offering in Israel and in the Ancient Near East," *IEJ* 22, no. 1 (1972): 33–38.

106 See Aaron's gesture in Lev 9:22.

107 Second Kgs 5:9–14.

108 See 2 Kgs 2:1–14; and Isabel Cranz, "Naaman's Healing and Gehazi's Affliction: The Magical Background of 2 Kgs 5," *VT* 68, no. 4 (2018): 548–549.

109 Judg 11:34; 1 Sam 18:6–7; 2 Sam 6:6, 14–15; Eccl 3:4; Bruce Rosenstock, "David's Play: Fertility Rituals and the Glory of God in 2 Samuel 6," *JSOT* 31, no. 1 (2006): 63–80.

110 Ps 150:3–5.

111 Jack Lennon, "Contaminating Touch in the Roman World," in Purves, *Touch and the Ancient Senses*, 128–129, ties the potential of contamination from blood or corpses to specific professions in ancient Rome, including executioners and undertakers.

112 See the legal phrase in Lev 11:24–28 and Num 5:2. A priestly judgment on this principle is found in Hag 2:13.

113 See Lam 4:14 and Hag 2:12–13 versus Ezek 44:19. See the discussion in Lena-Sofia Tiemeyer, "The Question of Indirect Touch: Lam 4,14; Ezek 44,19 and Hag 2,12–13," *Bib* 87, no. 1 (2006): 64–74.

114 Matt 9:20–22; Mark 5:24–34; Luke 8:43–48.

115 Relevant legislation regarding a woman who has a discharge of blood distinct from her menstrual cycle, which deems her as well as anything she has touched unclean, is found in Lev 15:25–30. Ordinarily, someone who has been contaminated then must wash themselves and remain impure until the evening.

116 See Mark 3:10. See also Joel Marcus, *Mark 1–8: A New Translation with Introduction and Commentary* (New York: Doubleday, 1999), 359.

117 See Susan Haber, "A Woman's Touch: Feminist Encounters with the Hemorrhaging Woman in Mark 5.24–34," *JSNT* 26, no. 2 (2003): 183–184.

118 Lev 11:43–45.

119 Jacob Milgrom, "The Rationale for Biblical Impurity," *JANES* 22 (1993): 109–110.

120 See Jonathan D. Lawrence, *Washing in Water: Trajectories of Ritual Bathing in the Hebrew Bible and Second Temple Literature* (Atlanta: SBL, 2006), 158–183, for a summary of excavated ritual baths (*miqva'ot*), including details about their styles and volume.

121 Eilat Mazar and Benjamin Mazar, *Excavations in the South of the Temple Mount: The Ophel of Biblical Jerusalem* (Jerusalem: Hebrew University Press, 1989); Stephen O. Ricks, "*Miqvaot*: Ritual Immersion Baths in Second Temple (Intertestamental) Jewish History," in *Masada and the World of the New Testament*, ed. John F. Hall and John W. Welch (Provo, UT: Brigham Young University Press, 1997), 277–286.

122 See Lev 12–15; and Yonatan Adler, "The Ritual Baths near the Temple Mount and Extra-Purification before Entering the Temple Courts: A Reply to Eyal Regev," *IEJ* 56, no. 2 (2006): 211.

123 Num 9:6–12; Johnson, *Sovereign Authority*, 165–170.

124 See Exod 12:1–28 and subsequent celebrations in Num 9:1–5; Josh 5:10; 2 Kgs 23:21; 2 Chr 7:8–9; and Ezra 6:19–22. See also Roland Barthes, "Toward a Psychosociology of Contemporary Food Consumption," in *Food and Culture: A Reader*, ed. C. Counihan and P. van Esterik (New York: Routledge, 2008), 29–30.

125 See Joel Marcus, "Passover and Last Supper Revisited," *NTS* 59, no. 3 (2013): 303–324.

126 Ezek 45:18–25; Tova Ganzel, "First-Month Rituals in Ezekiel's Temple Vision: A Pentateuchal and Babylonian Comparison," *CBQ* 83, no. 3 (2021): 402.

127 Gregory J. Polan, "The Passover: A Memorial Meal," *TBT* 57 (2019): 353–358.

128 Isa 25:6–8. See Zech 14:16–17 for a celebration of YHWH's enthronement as king. See also Blenkinsopp, *Isaiah 1–39*, 358–359.

129 See the discussion of how the senses work together to create a total sensory impression in Lee, "Gospel of John," 115–127.

130 See Lev 2:1–3 for the standard grain offering.

131 See the tie between the written words of the curse and the enactment of the ritual in Briggs, "Reading the *Sotah* Text," 298.

132 Num 5:11–28; Milgrom, *Numbers*, 38–42.

133 Stiebert, "Divinely Sanctioned Violence," 95.

134 As Jacqueline Winspear, *An Incomplete Revenge* (New York: Henry Holt, 2008), 255–256, notes, "It is in the senses that memories are summoned, so that a sound, a scent, or the way the wind blows brings a reminder of what happened and when."

Conclusion

1 See Ruth 3:2; 2 Kgs 13:7; and Job 5:26.

2 See the raid on Ziklag in 1 Sam 30:1–2.

3 This is illustrated by Abraham's reaction to the unexpected travelers who approach his tent "in the heat of the day" in Gen 18:1–5.

4 See Matt 11:16.

5 Jer 18:2–4.

6 See the food brought into Jerusalem in Neh 13:15–16. See also merchants like Abram's nephew Lot sitting in the city gate in Gen 19:1.

7 See the pitiful groaning and cries of the people in a captured city in Job 24:12.

8 See Cornelius, "Image of Assyria," 55–74.

9 See 1 Sam 17:2 and Job 39:19–25.

10 See the ritual associated with the Sotah in Num 5:11–31. See also the sacrifice made by the elders of a town to restore the purity of the land after a homicide in Deut 21:1–9.

Appendix

1 Exod 19:9; Deut 5:4–5. See Patrick D. Miller, *The Ten Commandments* (Louisville, KY: Westminster John Knox, 2009), 3.

2 William S. Morrow, *Introduction to Biblical Law* (Grand Rapids, MI: Eerdmans, 2017), 73–74.

3 Morrow, 203–205; Raymond Westbrook and Bruce Wells, *Everyday Law in Biblical Israel: An Introduction* (Louisville, KY: Westminster John Knox, 2009), 12.

4 See Dale Patrick, *Old Testament Law* (Atlanta: John Knox, 1985), 145–188; and Jakob Wöhrle, "The Priestly Writing(s): Scope and Nature," in *The Oxford Handbook of the Pentateuch*, ed. Joel S. Baden and Jeffrey Stackert (New York: Oxford University Press, 2021), 262–266.

Selected Bibliography

Ackerman, Diane. *A Natural History of the Senses*. New York: Vintage, 2011.

Adams, Colin E. P. "Supplying the Roman Army: 'Q. Petr.' 245." *ZPE* 109 (1995): 119–124.

Adler, Yonatan. "The Ritual Baths near the Temple Mount and Extra-Purification before Entering the Temple Courts: A Reply to Eyal Regev." *IEJ* 56, no. 2 (2006): 209–215.

Amato, Joseph. "Thoughts on a Cultural History of Touch." *Fides et Historia* 46, no. 1 (2014): 76–81.

Amit, Yairah. "Araunah's Threshing-Floor: A Lesson in Shaping Historical Memory." In Brenner and Polak, *Performing Memory*, 13–23.

Amzallag, Nissim. "Foreign Yahwistic Singers in the Jerusalem Temple? Evidence from Psalm 92." *SJOT* 31, no. 2 (2017): 213–235.

Anderson, Cheryl B. *Women, Ideology, and Violence: Critical Theory and the Construction of Gender in the Book of the Covenant and the Deuteronomic Law.* London: T&T Clark, 2004.

Anderson, G. A. *A Time to Mourn, a Time to Dance: The Expression of Grief and Joy in Israelite Religion.* University Park: Pennsylvania State University Press, 1991.

Arie, Eran, Baruch Rosen, and Dvory Namdar. "Cannabis and Frankincense at the Judahite Shrine of Arad." *TA* 47, no. 1 (2020): 5–28.

Assis, Elie. "'For It Shall Be a Witness between Us': A Literary Reading of Josh 22." *SJOT* 18, no. 2 (2004): 208–231.

Auld, A. Graeme. "Cities of Refuge in Israelite Tradition." *JSOT* 10, no. 4 (1978): 26–40.

Avalos, Hector. *Illness and Health Care in the Ancient Near East: The Role of Greece, Mesopotamia, and Israel.* Atlanta: Scholars Press, 1995.

———. "Introducing Sensory Criticism in Biblical Studies: Audiocentricity and Visiocentricity." In *This Abled Body: Rethinking Disabilities in Biblical Studies*, edited by Hector Avalos, Sarah Melcher, and Jeremy Schipper, 47–60. Semeia Studies 55. Atlanta: SBL, 2007.

Avigad, Nahman. "The Contribution of Hebrew Seals to an Understanding of Israelite Religion and Society." In *Ancient Israelite Religion: Essays in Honor of Frank Moore Cross*, edited by Patrick D. Miller, Paul D. Hanson, and S. Dean McBride, 195–208. Philadelphia: Fortress, 1987.

———. "Two Phoenician Votive Seals." *IEJ* 16, no. 4 (1966): 243–251.

Avioz, Michael. "A Rhetorical Analysis of Jeremiah 7:1–15." *TynBul* 57, no. 2 (2006): 173–189.

———. "Why Did Joseph Kiss His Father (Genesis 50, 1)? A New Proposal." *SJOT* 29, no. 2 (2015): 3–24.

Avrahami, Yael. "Foul Grapes: Figurative Smells and the Message of the Song of the Vineyard (Isa 5:1–7)." *VT* 67, no. 3 (2017): 341–356.

———. *The Senses of Scripture: Sensory Perception in the Hebrew Bible.* New York: T&T Clark, 2012.

———. "The Study of Sensory Perception in the Hebrew Bible: Notes on Method." *HBAI* 5, no. 1 (2016): 3–22.

Bacci, Francesca, and David Melcher, eds. *Art and the Senses.* New York: Oxford University Press, 2011.

Baden, Joel S., and Jeffrey Stackert, eds. *The Oxford Handbook of the Pentateuch.* New York: Oxford University Press, 2021.

Bailey, Kenneth E., and William L. Holladay. "Young Camel and Wild Ass in Jer 2:23–25." *VT* 18, no. 2 (1968): 256–260.

Bang, Seung Ho, and Oded Borowski. "Local Production of a Small Rectangular Limestone Incense Altar at Tell Halif, Israel: Iconographic Considerations." *BASOR* 377 (2017): 49–67.

Barmash, Pamela. "Blood Feud and State Control: Differing Legal Institutions for the Remedy of Homicide during the Second and First Millennia B.C.E." *JNES* 63, no. 3 (2004): 183–199.

Barré, Michael. "Yahweh Gears Up for Battle: Habakkuk 3,9a." *Bib* 87, no. 1 (2006): 75–84.

Barthes, Roland. "Toward a Psychosociology of Contemporary Food Consumption." In *Food and Culture: A Reader*, edited by C. Counihan and P. van Esterik, 21–27. New York: Routledge, 2008.

Barton, John, Robert P. Carroll, and J. P. Fokkelman, eds. *Prophets, Worship and Theodicy: Studies in Prophetism, Biblical Theology, and Structural and Rhetorical Analysis, and on the Place of Music in Worship.* OTS 23. Leiden: Brill, 1984.

Bartor, Assnat. "The Representation of Speech in the Casuistic Laws of the Pentateuch: The Phenomenon of Combined Discourse." *JBL* 126, no. 2 (2007): 231–249.

Batten, Alicia J. "Clothing and Adornment." *BTB* 40, no. 3 (2010): 148–159.

Bechar, Shlomit. "Take a Stone and Set It Up as a Maṣṣēbā: The Tradition of Standing Stones at Hazor." *ZDPV* 134, no. 1 (2018): 28–45.

Beck, B. E. F. "The Metaphor as Mediator between Semantic and Analogic Modes of Thought." *Current Anthropology* 19, no. 1 (1978): 83–97.

Beck, John A. "David and Goliath, a Story of Place: The Narrative-Geographical Shaping of 1 Samuel 17." *WTJ* 68, no. 2 (2006): 321–330.

Becking, Bob. "Sour Fruit and Blunt Teeth: The Metaphorical Meaning of the Masal in Jeremiah 31,29." *SJOT* 17, no. 1 (2003): 7–21.

———. "'Touch for Health . . .': Magic in II Reg 4,31–37 with a Remark on the History of Yahwism." *ZAW* 108, no. 1 (1996): 34–54.

Beentjes, Pancratius C. "'Sweet Is His Memory, like Honey to the Palate': King Josiah in Ben Sira 49:1–4." *BZ* 34, no. 2 (1990): 262–266.

Bellinger, William H., Jr. *Psalms as a Grammar for Faith: Prayer and Praise.* Waco, TX: Baylor University Press, 2019.

Ben-Ami, Doron. "Mysterious Standing Stones: What Do These Ubiquitous Things Mean?" *BAR* 32, no. 2 (2006): 38–45.

Benjamin, Don C. *The Old Testament Story: An Introduction.* Minneapolis: Fortress, 2004.

———. *The Social World of Deuteronomy: A New Feminist Commentary.* Eugene, OR: Cascade, 2015.

———. *Stones and Stories: An Introduction to Archaeology and the Bible.* Minneapolis: Fortress, 2010.

Ben-Joseph, Jacob. "The Climate in Eretz Israel during Biblical Times." *HS* 26, no. 2 (1985): 225–239.

Ben-Tor, Amnon. *Hazor: Canaanite Metropolis, Israelite City.* Jerusalem: Israel Exploration Society, 2016.

Ben Zvi, Ehud. "Who Wrote the Speech of Rabshakeh and When?" *JBL* 109, no. 1 (1990): 79–92.

Berlin, Adele. "Hannah and Her Prayers." *Scriptura* 87 (2004): 227–232.

Berlinerblau, Jacques. "The Israelite Vow: Distress or Daily Life?" *Bib* 72, no. 4 (1991): 549–555.

———. *The Vow and the Popular Religious Groups of Ancient Israel: A Philological and Sociological Inquiry.* Sheffield: Sheffield Academic, 1996.

Betts, Eleanor. *Senses of the Empire: Multisensory Approaches to Roman Culture.* London: Routledge, 2017.

Bierling, Neal. *Giving Goliath His Due: New Archaeological Light on the Philistines.* Grand Rapids, MI: Baker Academic, 1992.

Biran, Avraham. *Biblical Dan.* Jerusalem: Israel Exploration Society, 1994.

Bleibtreu, Erika. "Grisly Assyrian Record of Torture and Death." *BAR* 17, no. 1 (1991): 53–61, 75.

Blenkinsopp, Joseph. "Deuteronomy and the Politics of Post-mortem Existence." *VT* 45, no. 1 (1995): 1–16.

———. *Isaiah 1–39.* New York: Doubleday, 2000.

Bloch-Smith, Elizabeth. "Massebot Standing for Yhwh: The Fall of a Yhwistic Cult Symbol." In *Worship, Women, and War: Essays in Honor of Susan Niditch*, edited by John J. Collins, T. M. Lemos, and Saul M. Olyan, 99–115. Providence: Brown University Press, 2015.

Block, Daniel I. *The Book of Ezekiel, Chapters 1–24.* Grand Rapids, MI: Eerdmans, 1997.

Bodner, Keith. "The Locutions of 1 Kings 22:28: A New Proposal." *JBL* 122, no. 3 (2003): 533–543.

Boer, Wietse de, and Christine Göttler, eds. *Religion and the Senses in Early Modern Europe.* Leiden: Brill, 2013.

Booij, Thomas. "Psalm 141: A Prayer for Discipline and Protection." *Bib* 86, no. 1 (2005): 97–106.

Bordreuil, Pierre. "On the Authenticity of Iron Age Northwest Semitic Inscribed Seals." In *"An Eye for Form": Epigraphic Essays in Honor of Frank Moore Cross,* edited by Jo Ann Hackett and Walter E. Aufrecht, 127–140. Winona Lake, IN: Eisenbrauns, 2014.

Borowski, Oded. *Agriculture in Iron Age Israel.* Winona Lake, IN: Eisenbrauns, 1987.

———. *Daily Life in Biblical Times.* Atlanta: SBL, 2003.

———. "Eat, Drink and Be Merry: The Mediterranean Diet." *NEA* 67, no. 2 (2004): 96–107.

Botner, Max. "The Fragrance of Life: Reconsidering the Sacrificial Logic of Ephesians 5:2." *BR* 64 (2019): 67–82.

Bradley, Mark. *Smell and the Ancient Senses.* London: Routledge, 2015.

Brenner, Athalya. "Aromatics and Perfumes in the Song of Songs." *JSOT* 25, no. 8 (1983): 75–81.

Brenner, Athalya, and Frank H. Polak, eds. *Performing Memory in Biblical Narrative and Beyond.* Sheffield: Sheffield Phoenix, 2009.

Briggs, Richard S. "Reading the *Sotah* Text (Numbers 5:11–31): Holiness and a Hermeneutic Fit for Suspicion." *BibInt* 17, no. 3 (2009): 288–319.

Britt, Brian M. "Curses Left and Right: Hate Speech and Biblical Tradition." *JAAR* 78, no. 3 (2010): 633–661.

Brongers, H. A. "Fasting in Israel in Biblical and Post-biblical Times." In *Instruction and Interpretation: Studies in Hebrew Language, Palestinian Archaeology and Biblical Exegesis,* edited by Hendrik A. Brongers, 1–21. OTS 20. Leiden: Brill, 1977.

Broshi, Magen. "The Population of Iron Age Palestine." In *Biblical Archaeology Today, 1990,* edited by Avraham Biran and Joseph Aviram, 14–18. Jerusalem: Israel Exploration Society, 1993.

Bunimovitz, Shelomoh, and Avraham Faust. "Ideology in Stone: Understanding the Four-Room House." *NEA* 28, no. 4 (2002): 33–41.

Burton, Margie. "Biomolecules, Bedouin, and the Bible: Reconstructing Ancient Foodways in Israel's Northern Negev." In Malena and Miano, *Milk and Honey,* 215–239.

Cahill, Jane M., Karl Reinhard, David Tarler, and Peter Warnock. "It Had to Happen: Scientists Examine Remains of Ancient Bathroom." *BAR* 17, no. 3 (1991): 64–69.

Candelora, Danielle. "Grisly Trophies: Severed Hands and the Egyptian Military." *NEA* 84, no. 3 (2021): 192–199.

Cantrell, Deborah O. *The Horsemen of Israel: Horses and Chariotry in Monarchic Israel (Ninth–Eighth Centuries B.C.E.).* Winona Lake, IN: Eisenbrauns, 2011.

Carmichael, Calum M. "Biblical Laws of Talion." *HAR* 9 (1985): 107–126.

———. "A Common Element in Five Supposedly Disparate Laws." *VT* 29, no. 2 (1979): 129–142.

———. "The Three Laws on the Release of Slaves (Ex 21, 2–11; Dtn 15,12–18; Lev 25,39–46)." *ZAW* 112, no. 4 (2000): 509–525.

Carretero, Carlos S. "A Study of Color: Uses of *Lābān* in the Hebrew Bible." *Sef* 77, no. 1 (2017): 39–64.

Carroll, Robert P. "Blindsight and the Vision Thing: Blindness and Insight in the Book of Isaiah." In *Writing and Reading the Scroll of Isaiah*, edited by Craig C. Broyles and Craig A. Evans, 79–93. Leiden: Brill, 1997.

———. "Removing an Ancient Landmark: Reading the Bible as Cultural Production." In *Borders, Boundaries and the Bible*, edited by Martin O'Kane, 6–14. London: Sheffield Academic, 2002.

———. "YHWH's Sour Grapes: Images of Food and Drink in the Prophetic Discourses of the Hebrew Bible." *Semeia* 86 (1999): 113–131.

Cartledge, Tony W. *1 and 2 Samuel*. Macon, GA: Smyth & Helwys, 2001.

Catchpole, David R. "The 'Triumphal' Entry." In *Jesus and the Politics of His Day*, edited by Ernst Bammel and C. F. D. Moule, 319–334. New York: Cambridge University Press, 1984.

Chadwick, Jeffrey R., and Aren M. Maeir. "Judahite Gath in the Eighth Century B.C.E.: Finds in Area F from the Earthquake to the Assyrians." *NEA* 81, no. 1 (2018): 48–54.

Chaney, Marvin L. "Whose Sour Grapes? The Addressees of Isaiah 5:1–7 in the Light of Political Economy." *Semeia* 87 (1999): 105–122.

Chen, Anna. "Perfume and Vinegar: Olfactory Knowledge, Remembrance, and Recordkeeping." *American Archivist* 79, no. 1 (2016): 103–120.

Chun, S. Min. *Ethics and Biblical Narrative: A Literary and Discourse-Analytical Approach to the Story of Josiah*. Oxford: Oxford University Press, 2014.

Clark, Douglas R. "Bricks, Sweat and Tears: The Human Investment in Constructing a 'Four-Room' House." *NEA* 66, nos. 1–2 (2003): 34–43.

Classen, Constance. "Other Ways to Wisdom: Learning through the Senses across Cultures." *International Review of Education* 45 (1999): 269–280.

———. *Worlds of Sense: Exploring the Senses in History and across Cultures*. London: Routledge, 1993.

Classen, Constance, and David Howes. "Making Sense of Culture: Anthropology as a Sensual Experience." *Etnofoor* 9, no. 2 (1996): 86–96.

Classen, Constance, David Howes, and Anthony Synnott. *Aroma: The Cultural History of Smell*. London: Routledge, 1994.

Cocco, Francesco. *Women in the Wilderness: The "Female Legislation" of the Book of Numbers (Num 5,11–31; 27,1–11; 30,2–17)*. Tübingen: Mohr Siebeck, 2020.

Cogan, Mordechai. "'Ripping Open Pregnant Women' in Light of an Assyrian Analogue." *JAOS* 103, no. 4 (1983): 755–757.

Cogan, Mordechai, and Hayim Tadmor. *II Kings*. New York: Doubleday, 1988.

Cohen, Chaim, and Vladimir M. Berginer. "The Nature of Goliath's Visual Disorder and the Actual Role of His Personal Bodyguard: Nose Hatstsinnah (1 Sam 17:7,41)." *ANES* 43 (2006): 27–44.

Cohen, Jeffrey M. "An Unrecognized Connotation of *Nsq Peh* [Kiss] with Special Reference to Three Biblical Occurrences." *VT* 32, no. 4 (1982): 416–424.

Collins, Terence. "Physiology of Tears in the Old Testament." *CBQ* 33, no. 1 (1971): 18–36.

Cooper, Alan. "Once Again Seething a Kid in Its Mother's Milk." *JSIJ* 10 (2012): 109–143. http://jewish-faculty.biu.ac.il/en/JSIJ.

Corbin, Alain. "Charting the Cultural History of the Senses." In Howes, *Empire of the Senses*, 128–139.

———. "A History and Anthropology of the Senses." In *Time, Desire and Horror: Towards a History of the Senses*, 183–189. Cambridge: Polity, 1995.

Cornelius, Izak. "The Image of Assyria: An Iconographic Approach by Way of a Study of Selected Material on the Theme of 'Power and Propaganda' in the Neo-Assyrian Palace Reliefs." *OTE* 2, no. 1 (1989): 41–60.

Cortez, Marc. "The Law on Violent Intervention: Deuteronomy 25:11–12 Revisited." *JSOT* 30, no. 4 (2006): 431–447.

Couey, J. Blake. "Isaiah, Jeremiah, Ezekiel, Daniel, and the Twelve." In Melcher, Parsons, and Yong, *Bible and Disability*, 215–273.

Coverley, Merlin. *Psychogeography*. Harpenden, UK: Oldcastle, 2018.

Cowan, Alexander, and Jill Steward, eds. *The City and the Senses: Urban Culture since 1500*. Aldershot, UK: Ashgate, 2007.

Craffert, Pieter F. "Coming to (Terms with) Our Senses: Seeing, Hearing and Smelling the Gods." *Journal of Early Christian History* 7, no. 3 (2017): 25–56.

Cranz, Isabel. "Naaman's Healing and Gehazi's Affliction: The Magical Background of 2 Kgs 5." *VT* 68, no. 4 (2018): 540–555.

Crisler, B. Cobbey. "The Acoustics and Crowd Capacity of Natural Theaters in Palestine." *BA* 39, no. 4 (1976): 128–141.

Cross, Frank M. *Canaanite Myth and Hebrew Epic*. Cambridge, MA: Harvard University Press, 1973.

Crow, Loren. *The Songs of Ascents (Psalms 120–134)*. Atlanta: Scholars Press, 1996.

Currid, John D. "The Deforestation of the Foothills of Palestine." *PEQ* 116 (1984): 1–11.

Currid, John D., and Avi Navon. "Iron Age Pits and the Lahav (Tell Halif) Grain Storage Project." *BASOR* 273 (1989): 67–78.

Davidson, Joyce, Mick Smith, and Liz Bondi, eds. *Emotional Geographies*. Farnham, UK: Ashgate, 2007.

Davidson, Steed V. "'Every Green Tree and the Streets of Jerusalem': Counter Constructions of Gendered Sacred Space in the Book of Jeremiah." In *Constructions of Space IV: Further Developments in Examining Ancient Israel's Social Space*, edited by Mark K. George, 111–131. New York: Bloomsbury, 2013.

Davies, Vanessa. "The Treatment of Foreigners in Seti's Battle Reliefs." *JEA* 98 (2012): 73–85.

Day, John, ed. *Temple and Worship in Biblical Israel*. New York: T&T Clark, 2005.

de Geus, C. H. J. *Towns in Ancient Israel and in the Southern Levant*. Leuven, Belgium: Peeters, 2003.

Derby, Josiah. "'. . . Upon the Doorposts . . .'." *JBQ* 27, no. 1 (1999): 40–44.

Dion, Paul E. "The Horned Prophet (1 Kings XXII 11)." *VT* 49, no. 2 (1999): 259–261.

Dobbs-Allsopp, F. W. "The Genre of the Meṣad Ḥashavyahu Ostracon." *BASOR* 295 (1994): 49–55.

Donahou, Michael S. *A Comparison of the Egyptian Execration Ritual to Exodus 32:19 and Jeremiah 19*. Piscataway, NJ: Gorgias, 2010.

Dozeman, Thomas B. *Exodus*. Grand Rapids, MI: Eerdmans, 2009.

Dubin, Steven C. "Visual Onomatopoeia." *Symbolic Interaction* 13, no. 2 (1990): 185–216.

Dubovsky, Peter. "Ripping Open Pregnant Arab Women: Reliefs in Room L of Ashurbanipal's North Palace." *Or* 78, no. 3 (2009): 394–419.

Duggan, Michael W. *The Covenant Renewal in Ezra–Nehemiah (Neh 7:72B–10:40): An Exegetical, Literary and Theological Study*. Atlanta: SBL, 2001.

Eaton, John H. "Music's Place in Worship: A Contribution from the Psalms." In Barton, Carroll, and Fokkelman, *Prophets, Worship and Theodicy*, 85–107.

Ebeling, Jennie R. "Engendering the Israelite Harvests." *NEA* 79, no. 3 (2016): 186–194.

———. *Women's Lives in Biblical Times*. London: T&T Clark, 2010.

Eidevall, Gören. "Sounds of Silence in Biblical Hebrew: A Lexical Study." *VT* 62, no. 2 (2012): 159–174.

Elman, Pearl. "Deuteronomy 21:10–14: The Beautiful Captive Woman." *Women in Judaism* 1, no. 1 (1997). http://wjudaism.library.utoronto.ca/index.php/wjudaism.

Emerton, John A. "The Value of the Moabite Stone as an Historical Source." *VT* 52, no. 4 (2002): 483–492.

Evans, Craig A. "Ephesians 5:18–19 and Religious Intoxication in the World of Paul." In *Paul's World*, edited by Stanley E. Porter, 181–200. Leiden: Brill, 2008.

Faust, Avraham. *The Archaeology of Israelite Society in Iron Age II*. Winona Lake, IN: Eisenbrauns, 2012.

———. "The Four Room House: Embodying Iron Age Israelite Society." *NEA* 66, nos. 1–2 (2003): 22–31.

———. "Residential Patterns in the Ancient Israelite City." *Levant* 35 (2003): 123–138.

Feder, Yitzhaq. "Pentateuchal and Ancient Near Eastern Ritual." In Baden and Stackert, *Oxford Handbook of the Pentateuch*, 421–442.

Fensham, F. Charles. "The Battle between the Men of Joab and Abner as a Possible Ordeal by Battle?" *VT* 20, no. 3 (1970): 356–357.

Ferlo, Roger. *Sensing God: Reading Scripture with All Our Senses*. Cambridge, MA: Cowley, 2001.

Fidler, Ruth. "A Wife's Vow—the Husband's Woe? The Case of Hannah and Elkanah (1 Samuel 1.21, 23)." *ZAW* 118, no. 3 (2006): 374–388.

Finkel, Irving L. "On Late Babylonian Medical Training." In *Wisdom, Gods and Literature: Studies in Assyriology in Honour of W. G. Lambert*, edited by Andrew R. George and Irving L. Finkel, 137–223. Winona Lake, IN: Eisenbrauns, 2000.

Finkelstein, J. J. *The Ox That Gored*. Philadelphia: American Philosophical Society, 1981.

Fitzpatrick-McKinley, Anne. *The Transformation of Torah from Scribal Advice to Law*. Sheffield: Sheffield Academic, 1999.

Fleishman, Joseph. "Legal Innovation in Deuteronomy XXI 18–20." *VT* 53, no. 3 (2003): 311–327.

Fleming, Daniel E. "David and the Ark: A Jerusalem Festival Reflected in Royal Narrative." In Vanderhooft and Winitzer, *Literature as Politics*, 75–95.

Fowler, Barbara H. *Love Lyrics of Ancient Egypt*. Chapel Hill: University of North Carolina Press, 1994.

Fox, Nili S. "Biblical Sanctification of Dress: Tassels on Garments." In *Built by Wisdom, Established by Understanding: Essays on Biblical and Near Eastern Literature in Honor of Adele Berlin*, edited by Maxime L. Grossman, 89–107. Bethesda: University Press of Maryland, 2013.

———. "Clapping Hands as a Gesture of Anguish and Anger in Mesopotamia and in Israel." *JANES* 23 (1995): 49–60.

Frechette, Christopher G. *Mesopotamian Ritual-Prayers of "Hand-Lifting" (Akkadian Šuillas): An Investigation of Function in Light of the Idiomatic Meaning of the Rubric*. Münster: Ugarit-Verlag, 2012.

Freund, Richard A. "Individual vs. Collective Responsibility: From the Ancient Near East and the Bible to the Greco-Roman World." *SJOT* 11, no. 2 (1997): 279–304.

Fried, Lisbeth S. "The High Places (*Bāmôt*) and the Reforms of Hezekiah and Josiah: An Archaeological Investigation." *JAOS* 122, no. 3 (2002): 437–465.

Friedmann, Jonathan L. "The Magical Sound of Priestly Bells." *JQR* 46, no. 1 (2018): 41–46.

Frieman, Catherine, and Mark Gillings. "Seeing Is Perceiving?" *World Archaeology* 39, no. 1 (2007): 4–16.

Fritz, Volkmar. *The City in Ancient Israel*. Sheffield: Sheffield Academic, 1995.

Frymer-Kensky, Tikva. "Virginity in the Bible." In *Gender and Law in the Hebrew Bible and the Ancient Near East*, edited by Victor H. Matthews, Bernard M. Levinson, and Tikva Frymer-Kensky, 79–96. Sheffield: Sheffield Academic, 1998.

Ganzel, Tova. "First-Month Rituals in Ezekiel's Temple Vision: A Pentateuchal and Babylonian Comparison." *CBQ* 83, no. 3 (2021): 390–406.

Garroway, Kristine H. *Growing Up in Ancient Israel: Children in Material Culture and Biblical Texts*. Atlanta: SBL, 2018.

Garsiel, Moshe. "The Valley of Elah Battle and the Duel of David with Goliath: Between History and Artistic Theological Historiography." In *Homeland and Exile: Biblical and Ancient Near Eastern Studies in Honour of Bustenay Oded*, edited by Gershon Galil, Mark Geller, and Alan R. Millard, 391–426. Leiden: Brill, 2009.

Gass, Erasmus. "The Deborah-Barak Composition (Jdg 4–5): Some Topographical Reflections." *PEQ* 149, no. 4 (2017): 326–335.

Gelb, Ignace J. "Prisoners of War in Early Mesopotamia." *JNES* 32, nos. 1–2 (1973): 70–98.

Geoghegan, Jeffrey C. "Israelite Sheepshearing and David's Rise to Power." *Bib* 87, no. 1 (2006): 55–63.

George, Mark K. "Watch Your Step! Excrement and Governmentality in Deuteronomy." *BibInt* 26, no. 3 (2018): 291–315.

Gerstenberger, Erhard. "Non-temple Psalms: The Cultic Setting Revisited." In *The Oxford Handbook of the Psalms*, edited by William P. Brown, 338–349. New York: Oxford University Press, 2014.

———. "The Power of Praise in the Psalter: Human-Divine Synergies in the Ancient Near East and the Hebrew Scriptures." In *Between Israelite Religion and Old Testament Theology: Essays on Archaeology, History, and Hermeneutics*, edited by Robert D. Miller, 31–48. Leuven, Belgium: Peeters, 2016.

———. *Psalms, Part 2, and Lamentations*. Grand Rapids, MI: Eerdmans, 2001.

Giannetti, Laura. "Of Eels and Pears: A Sixteenth-Century Debate on Taste, Temperance, and the Pleasures of the Senses." In Boer and Göttler, *Religion and the Senses*, 289–305.

Gijbels, Jolien. "Tangible Memories: Waterloo Relics in the Nineteenth Century." *Rijksmuseum Bulletin* 63, no. 3 (2015): 228–257.

Gillingham, Susan. "The Zion Tradition and the Editing of the Hebrew Psalter." In Day, *Temple and Worship*, 308–341.

Glazov, Gregory Y. "The Significance of the 'Hand on the Mouth' Gesture in Job XL 4." *VT* 52, no. 1 (2002): 30–41.

Glück, Janus J. "Assonance in Ancient Hebrew Poetry: Sound Patterns as a Literary Device." In *De Fructu oris sui: Essays in Honour of Adrianus van Selms*, edited by Ian H. Eybers, 69–84. Leiden: Brill, 1971.

Goering, Greg S. "Attentive Ears and Forward-Looking Eyes: Disciplining the Senses and Forming the Self in the Book of Proverbs." *JJS* 66, no. 2 (2015): 242–264.

———. "Honey and Wormwood: Taste and Embodiment of Wisdom in the Book of Proverbs." *HBAI* 5, no. 1 (2016): 23–41.

Golani, Amir. "Revealed by Their Jewelry: Ethnic Identity of Israelites during the Iron Age in the Southern Levant." In *Beyond Ornamentation: Jewelry as an Aspect of Material Culture in the Ancient Near East*, edited by Amir Golani and Zuzanna Wygnańska, 269–296. Warsaw: University of Warsaw Press, 2014.

Goldsmith, Dora. "Fish, Fowl, and Stench in Ancient Egypt." In Schellenberg and Krüger, *Sounding Sensory Profiles*, 335–360.

Gomes, Jules F. *The Sanctuary of Bethel and the Configuration of Israelite Identity*. Berlin: Walter de Gruyter, 2006.

Gonzalez-Grandon, Ximena. "How Music Connects: Social Sensory Consciousness in Musical Ritual." *Material Religion* 14, no. 3 (2018): 423–425.

Gosbell, Louise. *"The Poor, the Crippled, the Blind, and the Lame": Physical and Sensory Disability in the Gospels of the New Testament*. Tübingen: Mohr Siebeck, 2018.

Goulder, Michael D. "Asaph's History of Israel (Elohist Press, Bethel, 725 BCE)." *JSOT* 65, no. 20 (1995): 71–81.

Graybill, Rhiannon. "'Hear and Give Ear!' The Soundscape of Jeremiah." *JSOT* 40, no. 4 (2016): 467–490.

Green, Deborah. *Aroma of Righteousness: Scent and Seduction in Rabbinic Life and Literature*. University Park: Pennsylvania State University Press, 2011.

Greenspahn, Frederick E. "Deuteronomy and Centralization." *VT* 64, no. 2 (2014): 227–235.

———. "Primogeniture in Ancient Israel." In *"Go to the Land I Will Show You": Studies in Honor of Dwight W. Young*, edited by Joseph Coleson and Victor H. Matthews, 69–79. Winona Lake, IN: Eisenbrauns, 1996.

Greenstein, Edward L. "Recovering 'the Women Who Served at the Entrance.'" In *Studies in Historical Geography and Biblical Historiography: Presented to Zecharia Kallai*, edited by Gershon Galil and Moshe Weinfeld, 165–173. Leiden: Brill, 2000.

Grossman, Yonatan. "Divine Command and Human Initiative: A Literary View on
    Numbers 25–31." *BibInt* 15, no. 1 (2007): 54–79.
Gudme, Anne Katrine de Hemmer. "A Pleasing Odour for Yahweh: The Smell of
    Sacrifices on Mount Gerizim and in the Hebrew Bible." *Body and Religion* 2,
    no. 1 (2018): 7–24.
Guijarro Oporto, Santiago. "Healing Stories and Medical Anthropology: A Reading
    of Mark 10:46–52." *BTB* 30, no. 3 (2000): 102–112.
Guzman, Emmanuel S. de. "The Scent of Marginality: Odorizing Difference
    in Migratory Relations." In *Intercultural Church: Bridge of Solidarity in the
    Migration Context*, edited by Agnes Brazal and Emmanuel S. de Guzman,
    19–43. n.p.: Borderless, 2015.
Haas, Peter. "'Die He Shall Surely Die': The Structure of Homicide in Biblical
    Law." *Semeia* 45 (1989): 67–87.
Haber, Susan. "A Woman's Touch: Feminist Encounters with the Hemorrhaging
    Woman in Mark 5.24–34." *JSNT* 26, no. 2 (2003): 171–192.
Haberman, Bonna D. "The Suspected Adulteress: A Study of Textual
    Embodiment." *Proof* 20, nos. 1–2 (2000): 12–42.
Hamilakis, Yannis. "Archaeologies of the Senses." In *Oxford Handbook of the
    Archaeology of Ritual and Religion*, edited by Timothy Insoll, 208–225. New
    York: Oxford University Press, 2011.
Harris, Marvin. "The Abominable Pig." In *Community, Identity, and Ideology*, edited
    by Charles Carter, 135–151. Winona Lake, IN: Eisenbrauns, 1996.
Hartley, John E. *Leviticus*. Dallas: Thomas Nelson, 1992.
Harvey, Graham, and Jessica Hughes, eds. *Sensual Religion: Religion and the Five
    Senses*. Sheffield: Equinox, 2018.
Harvey, Susan A. *Scenting Salvation: Ancient Christianity and the Olfactory
    Imagination*. Transformations of the Classical Heritage, vol. 42. Berkeley:
    University of California Press, 2006.
Healey, John F. "Ancient Agriculture and the Old Testament (with Special
    Reference to Isaiah XXVIII 23–29)." In Barton, Carroll, and Fokkelman,
    Prophets, Worship and Theodicy, 108–119.
Hecke, Pierre van. "Tasting Metaphor in Ancient Israel." In Schellenberg and Krüger,
    Sounding Sensory Profiles, 99–118.
Hepper, F. Nigel. *Baker Encyclopedia of Bible Plants*. Grand Rapids, MI: Baker, 1992.
Holladay, William L. *A Commentary on the Book of the Prophet Jeremiah Chapters
    1–25*. Philadelphia: Fortress, 1986.
Holman, Michael M. "Beer Production by Throwing Bread into Water: A New
    Interpretation of Qoh. XI 1–2." *VT* 52, no. 2 (2002): 275–278.
———. "Did the Ancient Israelites Drink Beer?" *BAR* 36, no. 5 (2010): 48–56, 78.
Hopkins, David C. "'All Sorts of Field Work': Agricultural Labor in Ancient
    Palestine." In *To Break Every Yoke: Essays in Honor of Marvin L. Chaney*, edited
    by Robert B. Coote and Norman K. Gottwald, 149–172. Sheffield: Sheffield
    Phoenix, 2007.
Horowitz, Seth S. *The Universal Sense: How Hearing Shapes the Mind*. New York:
    Bloomsbury, 2012.
Hossfeld, Frank-Lothar, and Erich Zenger. *A Commentary on Psalms 101–150*.
    Minneapolis: Fortress, 2011.

Houtman, Cornelius. "On the Function of the Holy Incense (Exodus XXX 34–8) and the Sacred Anointing Oil (Exodus XXX 22–33)." *VT* 42, no. 4 (1992): 458–465.

———. "On the Pomegranates and the Golden Bells of the High Priest's Mantle." *VT* 40, no. 2 (1990): 223–229.

Howes, David. "Can These Dry Bones Live? An Anthropological Approach to the History of the Senses." *Journal of American History* 95, no. 2 (2008): 442–451.

———, ed. *Empire of the Senses: The Sensual Culture Reader.* New York: Berg, 2005.

———. "Forming Perceptions." In Howes, *Empire of the Senses*, 399–402.

———. "Olfaction and Transition: An Essay on the Ritual Use of Smell." *Canadian Review of Sociology and Anthropology* 24, no. 3 (1987): 398–416.

———. "Resounding Sensory Profiles: Sensory Studies Methodologies." In Schellenberg and Krüger, *Sounding Sensory Profiles*, 43–54.

———. "Sensation." *Material Religion* 7, no. 1 (2011): 92–98.

———. *Sensory Relations: Engaging the Senses in Culture and Social Theory.* Ann Arbor: University of Michigan Press, 2003.

———, ed. *The Varieties of Sensory Experience: A Sourcebook in the Anthropology of the Senses.* Toronto: University of Toronto Press, 1991.

Huggins-Cooper, Lynn. *Spinning and Weaving.* Yorkshire: Pen & Sword History, 2019.

Hunt, Patrick. "Sensory Images in Song of Songs 1:12–2:16." In *"Dort ziehen Schiffe dahin . . .": Collected Communications to the XIVth Congress of the International Organization for the Study of the Old Testament, Paris 1992*, edited by Matthias Augustin and Klaus D. Schunck, 69–78. Frankfurt am Main: Peter Lang, 1996.

Hurowitz, Victor A. "'His Master Shall Pierce His Ear with an Awl' (Exodus 21:6)—Marking Slaves in the Bible in Light of Akkadian Sources." *American Academy for Jewish Research* 58 (1992): 47–77.

———. "YHWH's Exalted House—Aspects of the Design and Symbolism of Solomon's Temple." In Day, *Temple and Worship*, 63–110.

Hutton, Jeremy M. "Amos 1:3–2:8 and the International Economy of Iron Age II Israel." *HTR* 107, no. 1 (2014): 81–113.

Isser, Stanley J. *The Sword of Goliath: David in Heroic Literature.* Atlanta: SBL, 2003.

Jackson, Bernard S. "The Prophet and the Law in Early Judaism and the New Testament." *Jewish Law Association Studies* 7 (1994): 67–112.

———. *Theft in Early Jewish Law.* Oxford: Clarendon, 1972.

———. *Wisdom Laws: A Study of the Mishpatim of Exodus 21:1–22:16.* New York: Oxford University Press, 2006.

Jacob, Irene, and Walter Jacob, eds. *The Healing Past: Pharmaceuticals in the Biblical and Rabbinic World.* Leiden: Brill, 1993.

Jacoby, Ruth. "The Representation and Identification of Cities on Assyrian Reliefs." *IEJ* 41, nos. 1–3 (1991): 112–131.

Janzen, J. Gerald. "Prayer and/as Self-Address: The Case of Hannah." In *A God So Near: Essays on Old Testament Theology in Honor of Patrick D. Miller*, edited by Brent A. Strawn and Nancy R. Bowen, 113–127. Winona Lake, IN: Eisenbrauns, 2003.

Jay, Martin. "In the Realm of the Senses: An Introduction." *AHR* 116, no. 2 (2011): 307–315.

Jeffers, Joshua. "Fifth-Campaign Reliefs in Sennacherib's 'Palace without Rival' at Nineveh." *Iraq* 73 (2011): 87–116.

Jenner, Mark S. R. "Follow Your Nose? Smell, Smelling, and Their Histories." *AHR* 116, no. 2 (2011): 335–351.

Jeon, Jaeyoung. "Two Laws in the *Sotah* Passage (Num V 11–31)." *VT* 57, no. 2 (2007): 181–207.

Johnson, Dylan R. *Sovereign Authority and the Elaboration of Law in the Bible and the Ancient Near East.* Tübingen: Mohr Siebeck, 2020.

Kalimi, Isaac. "Human and Musical Sounds and Their Hearing Elsewhere as a Literary Device in the Biblical Narratives." *VT* 60, no. 4 (2010): 565–570.

Keating, Elizabeth, and R. Neill Hadder. "Sensory Impairment." *ARA* 39, no. 1 (2010): 115–129.

Keller, Marie Noël. "Opening Blind Eyes: A Revisioning of Mark 8:22–10:52." *BTB* 31, no. 4 (2001): 151–157.

Kilchör, Benjamin. "Levirate Marriage in Deuteronomy 25:5–10 and Its Precursors in Leviticus and Numbers: A Test Case for the Relationship between P/H and D." *CBQ* 77, no. 3 (2015): 429–440.

King, Philip J., and Lawrence E. Stager. *Life in Biblical Israel.* Louisville, KY: Westminster John Knox, 2001.

Kinman, Brent. *Jesus' Entry into Jerusalem: In the Context of Lukan Theology and the Politics of His Day.* Leiden: Brill, 1995.

Kitts, Margo. "Discursive, Iconic, and Somatic Perspectives on Ritual." *JRitSt* 31, no. 1 (2017): 296–304.

Klassen, William. "The Sacred Kiss in the New Testament: An Example of Social Boundary Lines." *NTS* 39, no. 1 (1993): 122–135.

Kloppenborg, John S. "Joshua 22: The Priestly Editing of an Ancient Tradition." *Bib* 62, no. 3 (1981): 347–371.

Koh, Andrew J., Andrea M. Berlin, and Sharon C. Herbert. "Phoenician Cedar Oil from Amphoriskoi at Tel Kedesh: Implications concerning Its Production, Use, and Export during the Hellenistic Age." *BASOR* 385 (2020): 99–117.

Korsmeyer, Caroline. *Making Sense of Taste: Food and Philosophy.* Ithaca, NY: Cornell University Press, 1999.

Kotze, Zacharias. "A Case of the Evil Eye in Genesis 16:4–5: A Social-Scientific Perspective." *HvTSt* 73, no. 3 (2017): 1–6.

Kropp, Andreas J. M., and Daniel Lohmann. "'Master, Look at the Size of Those Stones! Look at the Size of Those Buildings!': Analogies in Construction Techniques between the Temples at Heliopolis (Baalbek) and Jerusalem." *Levant* 43 (2011): 38–50.

Krüger, Thomas. "The Face and Emotions in the Hebrew Bible." *OTE* 18 (2005): 651–663.

———. "On the Sense of Balance in the Hebrew Bible." In Schellenberg and Krüger, *Sounding Sensory Profiles*, 87–97.

Kurek-Chomycz, Dominika A. "The Fragrance of Her Perfume: The Significance of Sense Imagery in John's Account of the Anointing in Bethany." *NovT* 52, no. 4 (2010): 334–354.

LaFont, Sophie. "Ancient Near Eastern Laws: Continuity and Pluralism." In *Theory and Method in Biblical and Cuneiform Law: Revision, Interpolation and Development*, edited by Bernard M. Levinson, 91–118. Sheffield: Sheffield Academic, 1994.

Lamberg, Marko, Marko Hakanen, and Janne Haikari, eds. *Physical and Cultural Space in Pre-industrial Europe: Methodological Approaches to Spatiality*. Lund: Nordic Academic, 2011.

Lamberg, Marko, Minna Mäkinen, and Merja Uotila. "A Rural Living Sphere." In Lamberg, Hakanen, and Haikari, *Physical and Cultural Space*, 289–318.

Landsberger, Franz. "The Origin of the Decorated Mezuzah." *HUCA* 31 (1960): 149–166.

Langer, Susanne K. *Philosophy in a New Key*. New York: Mentor, 1958.

Lass, Egon H. E. "Flotation Procedures in the Southern Levant: A Summary of 20 Years of Work, Part II." *Strata* 29 (2011): 103–120.

Lawrence, Jonathan D. *Washing in Water: Trajectories of Ritual Bathing in the Hebrew Bible and Second Temple Literature*. Atlanta: SBL, 2006.

Le Breton, David. *Sensing the World: An Anthropology of the Senses*. London: Bloomsbury, 2017.

Lee, Dorothy. "The Gospel of John and the Five Senses." *JBL* 129, no. 1 (2010): 115–127.

Leith, Mary Joan W. "Divine Scents: God Doesn't Just See and Hear the Israelites, He Can Smell Them Too." *BRev* 19, no. 4 (2003): 8, 61.

Lemaire, André. "The Evolution of the 8th Century B.C.E. Jerusalem Temple." In *The Fire Signals of Lachish: Studies in the Archaeology and History of Israel in the Late Bronze Age, Iron Age, and Persian Period in Honor of David Ussishkin*, edited by Israel Finkelstein and Nadav Na'aman, 195–202. Winona Lake, IN: Eisenbrauns, 2011.

Lemos, T. M. *Marriage Gifts and Social Change in Ancient Palestine*. Cambridge: Cambridge University Press, 2010.

———. "Shame and Mutilation of Enemies in the Hebrew Bible." *JBL* 125, no. 2 (2006): 225–241.

Lennon, Jack. "Contaminating Touch in the Roman World." In Purves, *Touch and the Ancient Senses*, 121–133.

Leon, Mark. "Characterising the Senses." In Macpherson, *Senses*, 156–183.

Leone, Massimo. "Transcendence and Transgression in Religious Processions." *Signs and Society* 2, no. 2 (2014): 314–349.

Leslie, Francis, Duncan Strathie, and Christopher F. J. Ross. "Reading the Beatitudes (Mt 5:1–10) through the Lenses of Introverted Intuition and Introverted Sensing: Perceiving Text Differently." *HvTSt* 75, no. 4 (2019): 1–8.

Levine, Baruch A. *JPS Torah Commentary: Leviticus*. Philadelphia: Jewish Publication Society, 1989.

———. "Silence, Sound, and the Phenomenology of Mourning in Biblical Israel." *JANES* 22 (1993): 89–106.

Levinson, Bernard M. *Deuteronomy and the Hermeneutics of Legal Innovation*. New York: Oxford University Press, 1997.

Lier, Gudrun E. "The Travail of Pain: An Interpretative Perspective from Scripture." *OTE* 32 (2019): 869–894.

Luc, Alex. "Storm and the Message of Job." *JSOT* 87, no. 25 (2000): 116–122.

Maaranen, Päivi. "Landscapes of Power." In Lamberg, Hakanen, and Haikari, *Physical and Cultural Space*, 239–272.

MacDonald, Nathan. "The Date of the Shema (Deuteronomy 6:4–5)." *JBL* 136, no. 4 (2017): 765–782.

———. *What Did the Ancient Israelites Eat? Diet in Biblical Times.* Grand Rapids, MI: Eerdmans, 2008.

Macpherson, Fiona, ed. "Individuating the Senses." In Macpherson, *Senses*, 3–43.

———. *The Senses: Classical and Contemporary Philosophical Perspectives.* Oxford: Oxford University Press, 2011.

Maerker, Anna. "Towards a Comparative History of Touch and Spaces of Display: The Body as Epistemic Object." *Historical Social Research* 40, no. 1 (2015): 284–300.

Magness, Jodi. *Stone and Dung, Oil and Spit: Jewish Daily Life in the Time of Jesus.* Grand Rapids, MI: Eerdmans, 2011.

———. "What's the Poop on Ancient Toilets and Toilet Habits?" *NEA* 75, no. 2 (2012): 80–87.

Makujina, John. "Additional Considerations for Determining the Meaning of *'Ănôt* and *'Annôt* in Exod XXXII 18." *VT* 55, no. 1 (2005): 39–46.

Malena, Sarah. "Spice Roots in the Song of Songs." In Malena and Miano, *Milk and Honey*, 165–184.

Malena, Sarah, and David Miano, eds. *Milk and Honey: Essays on Ancient Israel and the Bible in Appreciation of the Judaic Studies Program at the University of California, San Diego.* Winona Lake, IN: Eisenbrauns, 2007.

Malul, Meir. *The Comparative Method in Ancient Near Eastern and Biblical Legal Studies.* Kevelaer, Germany: Butzon & Bercker, 1990.

———. "More on *Paḥad Yiṣḥāq* (Genesis 31:42,53) and the Oath by the Thigh." *VT* 35, no. 2 (1985): 192–200.

Mandell, Alice, and Jeremy D. Smoak. "Reading beyond Literacy, Writing beyond Epigraphy: Multimodality and the Monumental Inscriptions at Ekron and Tel Dan." *Maarav* 22, nos. 1–2 (2018): 79–112, 134–135.

Manniche, Lise. *Sacred Luxuries: Fragrance, Aromatherapy, and Cosmetics in Ancient Egypt.* Ithaca, NY: Cornell University Press, 1999.

Marcus, Joel. *Mark 1–8: A New Translation with Introduction and Commentary.* New York: Doubleday, 1999.

———. "Passover and Last Supper Revisited." *NTS* 59, no. 3 (2013): 303–324.

Marriott, John, and Karen Radner. "Sustaining the Assyrian Army among Friends and Enemies in 714 BCE." *JCS* 67 (2015): 127–143.

Martin, M. G. F. "Sight and Touch." In Macpherson, *Senses*, 201–219.

Marwil, David. "A Soothing Savor." *JBQ* 42, no. 3 (2014): 169–172.

Massey, Doreen. *For Space.* London: Sage, 2005.

Matthews, Victor H. "The Art of Lying at King David's Court." *BTB* 47, no. 2 (2017): 80–86.

———. "Government Involvement in the Religion of the Mari Kingdom." *RA* 72, no. 2 (1978): 151–156.

———. *The Hebrew Prophets and Their Social World.* Grand Rapids, MI: Baker Academic, 2012.

——. *The History of Bronze and Iron Age Israel*. New York: Oxford University Press, 2019.

——. "Hospitality and Hostility in Genesis 19 and Judges 19." *BTB* 22, no. 1 (1992): 3–11.

——. Introduction to *Writing and Reading War: Rhetoric, Gender, and Ethics in Biblical and Modern Contexts*, edited by Brad E. Kelle and Frank R. Ames, 1–15. Atlanta: SBL, 2008.

——. "Messengers and the Transmission of Information in the Mari Kingdom." In *Go to the Land I Will Show You: Studies in Honor of Dwight W. Young*, edited by Victor H. Matthews and Joseph Coleson, 267–274. Winona Lake, IN: Eisenbrauns, 1996.

——. *More Than Meets the Ear: Discovering the Hidden Contexts of Old Testament Conversations*. Grand Rapids, MI: Eerdmans, 2008.

——. "Physical Space, Imagined Space, and 'Lived Space' in Ancient Israel." *BTB* 33, no. 1 (2003): 12–20.

——. "Spatial and Sensory Aspects of Battle in Biblical and Ancient Near Eastern Texts." *BTB* 49, no. 2 (2019): 82–87.

——. "Taking Calculated Risks: The Story of the Cannibal Mothers (2 Kgs 6:24–7:20)." *BTB* 43, no. 1 (2013): 4–13.

Matthews, Victor H., and Don C. Benjamin. *Old Testament Parallels: Laws and Stories from the Ancient Near East*. 4th ed. Mahwah, NJ: Paulist, 2016.

May, Natalie N., and Ulrike Steinert, eds. *The Fabric of Cities: Aspects of Urbanism, Urban Topography and Society in Mesopotamia, Greece, and Rome*. Leiden: Brill, 2014.

Mazar, Eilat, and Benjamin Mazar. *Excavations in the South of the Temple Mount: The Ophel of Biblical Jerusalem*. Jerusalem: Hebrew University Press, 1989.

Mazow, Laura B. "The Root of the Problem: On the Relationship between Wool Processing and Lanoline Production." *Journal of Mediterranean Archaeology* 27, no. 1 (2014): 33–50.

McCarter, P. Kyle. *1 Samuel*. New York: Doubleday, 1980.

McGuire, Meredith B. "Individual Sensory Experiences, Socialized Senses, and Everyday Lived Religion in Practice." *Social Compass* 63, no. 2 (2016): 152–162.

McHugh, James. "The Classification of Smells and the Order of the Senses in Indian Religious Traditions." *Numen* 54, no. 4 (2007): 374–419.

McKay, Heather A. "Through the Eyes of Horses: Representation of the Horse Family in the Hebrew Bible." In *Sense and Sensitivity: Essays on Reading the Bible in Memory of Robert Carroll*, edited by Alastair G. Hunter and Philip R. Davies, 127–141. London: Sheffield, 2002.

McKeating, Henry. "Development of the Law on Homicide in Ancient Israel." *VT* 25, no. 1 (1975): 46–68.

McNeill, William H. *Keeping Together in Time: Dance and Drill in Human History*. Cambridge, MA: Harvard University Press, 1995.

Mealy, J. Webb. "You Shall Not Boil a Kid in Its Mother's Milk (Exod. 23:19b; Exod. 34:26b; Deut. 14:21b): A Figure of Speech?" *BibInt* 20, nos. 1–2 (2012): 35–72.

Mearheimer, John J. *Why Leaders Lie: The Truth about Lying in International Politics*. New York: Oxford University Press, 2011.

Meiring, Jacob. "How Does Justice Smell? Reflections on Space and Place, Justice and the Body." *HvTSt* 72, no. 1 (2016): 1–7.

Melcher, Sarah J. "Genesis and Exodus." In Melcher, Parsons, and Yong, *Bible and Disability*, 29–56.

Melcher, Sarah J., Mikeal C. Parsons, and Amos Yong, eds. *The Bible and Disability: A Commentary.* Waco, TX: Baylor University Press, 2017.

Meyer, Birgit, ed. *Aesthetic Formations: Media, Religion and the Senses.* New York: Palgrave Macmillan, 2009.

Meyers, Carol L. *Exodus.* Cambridge: Cambridge University Press, 2005.

———. "Fumes, Flames, or Fluids: Reframing the Cup-and-Bowl Question." In *Boundaries of the Ancient Near Eastern World: A Tribute to Cyrus H. Gordon,* edited by Meir Lubetski, Claire Gottlieb, and Sharon Keller, 30–39. Sheffield: Sheffield Academic, 1998.

———. "Having Their Space and Eating There Too: Bread Production and Female Power in Ancient Israelite Households." *Nashim: A Journal of Jewish Women's Studies and Gender Issues* 5 (2002): 14–44.

———. "Material Remains and Social Relations: Women's Culture in Agrarian Households of the Iron Age." In *Symbiosis, Symbolism, and the Power of the Past: Canaan, Ancient Israel, and Their Neighbors from the Late Bronze Age through Roman Palaestina,* edited by William G. Dever and Seymour Gitin, 425–444. Winona Lake, IN: Eisenbrauns, 2003.

Milano, L., S. de Martino, Frederick Mario, and G. B. Lanfranchi, eds. *Landscapes: Territories, Frontiers and Horizons in the Ancient Near East.* HANE/M, vol. 3. Padova, Italy: Tipografia Edicta, 2000.

Milgrom, Jacob. "The Alleged Wave-Offering in Israel and in the Ancient Near East." *IEJ* 22, no. 1 (1972): 33–38.

———. *JPS Torah Commentary: Numbers.* Philadelphia: Jewish Publication Society, 1990.

———. *Leviticus 1–16.* New York: Doubleday, 1991.

———. "The Rationale for Biblical Impurity." *JANES* 22 (1993): 107–111.

Miller, Patrick D. *The Ten Commandments.* Louisville, KY: Westminster John Knox, 2009.

Milner, Matthew. *The Senses and the English Reformation.* Abingdon, UK: Routledge, 2016.

Minen, Francesca. "Flaying the Enemy in Assyria." In *Proceedings of the 11th International Congress on the Archaeology of the Ancient Near East,* 233–244. Vol. 1. Wiesbaden, Germany: Harrassowitz, 2020.

Mitchell, Terence C. "The Music of the Old Testament Reconsidered." *PEQ* 124 (1992): 124–143.

Morrow, William S. *Introduction to Biblical Law.* Grand Rapids, MI: Eerdmans, 2017.

Moss, Candida R. "The Man with the Flow of Power: Porous Bodies in Mark 5:25–34." *JBL* 129, no. 3 (2010): 507–519.

Munt, Sally R. "Sensory Geographies and Defamiliarisation: Migrant Women Encounter Brighton Beach." *Gender, Place & Culture: A Journal of Feminist Geography* 23, no. 8 (2016): 1093–1106.

Murnane, William J. "Rhetorical History? The Beginning of Thutmose III's First
   Campaign in Western Asia." *JARCE* 26 (1989): 183–189.
Musselman, Lytton J. *A Dictionary of Bible Plants.* Cambridge: Cambridge
   University Press, 2012.
Na'aman, Nadav. "Hezekiah's Fortified Cities and the LMLK Stamps." *BASOR* 261
   (1986): 5–21.
Nadali, Davide. "Esarhaddon's Glazed Bricks from Nimrud: The Egyptian
   Campaign Depicted." *Iraq* 68 (2006): 109–119.
Navon, Mois A. "The Kiss of Esau." *JBQ* 35, no. 2 (2007): 127–131.
Needham, Rodney. "Percussion and Transition." *Man* 2, no. 4 (1967): 606–614.
Neufeld, Edward. "Hygiene Conditions in Ancient Israel (Iron Age)." *BA* 34, no. 2
   (1971): 42–66.
Neumann, Kiersten. "Reading the Temple of Nabu as a Coded Sensory
   Experience." *Iraq* 80 (2018): 181–211.
Niditch, Susan. *War in the Hebrew Bible: A Study of the Ethics of Violence.* New York:
   Oxford University Press, 1993.
Nielsen, Kirsten. *Incense in Ancient Israel.* Leiden: Brill, 1986.
Nielsen, Kjeld. "Ancient Aromas: Good and Bad." *BRev* 7, no. 3 (1991): 26–33.
Nissan, Ephraim, and Abraham Ofir Shemesh. "Olfaction When Judging:
   According to Isaiah 11:3–4." *BeO* 59, nos. 1–4 (2017): 23–52.
Noegel, Scott B. "Evil Looms: Delilah—Weaver of Wicked Wiles." *CBQ* 79, no. 2
   (2017): 187–204.
Odell, David. "Images of Violence in the Horse in Job 39:18–25." *Proof* 13, no. 2
   (1993): 163–173.
Olyan, Saul M. "Honor, Shame, and Covenant Relations in Ancient Israel and Its
   Environment." *JBL* 115, no. 2 (1996): 201–218.
Orlick, Jeffrey K. *The Politics of Regret: On Collective Memory and Historical
   Responsibility.* New York: Routledge, 2007.
Palyvou, Klaire. "Skylines: Borders of Materiality, Thresholds of Heaven." *Journal of
   Egyptian Interconnections* 7, no. 3 (2015): 65–75.
Paterson, Mark. *The Senses of Touch: Haptics, Affects and Technologies.* Oxford:
   Routledge, 2007.
Patrick, Dale. *Old Testament Law.* Atlanta: John Knox, 1985.
Patton, Corinne L. "Psalm 132: A Methodological Inquiry." *CBQ* 57, no. 4 (1995):
   643–654.
Paz, Sarit. *Drums, Women, and Goddesses: Drumming and Gender in Iron Age Israel.*
   Fribourg: Vandenhoeck & Ruprecht, 2007.
Perullo, Nicola. *Taste as Experience: The Philosophy and Aesthetics of Food.* New York:
   Columbia University Press, 2016.
Phillips, Anthony. "Another Look at Adultery." *JSOT* 20, no. 6 (1981): 3–25.
Pilch, John J. *Healing in the New Testament: Insights from Medical and
   Mediterranean Anthropology.* Minneapolis: Fortress, 2000.
———. "Smells and Tastes." *TBT* 34 (1996): 246–251.
Pink, Sarah. *Doing Sensory Ethnography.* London: Sage, 2009.
———. "The Future of Sensory Anthropology / the Anthropology of the Senses."
   Social Anthropology 18 (2010): 331–340.

Polak, Frank H. "Negotiations, Social Drama and Voices of Memory in Some Samuel Tales." In Brenner and Polak, *Performing Memory*, 46–69.

Polan, Gregory J. "The Passover: A Memorial Meal." *TBT* 57 (2019): 353–358.

Pressler, Carolyn. *The View of Women Found in the Deuteronomic Family Laws.* Berlin: Walter de Gruyter, 1993.

Price, Max D. *Evolution of a Taboo: Pigs and People in the Ancient Near East.* New York: Oxford University Press, 2020.

Prince, Deborah T. "Seeing Visions: The Pervasive Power of Sight in the Acts of the Apostles." *JSNT* 40, no. 3 (2018): 337–359.

Promey, Sally M., ed. *Sensational Religion.* New Haven, CT: Yale University Press, 2014.

Purnell, Carolyn. *The Sensational Past: How the Enlightenment Changed the Way We Use Our Senses.* New York: W. W. Norton, 2017.

Purves, Alex. "Introduction: What and Where Is Touch?" In Purves, *Touch and the Ancient Senses*, 1–20.

———. *Touch and the Ancient Senses.* London: Routledge, 2018.

Radstone, Susannah, and Bill Schwarz, eds. *Memory: Histories, Theories, Debates.* New York: Fordham University Press, 2010.

Rao, D. Vijaya. *Armies, Wars and Their Food.* New Delhi: Cambridge University Press India, 2012.

Reich, Ronny. "A Note on the Population Size of Jerusalem in the Second Temple Period." *RB* 121, no. 2 (2014): 298–305.

Renfrew, Colin, and Paul Bahn. *Archaeology: Theories, Methods and Practice.* London: Thames & Hudson, 2004.

Richey, Madadh. "Goliath among the Giants: Monster Decapitation and Capital Display in 1 Samuel 17 and Beyond." *JSOT* 45, no. 3 (2021): 336–356.

Ricks, Stephen O. "*Miqvaot*: Ritual Immersion Baths in Second Temple (Intertestamental) Jewish History." In *Masada and the World of the New Testament*, edited by John F. Hall and John W. Welch, 277–286. Provo, UT: Brigham Young University Press, 1997.

Ritchie, Ian D. "The Nose Knows: Bodily Knowing in Isaiah 11.3." *JSOT* 87, no. 25 (2000): 59–73.

Ritner, Robert K. "Innovations and Adaptations in Ancient Egyptian Medicine." *JNES* 59, no. 2 (2000): 107–117.

Robbins, Ellen. "The Pleiades, the Flood, and the Jewish New Year." In *Ki Baruch Hu: Ancient Near Eastern, Biblical, and Judaic Studies in Honor of Baruch A. Levine*, edited by Robert Chazan, William W. Hallo, and Lawrence H. Schiffman, 329–344. Winona Lake, IN: Eisenbrauns, 1999.

Robbins, Vernon K. "The Woman Who Touched Jesus' Garment: Socio-rhetorical Analysis of the Synoptic Accounts." *NTS* 33, no. 4 (1987): 502–515.

Robinson, Geoffrey D. "The Motif of Deafness and Blindness in Isaiah 6:9–10: A Contextual, Literary, and Theological Analysis." *BBR* 8 (1998): 167–186.

Rolls, Edmund T. "The Texture and Taste of Food in the Brain." *Journal of Texture Studies* 51, no. 1 (2020): 23–44.

Rollston, Christopher A. "Scribal Education in Ancient Israel: The Old Hebrew Epigraphic Evidence." *BASOR* 344 (1998): 47–68.

Rosenstock, Bruce. "David's Play: Fertility Rituals and the Glory of God in 2 Samuel 6." *JSOT* 31, no. 1 (2006): 63–80.

Roth, Martha T. "Errant Oxen or the Goring Ox Redux." In Vanderhooft and Winitzer, *Literature as Politics*, 397–404.

———. *Law Collections from Mesopotamia and Asia Minor*. Atlanta: Scholars Press, 1995.

Rudolph, Kelli C. *Taste and the Ancient Senses*. London: Routledge, 2018.

Samat, Nili. "On Agricultural Imagery in Biblical Descriptions of Catastrophes." *Journal of Ancient Judaism* 3, no. 1 (2012): 2–12.

Sapir-Hen, Lidar. "Food, Pork Consumption, and Identity in Ancient Israel." *NEA* 82, no. 1 (2019): 52–59.

Sasson, Jack M. "The Eyes of Eli: An Essay in Motif Accretion." In *Inspired Speech: Prophecy in the Ancient Near East: Essays in Honor of Herbert B. Huffmon*, edited by John Kaltner and Louis Stulman, 171–190. New York: T&T Clark, 2004.

Schellenberg, Annette. "Senses, Sensuality, and Sensory Imagination: On the Role of the Senses in the Song of Songs." In Schellenberg and Krüger, *Sounding Sensory Profiles*, 199–214.

Schellenberg, Annette, and Thomas Krüger, eds. *Sounding Sensory Profiles in the Ancient Near East*. Atlanta: SBL, 2019.

Schenker, Adrian. "The Biblical Legislation on the Release of Slaves: The Road from Exodus to Leviticus." *JSOT* 78, no. 23 (1998): 23–41.

Schipper, Jeremy. "Reconsidering the Imagery of Disability in 2 Sam 5:8b." *CBQ* 67, no. 3 (2005): 422–434.

Schwartz, Joshua. "Dogs, 'Water' and Wall." *SJOT* 14, no. 1 (2000): 101–116.

Seely, David R. "The Raised Hand of God as an Oath Gesture." In *Fortunate the Eyes That See: Essays in Honor of David Noel Freedman in Celebration of His Seventieth Birthday*, edited by Astrid Beck, Andrew H. Bartelt, and Paul R. Raabe, 411–421. Grand Rapids, MI: Eerdmans, 1995.

Seidler, Ayelet. "The Law of Levirate and Forced Marriage—Widow vs. Levir in Deuteronomy 25.5–10." *JSOT* 42, no. 4 (2018): 435–456.

Shafer-Elliott, Cynthia. *Food in Ancient Judah: Domestic Cooking in the Time of the Hebrew Bible*. Abingdon, UK: Routledge, 2014.

Shemesh, Yael. "Rape Is Rape Is Rape: The Story of Dinah and Shechem (Genesis 34)." *ZAW* 119, no. 1 (2007): 2–21.

Shepperson, Mary. *Sunlight and Shade in the First Cities: A Sensory Archaeology of Early Iraq*. Bristol, CT: Vandenhoeck & Ruprecht, 2017.

Shifman, Arie. "'A Scent' of the Spirit: Exegesis of an Enigmatic Verse (Isaiah 11:3)." *JBL* 131, no. 2 (2012): 241–249.

Shiloh, Yigal. "The Casemate Wall, the Four Room House, and Early Planning in the Israelite City." *BASOR* 268 (1987): 3–15.

Shin, SuJung. "A 'Vital Materiality' of the Ark in Its Relativity to the Body of David in 2 Sam 6." *Bible and Critical Theory* 16, no. 2 (2020): 7–22.

Simkins, Ronald. "The Widow and Orphan in the Political Economy of Ancient Israel." *Journal of Religion and Society* 10 (2014): 20–33.

Śliwa, Joachim. "Some Remarks concerning Victorious Ruler Representations in Egyptian Art." In *Forschungen und Berichte*, 97–117. Archäologische Beiträge, Bd. 16. Berlin: Akademie-Verlag, 1974.

Smelik, Klaas A. D. "The Literary Structure of the Yavneh-Yam Ostracon." *IEJ* 42, nos. 1–2 (1992): 55–61.

Smith, John A. *Music in Religious Cults of the Ancient Near East.* London: Routledge, 2021.

Smith, Mark M. "Preface: Styling Sensory History." *Journal for Eighteenth-Century Studies* 35, no. 4 (2012): 469–472.

———. "Producing Sense, Consuming Sense, Making Sense: Perils and Prospects for Sensory History." *Journal of Social History* 40, no. 4 (2007): 841–858.

———. *Sensing the Past: Seeing, Hearing, Smelling, Tasting, and Touching in History.* Berkeley: University of California Press, 2007.

———. *The Smell of Battle, the Taste of Siege: A Sensory History of the Civil War.* Oxford: Oxford University Press, 2015.

Snyman, Gerrie. "Who Is Responsible for Uzzah's Death? Rhetoric in 1 Chronicles 13." In *Rhetoric, Scripture and Theology: Essays from the 1994 Pretoria Conference,* edited by Stanley E. Porter and Thomas H. Olbricht, 203–217. Sheffield: Sheffield Academic, 1996.

Sparks, Kenton L. "*Enuma Elish* and Priestly Mimesis: Elite Emulation in Nascent Judaism." *JBL* 126, no. 4 (2007): 625–648.

Stacey, David. "The Function of Prophetic Drama." In *"The Place Is Too Small for Us": The Israelite Prophets in Recent Scholarship,* edited by Robert P. Gordon, 112–132. Winona Lake, IN: Eisenbrauns, 1995.

———. "Seasonal Industries at Qumran." *BAIAS* 26 (2008): 7–29.

Stackert, Jeffrey. "Why Does Deuteronomy Legislate Cities of Refuge? Asylum in the Covenant Collection (Exodus 21:12–14) and Deuteronomy (19:1–13)." *JBL* 125, no. 1 (2006): 23–49.

Stager, Lawrence E. "The Archaeology of the Family in Ancient Israel." *BASOR* 260 (1985): 1–35.

Staubli, Thomas. *Werbung für die Götter: Heilsbringer aus 4000 Jahren.* Fribourg: Universitätsverlag, 2003.

Staubli, Thomas, Silvia Schroer, and Linda M. Maloney. *Body Symbolism in the Bible.* Collegeville, MN: Liturgical, 2001.

Stiebert, Johanna. "Divinely Sanctioned Violence against Women: Biblical Marriage and the Example of the *Sotah* of Numbers 5." *Bible and Critical Theory* 15, no. 2 (2019): 83–108.

Stol, Marten. *Women in the Ancient Near East.* Boston: Walter de Gruyter, 2016.

Stoller, Paul. *Sensuous Scholarship.* Philadelphia: University of Pennsylvania Press, 1997.

Stulman, Louis. "Encroachment in Deuteronomy: An Analysis of the Social World of the D Code." *JBL* 109, no. 4 (1990): 613–632.

Surralles, Alexandre. "On Contrastive Perception and Ineffability: Assessing Sensory Experience without Colour Terms in an Amazonian Society." *JRAI* 22, no. 4 (2016): 962–979.

Tally, Robert T., Jr. *Spatiality.* London: Routledge, 2013.

Tamney, Joseph B. "Fasting and Dieting: A Research Note." *RRelRes* 27, no. 3 (1986): 255–263.

Theocharous, Myrto. "Stealing Souls: Human Trafficking and Deuteronomy 24:7." In *For Our Good Always: Studies on the Message and Influence of Deuteronomy in Honor of Daniel I. Block,* edited by Jason S. DeRochie, Jason Gile, and Kenneth J. Turner, 495–509. Winona Lake, IN: Eisenbrauns, 2013.

Thompson, J. A. *The Book of Jeremiah*. Grand Rapids, MI: Eerdmans, 1980.

Tiemeyer, Lena-Sofia. "The Question of Indirect Touch: Lam 4,14; Ezek 44,19 and Hag 2,12–13." *Bib* 87, no. 1 (2006): 64–74.

Tigay, Jeffrey H. *The JPS Torah Commentary: Deuteronomy*. Philadelphia: Jewish Publication Society, 1996.

Tilford, Nicole L. *Sensing Word, Sensing Wisdom*. Atlanta: SBL, 2017.

———. "When People Have Gods: Sensory Mimicry and Divine Agency in the Book of Job." *HBAI* 5, no. 1 (2016): 42–58.

Tissi, Lucia M. "Sanctuary Doors, Vestibules, and *Adyta* in the Works of Neoplatonic Philosophers." In *Sacred Thresholds: The Door to the Sanctuary in Late Antiquity*, edited by Emilie M. van Opstall, 139–159. Leiden: Brill, 2018.

Toller, Steve van, and George Dodd, eds. *Perfumery: The Psychology and Biology of Fragrance*. London: Chapman & Hall, 1988.

Trimm, Charlie. *Fighting for the King and the Gods: A Survey of Warfare in the Ancient Near East*. Atlanta: SBL, 2017.

———. "God's Staff and Moses' Hand(s): The Battle against the Amalekites as a Turning Point in the Role of the Divine Warrior." *JSOT* 44, no. 1 (2019): 196–213.

Tuan, Yi-Fu. *Space and Place: The Perspective of Experience*. Minneapolis: University of Minnesota Press, 1977.

Ullendorff, Edward. "Thought Categories in the Hebrew Bible." In *Studies in Rationalism, Judaism and Universalism in Memory of Leon Roth*, edited by Raphael Loewe, 273–288. London: Routledge & Kegan Paul, 1966.

Unterman, Jeremiah. "The [Non]sense of Smell in Isaiah 11:3." *HS* 33 (1992): 17–23.

Ussishkin, David. *Megiddo-Armageddon: The Story of the Canaanite and Israelite City*. Jerusalem: Israel Exploration Society, 2018.

Van Beek, Gus W. "Frankincense and Myrrh." *BA* 23, no. 3 (1960): 70–95.

Vanderhooft, David S., and Abraham Winitzer, eds. *Literature as Politics, Politics as Literature: Essays on the Ancient Near East in Honor of Peter Machinist*. Winona Lake, IN: Eisenbrauns, 2013.

VanderKam, James C. "Joshua the High Priest and the Interpretation of Zechariah 3." *CBQ* 53, no. 4 (1991): 553–570.

van der Toorn, Karel, Bob Becking, and Pieter W. van der Horst, eds. *Dictionary of Deities and Demons in the Bible*. 2nd ed. Leiden: Brill, 1999.

van der Toorn, Karel, and Cornelius Houtman. "David and the Ark." *JBL* 113, no. 2 (1994): 209–231.

Walsh, Carl. "Kerma Ceramics, Commensality Practices, and Sensory Experiences in Egypt during the Late Middle Bronze Age." *Journal of Egyptian Interconnections* 20 (2018): 31–51.

Walsh, Cary E. "Under the Influence: Trust and Risk in Biblical Family Drinking." *JSOT* 90, no. 25 (2000): 13–29.

Wang, Sunny Kuan-Hui. *Sense Perception and Testimony in the Gospel according to John*. Tübingen: Mohr Siebeck, 2017.

———. "The Visual and Auditory Presentation of God on Mount Sinai." *Journal for the Evangelical Study of the Old Testament* 5, no. 1 (2016): 39–59.

Warren, Meredith. *Food and Transformation in Ancient Mediterranean Literature.*
    Atlanta: SBL, 2019.
———. "Tasting the Little Scroll: A Sensory Analysis of Divine Interaction in
    Revelation 10.8–10." *JSNT* 40, no. 1 (2017): 101–119.
Washington, Harold V. *Injustice Made Legal: Deuteronomic Law and the Plight
    of Widows, Strangers, and Orphans in Ancient Israel.* Grand Rapids, MI:
    Eerdmans, 2002.
Wasserman, Nathan. "'Sweeter Than Honey and Wine . . .': Semantic Domains and
    Old-Babylonian Imagery." In Milano, de Martino, Mario, and Lanfranchi,
    Landscapes, 191–195.
Watts, James, ed. *Sensing Sacred Texts.* Sheffield: Equinox, 2018.
Weissenrieder, Annette. "A Roadmap to Heaven: High-Priestly Vestments and
    the Jerusalem Temple in Flavius Josephus." In *Beyond Priesthood: Religious
    Entrepreneurs and Innovators in the Roman Empire,* edited by Richard Gordon,
    Georgia Petridou, and Jörg Rüpke, 157–183. Berlin: Walter de Gruyter, 2017.
Weitzman, Steven. "Sensory Reform in Deuteronomy." In *Religion and Self in
    Antiquity,* edited by David Brakke, Michael L. Satlow, and Steven Weitzman,
    123–139. Bloomington: Indiana University Press, 2005.
Wells, Bruce. *The Laws of Testimony in the Pentateuchal Codes.* Wiesbaden,
    Germany: Harrassowitz, 2004.
———. "Sex, Lies, and Virginal Rape: The Slandered Bride and False Accusation in
    Deuteronomy." *JBL* 124, no. 1 (2005): 41–72.
Wenkel, David H. "Sensory Experience and the Contrast between the Covenants in
    Hebrews 12." *BSac* 173, no. 690 (2016): 219–234.
Westbrook, Raymond. "Codex Hammurabi and the Ends of the Earth." In Milano,
    de Martino, Mario, and Lanfranchi, *Landscapes,* 101–103.
———. "Cuneiform Law Codes and the Origins of Legislation." *ZA* 79, no. 2
    (1989): 201–222.
Westbrook, Raymond, and Bruce Wells. *Everyday Law in Biblical Israel: An
    Introduction.* Louisville, KY: Westminster John Knox, 2009.
White, Marsha C. "Saul and Jonathan in 1 Samuel 1 and 14." In *Saul in Story
    and Tradition,* edited by Carl S. Ehrlich, 119–138. Tübingen: Mohr Siebeck,
    2006.
Whitelam, Keith. "The Symbols of Power: Aspects of Royal Propaganda in the
    United Monarchy." *BA* 49 (1986): 166–173.
Whittle, Chris L., Steven Fakharzade, Jason Eades, and George Preti. "Human
    Breath Odors and Their Use in Diagnosis." *Annals of the New York Academy of
    Sciences* 1098, no. 1 (2007): 252–266.
Wigoder, Devorah E. "A Biblical Spice Rack." *BRev* 13, no. 5 (1997): 32–35.
Willis, John T. "Anti-elide Narrative Tradition from a Prophetic Circle at the
    Ramah Sanctuary." *JBL* 90, no. 3 (1971): 288–308.
Willis, Timothy M. *The Elders of the City: A Study of the Elders-Laws in
    Deuteronomy.* Atlanta: SBL, 2001.
Wilson, Brittany E. "Hearing the Word and Seeing the Light: Voice and Vision in
    Acts." *JSNT* 38, no. 4 (2016): 456–481.
———. "Seeing Divine Speech: Sensory Intersections in Luke's Birth Narrative and
    Beyond." *JSNT* 42, no. 3 (2020): 251–273.

———. "The Smell of Sacrifice: Scenting the Christian Story in Luke-Acts." *CBQ* 83, no. 2 (2021): 257–275.

Winspear, Jacqueline. *An Incomplete Revenge*. New York: Henry Holt, 2008.

Winter, Irene. "Art in Empire: The Royal Images and the Visual Dimension of Assyrian Ideology." In *Assyria 1995*, edited by S. Parpola and R. M. Whiting, 359–381. Helsinki: Neo-Assyrian Text Corpus Project, 1997.

———. "Royal Rhetoric and Development of Historical Narrative." *Studies in Visual Communication* 7, no. 2 (1981): 2–38.

Wöhrle, Jakob. "The Priestly Writing(s): Scope and Nature." In Baden and Stackert, *Oxford Handbook of the Pentateuch*, 255–275.

Wright, David P. "Deuteronomy 21.1–9 as a Rite of Elimination." *CBQ* 49, no. 3 (1987): 387–403.

———. "The Gesture of Hand Placement in the Hebrew Bible and in Hittite Literature." *JAOS* 106 (1986): 433–446.

———. "Music and Dance in 2 Samuel 6." *JBL* 121, no. 2 (2002): 201–225.

Wu, Ping-Hsien. "How Do You Smell, Fragrance or Stench? Text: 2 Corinthians 2:5–17." *Asian American Theological Forum* 5, no. 2 (2018): 29–31.

Yadin, Yigael. *The Art of Warfare in Biblical Lands in the Light of Archaeological Discovery*. London: Weidenfeld & Nicolson, 1963.

Yasur-Landau, Assaf. "Behavioral Patterns in Transition: Eleventh-Century B.C.E. Innovation in Domestic Textile Production." In *Exploring the Longue Durée: Essays in Honor of Lawrence E. Stager*, edited by J. David Schloen, 507–515. Winona Lake, IN: Eisenbrauns, 2009.

Yee, Gale A. "'I Have Perfumed My Bed with Myrrh': The Foreign Woman (*'Issâ Zarâ*) in Proverbs 1–9." *JSOT* 43, no. 13 (1989): 53–68.

Young, Teron. "Psalm 18 and 2 Samuel 22: Two Versions of the Same Song." In *Seeking Out the Wisdom of the Ancients: Essays Offered to Honor Michael V. Fox on the Occasion of His Sixty-Fifth Birthday*, edited by Ronald L. Troxel, Kelvin G. Friebel, and Dennis R. Magary, 53–69. Winona Lake, IN: Eisenbrauns, 2005.

Zenger, Erich, and Klaus Baltzer. *A Commentary on Psalms 51–100*. Minneapolis: Fortress, 2005.

Zorn, Jeffrey R. "Estimating the Population Size of Ancient Settlements: Methods, Problems, Solutions, and a Case Study." *BASOR* 295 (1994): 31–48.

Zorzi, Nicia De. "'Rude Remarks Not Fit to Smell': Negative Value Judgements Relating to Sensory Perceptions in Ancient Mesopotamia." In Schellenberg and Krüger, *Sounding Sensory Profiles*, 217–252.

Zucconi, Laura M. *Ancient Medicine: From Mesopotamia to Rome*. Grand Rapids, MI: Eerdmans, 2019.

Scripture Index

Exodus

Leviticus

Leviticus (*continued*)

Deuteronomy

Deuteronomy (*continued*)

Joshua

Judges

Psalms

Author Index

Subject Index

Passover, 25, 52, 114, 120, 171, 186, 190
perfume, 1, 14, 27, 34, 44, 45, 46, 47, 146, 147, 162, 169, 176, 177, 184, 193, 195
Perseus, 152
Philistines, 43, 49, 62, 64, 68, 70, 76, 77, 84, 108, 151, 152, 153, 175
Phoenicia, 38, 45, 141, 146, 160, 174, 184
potter, 1, 7, 15, 22, 23, 26, 33, 41, 45, 110, 119, 141
prayer, 103, 106, 107, 120, 168, 170, 175, 176, 180, 183
priests, 11, 24, 26, 33, 37, 38, 42, 44, 45, 48, 67, 84, 86, 88, 89, 90, 92, 99, 101, 102, 103, 104, 105, 106, 108, 109, 110, 111, 112, 113, 114, 115, 116, 120, 121, 125, 128, 129, 131, 139, 141, 143, 145, 147, 159, 162, 165, 166, 167, 169, 171, 172, 180, 183, 184, 192, 193, 194, 195
procession, 42, 43, 101, 103, 104, 105, 109, 120, 166, 167, 185
propaganda, 33, 65, 68, 71, 141, 150, 178, 194
purity, 88, 96, 105, 106, 113, 114, 120, 128, 131, 172

Rabshakeh, 71, 150, 155, 175
Rachael, 20, 27
Rahab, 35, 141
Rebekah, 27, 39
Red Sea, 60, 137
rhythm, 12, 16, 17, 18, 20, 66, 70, 107, 118
Rome, 71, 171, 187, 195
Ruth, 8, 22, 81

Sabbath, 101, 108, 120, 124, 127
sacrifice, 11, 19, 25, 27, 33, 45, 46, 67, 74, 86, 101, 102, 107, 109, 110, 111, 120, 126, 128, 129, 139, 159, 169, 172, 182, 195
Samaria, 5, 32, 42, 63, 87, 142, 143
Samson, 15, 49, 67, 137, 149, 162

Samuel, 50, 84, 103, 148, 152, 190
Sargon II, 76, 153, 170
Saul, 37, 43, 50, 62, 64, 70, 76, 77, 138, 141, 143, 148, 151, 153, 154, 155, 157, 167, 194
scent, 21, 23, 26, 34, 44, 45, 46, 47, 48, 72, 146, 172, 181, 182, 185, 191, 195
Sea Peoples, 6
Sennacherib, 58, 61, 71, 73, 77, 154, 157, 170, 184
Shalmaneser III, 151
Shalmaneser V, 170
Shechem, 5, 59, 101, 144, 162, 191
Shephelah, 2, 57, 62
Shiloh, 2, 43, 84, 86, 106, 144, 160
siege, 35, 57, 58, 59, 62, 69, 71, 142, 150, 153, 192
singing, 15, 16, 18, 20, 67, 70, 104, 108, 109, 137, 143, 168, 169, 173
Sinuhe, 23
Sisera, 14, 20, 38, 60, 138, 148
Sodom, 34, 142
song, 1, 12, 13, 17, 18, 19, 20, 43, 47, 66, 106, 109, 120, 164, 169, 174, 178, 195
Sotah, 88, 115, 161, 172, 176, 184, 192
sour, 29, 50, 52, 175, 177
spice, 6, 9, 27, 28, 29, 45, 47, 52, 109, 119, 139, 140, 147, 149, 186, 194
standing stone (massebôt), 101, 165, 174, 175
Šuilla, 108, 168, 170, 180
sweet, 24, 29, 30, 48, 50, 51, 52, 76, 109, 115, 118, 149, 169, 170, 175, 194

Tamar, 7, 50, 81, 158
tanning, 22, 45, 119, 146
taste, 1, 3, 21, 29, 30, 34, 48, 50, 51, 52, 76, 77, 89, 96, 114, 115, 116, 117, 118, 127, 128, 130, 132, 140, 148, 149, 164, 181, 184, 190, 191, 192
Teachings of Ahiqar, 159